Refugee Children in the Classroom

Refugee Children in the Classroom

including a comprehensive information briefing on refugees in Britain

Jill Rutter

Education Officer,

Information and Policy Division, Refugee Council

tb

Trentham Books

First published in 1994 by Trentham Books Limited

Trentham Books Limited
Westview House
734 London Road
Oakhill
Stoke-on-Trent
Staffordshire
England ST4 5NP

British Cataloguing in Publication Data
A catalogue record for this book is available from the British Library.

ISBN: 1 85856 008 X

Cover photograph: Syrian Christian boy in New Zealand
by Howard J. Davies

Designed and typeset by Trentham Print Design Limited, Chester and printed in Great Britain by Bemrose Shafron Limited, Chester

Contents

Foreword

This authoritative book could hardly be more timely. At a time when central government has eroded local authority advisory services and support to schools and is cutting back on Section 11, refugee children are coming into British schools and are singularly in need of help. Despite increasing immigration controls, there are more recent refugees, from more countries — in Europe, Africa and Asia — and many are likely to have endured suffering and loss.

Jill Rutter is the Education Officer at the Refugee Council. The facts about the situation of refugees in Britain are at her fingertips. In her visits to schools she sees children who have lost their entire families, who have been tortured, who have witnessed events that no adult, still less a child, should have to see. The one hope for these children is to rebuild their lives and education is the only way to begin; the responsibility that rests on the shoulders of teachers is immense.

This book provides teachers with a guidance and support across all phases of education. It considers approaches and strategies in the classroom: how teachers can help children to hold on to what they have — including their language — and to deal with their loss. Rachel Warner contributes professional expertise about helping children with their acquisition of English — the first essential tool of survival and of learning.

The book is also an authoritative handbook on virtually everything anyone needs to know about refugee groups in Britain. It scythes a clear path through the tangle of restrictions to entry into the UK and explains clearly the status of refugees or, increasingly common, Exceptional Leave to Remain. Part Three is an encyclopaedia of information about over 30 major groups of refugees to Britain: their backgrounds, ethnicities, religions, languages and how these are written, and whether there are community organisations for the groups in the UK.

Specific, relevant information, readily accessed, in one publication means that schools and colleges now have a handbook which will enable them to enhance their refugee pupils' futures. There are over 23.000 refugee children in British schools and, if they are to contribute to our society in future, schools must embrace, understand and assist them now.

Gillian Klein

Acknowledgements

During the last five years I have participated in many training sessions for teachers and educationalists run by schools and LEAs. This book attempts to summarise and extend the issues raised by teachers and trainers alike. I could not have written it without the contributions of those who have attended these sessions: students, teachers, advisers and refugees themselves. My thanks goes to the many people who have helped and inspired me.

Others have made comments on the text or provided me with material. I would like to thank Rachel Warner, Education Officer, Minority Rights Group for her chapter on English as a Second Language Support. I used a great deal of information from Sarah Graham-Brown's publication on the Gulf. I am also grateful to Sheila Melzak and Jeremy Woodcock, Medical Foundation for the Care of Victims of Torture, for material and advice, Rocky Deans, Travellers and Displaced Person's Unit, Brent LEA for material and ideas on induction, Sheila Kasabova, Refugee Liaison Teacher, Camden LEA for all her support and friendship, Kath Formoy, Holland Park School, Caroline Lodge, George Orwell School, Athy Demitriades and other staff at Hampstead School, Bill Bolloten and Tim Spafford of Waltham Forest LEA, and Betty Davies at Anson School.

Colleagues at the Refugee Council have given me support and friendship while I have been writing the book, especially Susannah Cox, Allan Leas, Vasi Krishna, Clare Crawford and Jessica Yudilevich, David Hudson, the Advice Team Julia Purcell, Nish Matenjwa, Parizad Bathai, Vije, Toby

Buxton and Ros Finlay. Warwick Harris our librarian deserves special thanks: I could not have written the book without the use of our wonderful library.

The Development Education Fund of the Commission of European Communities provided me with funding for my salary. Without this funding the Refugee Council would not have been able to employ me. I would also like to thank Crispin Jones, my tutor at the Institute of Education who has patiently waited for overdue research. Finally I would like to thank Gillian Klein, my editor, for her work.

This book is dedicated to Guy Pilavsky, my husband.

PART ONE
Being a refugee in Britain

Chapter One

Who Are Refugees?

'I come from a village in Afghanistan. The war started when I was about three years old. I started school at seven. My education was in Kabul, the capital city, in a state school. It was a very good school, but we had problems from missiles called 'Scot missiles' fired from the villages into the city. Twice they hit our school when we were in class. One did not explode, the other smashed the trees outside. We did not have a bomb shelter and all the children were screaming. The school was a high building of four stories and everyone had to come down to the ground floor, but the building was not damaged.

Going to school and coming home was a dangerous time, especially in the last two or three years. Sometimes the teacher sent us home because the Scot missiles were coming. Now nobody can stay in Kabul, only fighters — mujahideen.

When I was fourteen years old in Afghanistan the government didn't accept me as a student because I refused to do military service. I didn't want to kill my brothers. After that I ran away. Because of the situation I had to leave the country. At midnight I went with the mujahideen *and together we walked in the mountains to Pakistan which was very dangerous because of the mines. We couldn't walk off the road because around the road there were bombs.*

We walked from midnight until the early morning. After this we had a rest, prayed and had breakfast. Then after a few hours we started to journey until midday. Then we had lunch and prayed. Sometimes the enemy attacked us and suddenly the fighting started. After two or three hours it stopped. Then we walked again, and again we rested and prayed. Sometimes we walked until 11 o'clock at night.

After three or four days we arrived at the Pakistani border. For one day we had a rest near the border. The next morning we started a journey to Peshawar. The journey took one day in a coach.

I like education here in England because they can teach properly and I understand. I had problems with English. When I was in my country I learnt German. Discipline is good here but in Afghanistan students don't talk loudly and use bad words — in my country students would be expelled from school for swearing. In my country we had much more homework too. I think that is better.

Some students make jokes about others who can't speak English. I think schools here need to give us an information book in different languages, general information about travel, local geography, useful facts about different places in Britain, laws, rights and responsibilities.'

14 year old student, Holland Park School, London.

Some 19 million people are refugees in today's world. Many others are living in refugee-like situations. The migration of refugees is a growing challenge to governments, NGOs and international agencies — the numbers of refugees has doubled in a decade. Even in Britain the number of refugees has increased substantially since the mid 1980s. Almost every London school now has refugee students, something that could not have been predicted ten years ago.

The word refugee is now part of everyday vocabulary. But it does have a precise legal meaning. A person with refugee status is defined as someone who has fled from his or her home country or is unable to return to it '*owing to a well founded fear of being persecuted for reasons of race, religion, nationality, membership of a particular social group or political opinion.*' An asylum-seeker is a person who has crossed an international border in search of safety, and refugee status, in another country. In Britain asylum-seekers are people who are awaiting a Home Office decision as to whether they can remain.

The definition of refugees is taken from the 1951 UN Convention and 1967 UN Protocol Relating to the Status of Refugees, international law now signed by 121 states, including the UK. These two legal instruments enshrine the rights of asylum-seekers and refugees, preventing them being returned to countries where they fear persecution.

Other international laws can be invoked to protect asylum-seekers and refugees. The European Convention on Human Rights has been used by some immigration lawyers in Europe, as it contains commitments preventing the return of people to countries where they would be subject to 'cruel or degrading treatment'.

The Organisation of African Unity has broadened the definition of refugees to include people compelled to leave their home countries by 'external aggression or domination' or 'by events seriously undermining public order'. In African countries protection is thus afforded to large groups of people who are living in generally dangerous or unstable conditions, for example because there is a civil war in their home countries. European countries are not so generous: an increasing number of people who have fled war are being refused refugee status, even when the conflict is of ethnic or religious nature.

In addition to asylum-seekers and those with refugee status at least 27 million other people are living in refugee-like situations. About 25 million people are internally displaced, having fled from their homes but not crossed an international border. Others may be '*de facto* refugees'. They may have fled from their countries, and are living in host countries with other forms of immigration status such as temporary residence permits, or they may be living in the host country without the correct documentation.

The UN High Commissioner for Refugees (UNHCR) is the organisation responsible for ensuring that the humanitarian principles outlined in the 1951 UN Convention and 1967 UN Protocol Relating to the Status of Refugees are observed by contracting states. The UNHCR began operations in 1951. Its headquarters are in Geneva, Switzerland, and it has offices in more than 70 countries. It is funded by donations from individual countries, and has three separate responsibilities:

— the legal protection of refugees and asylum-seekers, ensuring that they would not be returned to danger

— working with other organisations to enable aid reach refugees

— working for long-term solutions for refugees, which may include repatriation or resettlement.

☐ Persecution

Persecution takes many forms and people are forced to flee for many different reasons. Some people flee after long periods of political activity, others simply run away because they are frightened. The type, intensity and duration of persecution obviously influences how individuals and families cope and recover from that trauma.

The majority of the world's refugees have fled from war, escaping fighting, aerial attacks and the deliberate terrorisation of civilian populations. Today over 85 per cent of warfare's casualties are among civilians — conflicts rarely involve just the active combatants. Some 31 conflicts continue to claim casualties and produce refugees. These can be 'total' or 'high intensity' wars as experienced by those living in former Yugoslavia, Liberia, Angola and Sri Lanka. At the time of writing over four million people had fled from their homes in former Yugoslavia, most leaving under extreme duress. All sides have been accused of using methods reminiscent of the Nazis to drive people from their homes: this is 'ethnic cleansing'.

But most of the world's conflicts are 'low intensity wars' claiming less than 1,000 lives a year, and seldom receiving media attention. Conflicts raging in Guatemala, Colombia, Turkish Kurdistan and the Philippines are typical of this type of warfare, which may well have worse long term psychological effects on a population.

In other parts of the world persecution can mean the denial of the right to a chosen way of life: denial of the right to peaceful political organisation, or being denied religious or sexual freedom. Those who defy such rulings risk intimidation, losing their jobs, arrest, torture or execution. In 1992 Amnesty International concluded that torture and the beating of detainees and prisoners occurred in 96 countries. Torture is a method of political control, usually part of that state's mechanism for controlling dissent. A torturer may require specific information, but torture is also a way of inducing fear in a larger population. In some countries children are tortured.

It seems likely that most people who are tortured do not survive the experience. Those who do live may suffer acute, chronic or long term physical and psychological damage.

☐ Trauma

Within British schools a refugee child's exposure to traumatic events varies widely. Some children are kidnapped and tortured, some witness the killing of parents, siblings and friends, others are separated from their parents, or spend protracted periods of time in refugee camps. Some children come under fire while others watch the conflict on television. Not to be underestimated is the effect of poverty as a stressor.

The greater the duration and intensity of traumatic and stressful experiences, the greater the likelihood that a child will suffer from a psychiatric disorder. That child's healing mechanisms will not be able to overcome such events. Recent research in the Lebanon, Central America and south east Asia has attempted to quantify the traumatic experiences of childhoods disrupted by war and persecution (Maksoud 1992, McCallin 1992, Harvard Programme in Refugee Trauma 1992). The findings make shocking reading for those of us who have grown up in western Europe, and are, perhaps, testimony to the resilience of most children.

Mona Maksoud attempted to assess war trauma among Lebanese children. She distributed a questionnaire to the parents of 2,200 children in Greater Beirut. The children were aged between three and 16 years and the sample was selected to be representative of class, gender and religion. Parents were asked to report on the traumatic events experienced by their children. The results are shown below:

> 90.3 per cent of the children had been exposed to shelling or combat
>
> 68.4 per cent of the children had been forcibly displaced from home
>
> 54.5 per cent of the children had experienced grave shortages of food, water and other necessities
>
> 50.3 per cent of the children had witnessed violent acts such as murder

REFUGEES IN TODAYS WORLD

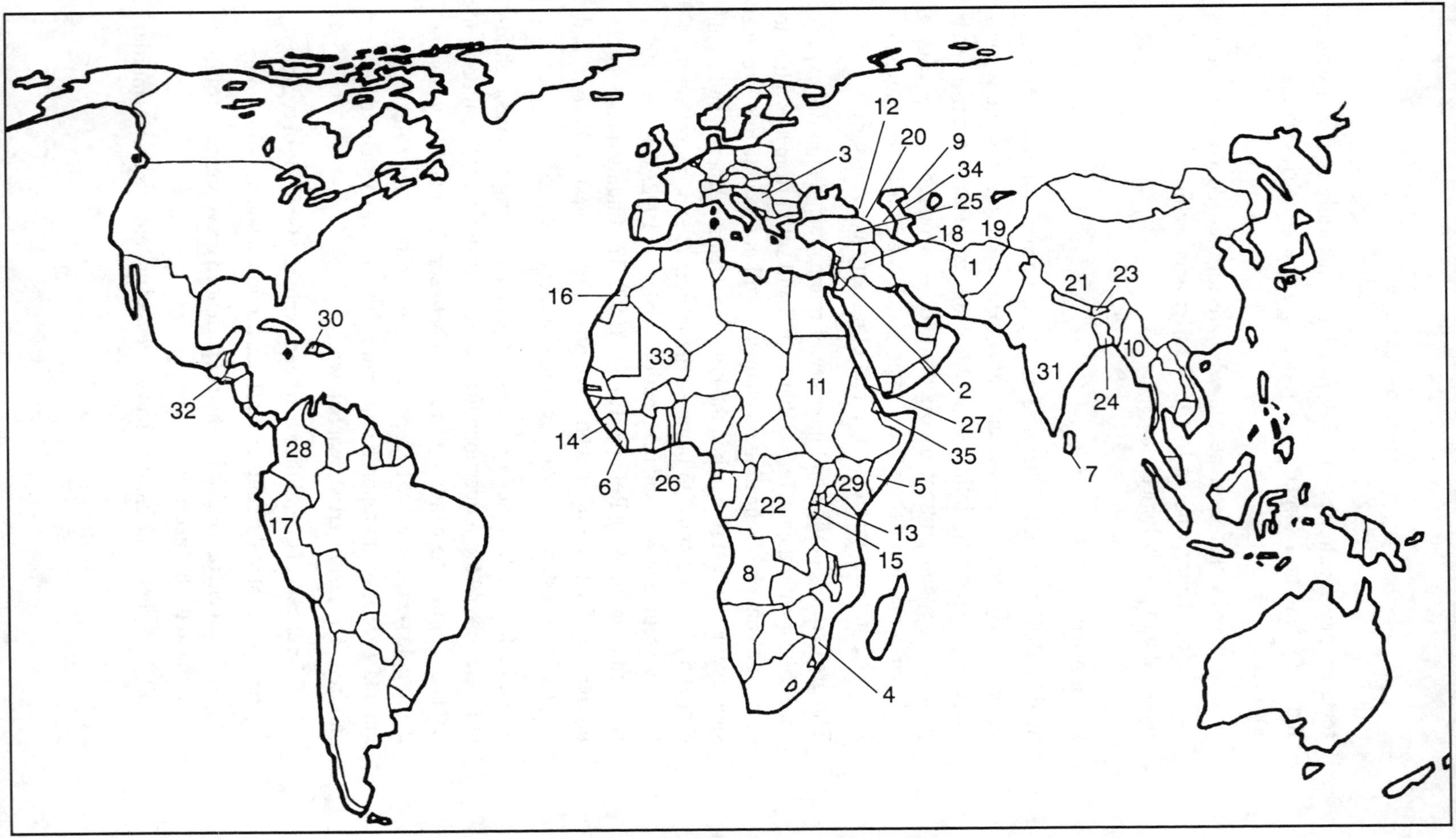

Source UNHCR and Refugee Council

1. Afghans 4,000,000 refugees and 500,000 internally displaced people
2. Palestinians 2,800,000 refugees
3. Refugees from former Yugoslavia 1,300,000 refugees and 1,300,000 internally displaced people
4. Mozambicans 700,000 refugees and 1,750,000 displaced people, many of whom will return in 1994.
5. Somalis 500,000 refugees and 700,000 internally displaced people.
6. Liberians 700,000 refugees and 1,000,000 internally displaced people.
7. Sri Lankans 500,000 refugees and 900,000 internally displaced people.
8. Angolans 500,000 refugees and 2,000,000 internally displaced people.
9. Azeris 300,000 refugees and 600,000 internally displaced people.
10. Burmese 330,000 refugees and 500,000 — 1,000,000 internally displaced people.
11. Sudanese 400,000 refugees and 4,000,000 internally displaced people.
12. Armenians 200,000 refugees.
13. Rwandans 3,000,000 refugees and 1,000,000 internally displaced people.
14. Sierra Leone 260,000 refugees and 400,000 displaced people.
15. Burundis 800,000 refugees and 500,000 internally displaced people
16. Sahrawis 170,000 refugees
17. Peruvians 600,000 displaced people
18. Iraqis and Iraqi Kurds 200,000 refugees and 400,000 displaced people.
19. Tajiks 150,000 refugees and 400,000 internally displaced people
20. Georgians 140,000 refugees and 250,000 internally displaced people
21. Tibetans 130,000 refugees
22. Zaireans 100,000 refugees and 700,000 internally displaced people.
23. Bhutanese 100,000 refugees
24. Bangladeshis 50,000 refugees
25. Turkish Kurds 70,000 refugees
26. Togolese 240,000 refugees and 150,000 internally displaced people
27. Eritreans 430,000 refugees
28. Colombians 300,000-600,000 internally displaced people
29. Kenya 300,000 internally displaced people
30. Haitians 30,000 refugees and 300,000 internally displaced people
31. Indians 250,000 internally displaced people
32. Guatemalans 150,000 refugees and 200,000 internally displaced people
33. Malians 80,000 refugees
34. Uzbeks 80,000 refugees
35. Djiboutis 140,000 internally displaced people

Sources UNHCR and the Refugee Council

26 per cent of the children had lost family and/or friends

21.3 per cent of the children had become separated from their families

5.9 per cent of the children had been injured

3.5 per cent of the children were the victims of violent acts such as arrest, detention and torture

0.2 per cent of children were forced to join militia.

Older children, boys and children from poorer families were more likely to have experienced multiple traumatic events; a richer family was more likely to have had the resources to send their children to a safer part of the country. Assessment of the experiences of refugee children from central America and Cambodia show that a similar proportion of children had experienced warfare, the loss of family and friends and extreme poverty.

☐ Life in Refugee Camps

Some groups of refugees have spent periods of time in camps for refugees or displaced people before arriving in Britain. Almost all Vietnamese refugees living in Britain have come via camps in Hong Kong or other south east Asian countries. Some Somalis, Eritreans, Ethiopians, Kurds, Afghans and Bosnians may also have lived in refugee camps.

Conditions in refugee camps can be very stressful or unsafe. Accommodation is usually overcrowded. Circumstances vary, but throughout the world refugee camps have many things in common:

- camps are often located in border areas where refugees are sometimes at risk from attacks and bombardment by the government from which they have fled
- refugees in camps are often deliberately segregated from local people, to prevent refugees from integrating into local society and becoming permanent migrants
- refugee camps are usually overcrowded
- domestic violence and family conflicts are more prevalent
- women and girls are more likely to be raped in a refugee camp than in outside society

— food, clean water and adequate shelter are not always in plentiful supply, and malnutrition is common

— many refugee camps lack adequate sanitation

— malnutrition combined with inadequate sanitation and overcrowding result in high mortality in refugee camps

— refugees often have limited access to schooling, further education, training, employment and leisure activities

— refugees who live in camps rarely have the opportunity to develop the skills they will need for return to their home country

— refugees rarely participate in decision making processes in camps and are usually dependent on the benevolence of camp officials and the host government. This can lead to people feeling that they have no control over their lives

— most refugees have little idea when they will leave the camp.

In Britain refugees do not live in camps. But in Hong Kong — a British Overseas Territory — about 40,000 Vietnamese 'boat people' are living in detention centres. Some detention centres are 'closed' and the inhabitants are effectively imprisoned. Other detention centres allow for the inhabitants to leave the camps. Living conditions are very overcrowded, with families living in containers that are stacked on top of each other. Research in Hong Kong shows that the majority of children reported feeling depressed and anxious — up to 90 per cent of children in some age groups. Anxieties were caused by fears for family at home and fears for safety in camps. Girls feared sexual assault and boys were fearful of violence and bullying. Nearly ten per cent of children had witnessed a successful suicide (McCallin, 1992).

Life in a refugee camp is at best a life in limbo. But in camps refugees, both adults and children, can be exposed to conditions as distressing as those from which they fled: rape, organised violence and shelling. The mental health of all refugees in camps deteriorates over time, regardless of other factors, a consideration which should be used to lobby for permanent solutions to refugee migrations.

☐ Flight

Most of the world's refugees are from poor countries and flee to neighbouring states: over 80 per cent of the world's refugees live in poor countries, and only six per cent in western Europe. But to whatever destination a refugee flees, flight is a time of enormous stress.

The decision to flee can be planned over a period of days or weeks, or a refugee may be forced to leave home at the spur of the moment. Those who had some time to prepare for exile may be more likely to cope with future events than refugees who did not anticipate their flight.

Desperate refugees use all available means to escape from danger. Almost all asylum-seekers who arrive in Britain have faced long and traumatic journeys: they have usually lived in hiding or walked for days through deserts or mountains. Almost all Vietnamese refugees in Hong Kong have made perilous journeys in small boats to Hong Kong and other south east Asian countries — journeys in which at least ten per cent of refugees perished from dehydration, drowning or pirate attacks. During flight fears of discovery, arrest, violence, return and family separation are common.

Most refugees have little choice in their destinations. The availability of flights to London is undoubtedly a major factor in determining the arrival of refugees in Britain. The few who have more time to plan their journeys have more choice over their eventual destination. Fluency in English, having made previous visits to Britain, or having friends and relatives in this country can all influence a refugee's decision to come to Britain.

But since the mid-1980s refugees who try to flee to Britain and other western European countries have had to contend with another hurdle: the enactment of legislation and policy designed to keep refugees out of 'fortress Europe'. The British Government has repeatedly imposed visa requirements on nationals of refugee producing countries. Britain, and five other EC countries, fine airlines and other carriers who transport passengers who do not have the correct travel documents. The visa barrier and carrier's sanctions cause additional stress to already traumatised people. At worst they present an impenetrable obstacle to refuge?

Chapter Two

Refugees in Britain

☐ Applying for Asylum

The following section outlines the process of applying for asylum in Britain. It is not a foolproof guide, and all asylum-seekers should seek expert legal advice.

The term 'asylum-seeker' refers to someone who has fled from his or her country of origin, and has made an application for asylum to the Home Office.

A person usually has to be in the UK in order to apply for asylum. They can apply on arrival in Britain, or after making legal entry to Britain. Illegal entrants, and people who have remained unlawfully in the UK after their leave to remain has expired are also allowed to apply for asylum. Occasionally, however, the British Government has accepted people as refugees before they arrived in Britain, as part of a Government resettlement programme, or to join existing family.

Applying on Arrival in Britain

People seeking asylum at a port of entry apply to the immigration officer, explaining the dangers they face in their home countries. Immigration officers work for the Immigration and Nationality Department of the Home Office.

☐ Refugees in Britain

Country of Origin	Main Date of Entry	Numbers
Eastern European Jews	1880-1914	200,000
Jews from Germany, Austria and Czechoslovakia	1933-1939	56,000
Poland	1939-1950	200,000
Czechoslovakia, Hungary and Romania	1945-1950	50,000
Hungary	1956	17,000
Czechoslovakia	1968	5,000
Uganda	1972-	36,000
Chile	1973-1979	3,000
Ethiopia	1973-	7,000
Eritrea	1973-	8,000
Cyprus	1974	24,000
Viet Nam	1975-1992	24,000
Iran	1978-	20,000
Iraq	1980-	12,000
Poland	1981	1,000
Ghana	1988-	9,000
Sri Lanka	1983-	22,000
Somalia	1988-	15,000
Turkey	1989-	12,000
Zaire	1989-	15,000
Sudan	1989-	4,000
Former Yugoslavia	1990-	8,000
Angola	1989-	10,000

Source: Refugee Council, 1994

There may be an initial interview at the port of entry so that the immigration officer can find details of the asylum-seeker's journey.

Asylum-seekers will be fingerprinted at the port of entry, and also issued with documentation that describes their status and which can be used to obtain benefits. Children under 16 should be fingerprinted in the presence of someone who is not an immigration officer or police officer.

The Standard Acknowledgement Letter states that the bearer has applied for asylum in Britain. It includes personal details of the asylum-seeker including an address and a photograph, and the names of dependant children. A separate form is issued to an asylum-seeker's partner. The Standard Acknowledgement Letter also lists the asylum-seeker's Home Office reference number. They are valid for varying periods of time, usually six months or one year.

The Standard Acknowledgement Letter is only issued when the Home Office is satisfied about the asylum-seeker's identity. Usually a person has to produce a passport or birth certificate or some other form of identification before obtaining a Standard Acknowledgement Letter. This may be a problem for many asylum-seekers who may arrived with forged passports, or flee without their belongings. Those who cannot prove their identity are issued with an interim letter called IS96. It gives the asylum-seeker 'temporary admission' to the UK. Temporary admission is granted for a set period of time, rarely over three months. In order to be granted temporary admission a person will have to provide an address in the UK, and comply with other conditions that the immigration officer may attach, such as reporting to a police station.

Someone with an IS96 form is told to return to the port of entry with additional documentation to prove their identity. An asylum-seeker with an IS96 is still entitled to apply for benefits.

Most asylum-seekers are now given a form to take away called a 'Political Asylum Questionnaire'. This forms the basis of the application for political asylum. In the Political Asylum Questionnaire the asylum-seeker has to detail the persecution faced at home. Secondary evidence can be attached to the Political Asylum Questionnaire, such as press clippings, medical reports to indicate torture or statements from Amnesty International.

The Political Asylum Questionnaire has to be returned to the immigration officers at the port of entry within a set time limit, usually four weeks. People who fail to return a complete form within the time limit may have their application for asylum refused under Immigration Rule 180.

Where a family arrives intact one asylum application is usually made per household. Unaccompanied refugee children have to complete the same documents as adults.

Sometimes asylum-seekers are interviewed in full, in order to complete the Political Asylum Questionnaire at the port. This practice gives concern to the Refugee Council, as the asylum-seeker may be forced to fill in the Political Asylum Questionnaire without receiving legal advice, or fully understanding the significance of some of the questions.

Asylum-seekers and their families may have to make many journeys to the port of entry to present evidence of identity, for fingerprinting and for interviews to determine their application for asylum.

All asylum-seekers should, if possible, obtain specialist legal advice before making an asylum application and take legal advisers with them to interviews. Agencies which offer legal advice are listed on page 266. It is also important that asylum-seekers inform the Home Office of any change of address. All correspondence with the Home Office should be sent by recorded delivery post, and copies should be kept of any letters.

Detention

Immigration officers have the power under the 1971 Immigration Act to detain asylum-seekers. An increasing number of asylum-seekers are being detained since the implementation of the 1993 Asylum and Immigration (Appeals) Act. Most detainees are newly-arrived asylum-seekers, held at the port of entry. In-country asylum applicants can also be detained if they have overstayed their leave to enter, or have illegally entered the UK. The Immigration and Nationality Department sometimes detains children, although it tries to avoid this practice.

The first hours of detention can be anywhere — on a ship, in an aircraft or in a police cell. For periods longer than five days three facilities are used: Harmondsworth Detention Centre, the Queen's Building at Heathrow Airport or the Beehive at Gatwick Airport. For longer periods detainees are moved to prisons such as HMP Pentonville or Holloway, or specialist detention centres such as those at Harmondsworth, HMP Haslar, or Campsfield House, Oxford.

The normally stated reasons for detention are:

- that the person is to be removed or deported
- that the person may abscond
- that the person entered Britain illegally or has overstayed their leave to enter
- people who are suspected or have been charged with an immigration offence
- that the person's application for asylum is 'without foundation'.

The 1971 Immigration Act gives immigration officers the power to detain without limit of time. Detainees are also given little information about their rights and about how to seek legal advice. It is not unknown for a detainee to spend one or two months without making contact with a solicitor. It is a profoundly disorientating experience, and detainees regularly inflict harm on themselves or suffer severe anxiety and depression.

A detainee can apply for bail if he or she meets certain conditions. Although large amounts of money are demanded as sureties (£2,000-£10,000), some human rights activists have started bail groups to guarantee surety for detainees. Alternatively, detainees can apply for temporary release.

The Detention Advisory Service, the Refugee Legal Centre, the Refugee Arrival's Project and the Refugee Council offer advice to detainees. They work in tandem with specialist immigration lawyers. Their addresses are listed in Part Three of this book.

The Fast Track

The 1993 Asylum and Immigration (Appeals) Act introduced accelerated procedures for some asylum-seekers. People who apply at a port of entry can now have their asylum application judged to be 'without foundation'. At the time of writing, over 50 per cent of Angolan and Zairian asylum-seekers arriving at UK airports were judged to have no claim to asylum. If immigration officers believe that the application is without foundation they will make a decision very quickly, within a few days or in some cases hours (although all cases must be referred to the Home Office). The main reasons that asylum-seekers are rejected without entering the full asylum determination procedures are that:

- they have come from a country which the Home Office believes does not persecute its citizens
- they have travelled to Britain via a country that the Home Office believes to be safe
- before coming to Britain they have lived in a country that the Home Office believes to be safe
- they have been refused asylum in another country which is signatory to the 1951 UN Convention and 1967 Protocol Relating to the Status of Refugees
- they are part of a group which the Home Office believes is not persecuted or not related to the UN Convention's criteria for refugee status.

Asylum-seekers who are refused in this way are usually held in detention at the port of entry or after being recalled to the port of entry. They are handed their decision in person. Some people may wish to appeal against this decision. They have two working days in which to lodge notice of appeal to the Appeal Adjudicator. This time limit makes it very difficult for potential appellants to obtain the necessary legal advice.

The appeals hearing has to be heard within seven days of receiving notice of appeal. There are no further rights of appeal against the Appeal Adjudicator's decision, except by judicial review. In reality most asylum-seekers who go through this fast track procedure are removed from Britain within a few days.

In-Country Applications

About 70 per cent of asylum applications are made 'in country', rather than at the port of entry. Most in-country asylum applications are made by people who have been in Britain for a few days. But in-country applications are also made by people with leave to remain in Britain (a student's visa or visitor's visa, for example), or by visa overstayers and those who have entered Britain illegally. In the past there was no evidence that asylum applications were considered weaker by the Immigration and

Nationality Department if they were made after entry. But new criteria introduced in the 1993 Immigration Rule changes make 'failure to apply forthwith on arrival' something which may lead to a refusal.

An asylum application is made by writing to the Immigration and Nationality Department of the Home Office, or by visiting the Immigration and Nationality Department in person to request asylum. The headquarters of the Immigration and Nationality Department is in Croydon, Surrey and there are regional offices in different parts of Britain.

After a person has stated that he or she wants to apply for asylum, he or she is then invited for interview, usually held within one week. The interview is given by officials working for the Asylum Screening Unit, and main its purpose is to establish that person's identity. Asylum-seekers are usually asked questions at this initial interview about their route to Britain. Wherever possible asylum-seekers should take a representative with them to the interview; occasionally asylum-seekers have been detained at the Asylum Screening Unit.

The interview will take place in an Asylum Screening Unit of the Home Office. These are located in Croydon, Surrey and in Birmingham and Glasgow. In other parts of the country asylum-seekers may be interviewed by immigration officers at airports. They should bring as much documentation as possible which confirms their identity — passports, birth or marriage certificates, rent books or letters from landlords. Once an asylum-seeker's identity is established he or she will be given a Standard Acknowledgement Letter.

The process of obtaining a Standard Acknowledgement Letter may take several weeks and involve a number of visits. To enable a person without this form to claim benefits another, interim document is usually issued. This is called a GEN32.

An asylum-seeker and his or her family will also be fingerprinted in the Asylum Screening Unit.

After a person's identity has been established and he or she has been fingerprinted, a Political Asylum Questionnaire will be issued. The asylum-seeker has four weeks in which to complete it and return it to the Home Office. From then onwards the case is dealt with by the Asylum Casework Section, located in Croydon.

Applying Overseas

In rare cases endangered people may apply overseas for permission to come to the UK. This may be for several reasons:

1. The person may be part of a Government resettlement programme for a certain number of refugees from one particular country. Such people are known as quota or programme refugees. In the past the British Government has accepted quotas of Chilean and Vietnamese programme refugees. These were all people who had been given refugee status abroad, and were accepted for resettlement in Britain. Chilean and Vietnamese programme refugees had the same entitlements as other people with refugee status.

In 1992 the British Government agreed to accepted a quota of 1,000 Bosnian men who had been interned in concentration camps. These men were allowed to bring their families with them, and were to be housed in reception centres run by the Refugee Council and the British Red Cross. Although the reception arrangements made for this group were very similar to those made for Vietnamese, this group were not, in strict legal terms, programme refugees. They did not have full refugee status; instead they were issued with visas which gave them one year's leave to enter Britain.

2. The person has close family already in the UK. If this is so he or she can apply for family reunion. Whether this is granted or not depends on the immigration status of the family in UK.

A person granted full refugee status is entitled to be joined by his or her spouse plus children under 18. Those asylum-seekers granted exceptional leave to remain (ELR) do not have this right. Normally they have to wait until they have had ELR for four years, although the Home Office can grant family reunion to people with ELR for humanitarian reasons. Asylum-seekers have no right to family reunion.

Children and spouses are normally granted the same immigration status as the head of household.

Any other relative who wishes to join family in Britain will usually be treated under the normal immigration rules covering dependant relatives.

Decisions

After submitting a Political Asylum Questionnaire an asylum-seeker may be invited for interview in order to provide further information. They should take a solicitor or legal adviser with them. But the majority of asylum-seekers receive a decision based on the written evidence provided on the Political Asylum Questionnaire.

It is impossible to predict how long an asylum-seeker will have to wait for a decision. Some who lodged an application in 1993 are receiving rapid decisions on their cases — within a few months. Others who applied prior to this may face a long wait, often up to two years.

Where an asylum-seeker has dependants, the decision given to the principal applicant applies to the whole family. For example if a child's father is given full refugee status, this decision applies to a spouse and any dependant children.

If an asylum-seeker is judged to have 'a well-founded fear of being persecuted for reasons of race, religion, nationality, membership of a particular social group or political opinion' he or she will be granted full refugee status (1951 UN Convention Relating to the Status of Refugees).

But there is no international accepted definition of what constitutes a 'well-founded fear' of persecution. Instead the interpretation of the UN Convention varies between different countries. In order to try to overcome this subjectivity, the UNHCR has prepared a book describing the interpretation of the UN Convention, called the *Handbook on Procedure and Criteria for Determining Refugee Status*. Its principles are accepted by the Home Office.

To be granted refugee status a person has to show that he or she is likely to suffer persecution in the home country. There must be threats to life or freedom, or an accumulation of discriminations and dangers which amount to persecution. Someone granted refugee status must be endangered individually, although the reason for this may be their membership of a particular group. People are not normally given refugee status if they are fleeing a generally unstable or dangerous condition, for example if there is a civil war in their home country. The UN Convention does not recognise persecution on grounds of gender or sexuality, although some lawyers argue that lesbians and gay men form a social group. The Home

Office has not accepted these arguments, and has refused full refuge status to gay men from countries such as Cyprus, Iran and Argentina.

When a person is granted refugee status they have certain entitlements, which are outlined on page 26.

The Home Office has another immigration status which, since 1984, has been granted to a much larger proportion of asylum-seekers who are allowed to remain in Britain. This status is called 'exceptional leave to remain' (ELR). It is outside the provisions of the Immigration Rules and is granted at the discretion of the Home Secretary for 'humane and administrative reasons'. People — such as a gay man fleeing Iran — whose persecution falls outside the terms of the UN Convention are often granted ELR. People who are escaping civil war and for whom return would be dangerous are often granted ELR. The Home Office has also granted ELR to certain groups of people who are forced to stay in Britain because of changing events in their home country. Chinese citizens who entered the UK before 4 June 1989 (Tiannamen Square massacre) were given ELR as a group. ELR can also be given for personal and compassionate reasons.

ELR does not afford the same rights as full refugee status. It is not a permanent status, and has to be renewed at intervals, usually of one year, three years and three years. Although rare, there are cases of extensions to ELR being refused.

After seven years indefinite leave to remain in the UK may be granted (permanent settlement). A person with ELR is not entitled to UN travel documents, and does not have the same rights to family reunion and education.

Critics of British asylum policy argue that ELR is now being granted to people who would have been granted refugee status ten years ago. They argue that as ELR does not afford the same rights and that its widespread use is a deliberate deterrent measure.

Asylum-seekers may also have their case refused. They may be subjected to the fast track procedures described above, and refused. Asylum-seekers may be refused under Immigration Rule 180, because they have failed to attend an interview, or failed to provide additional evidence to support an asylum application. Asylum-seekers may also be refused on the basis of the information in their Political Asylum Questionnaires and subsequent interviews.

Those who are refused because their case is without foundation have very limited rights of appeal, described on page 24.

All other asylum-seekers have a right to appeal in UK. Those who have been posted a notice of refusal will have ten working days in which to inform the Appeal Adjudicator of notice of appeal. This appeal must usually be heard within 42 days. The appellant has a right to a full oral hearing by the Appeal Adjudicator.

If the appeal to the Appeal Adjudicator is unsuccessful, a person may be able to request leave to appeal on a point of law to an Immigration Appeals Tribunal, and ultimately to a Court of Appeal. At present a number of people are being denied the right to appeal to an Immigration Appeals Tribunal. Asylum appeals are difficult, and there are very strict time limits. Any asylum-seeker who has been refused should be referred to the Refugee Legal Centre or to an immigration lawyer immediately.

Little information exists on what happens to asylum-seekers who are refused refugee status or ELR. Some appeal, although at present very few people are winning their appeals. Others leave the UK voluntarily. Other people are issued with deportation orders by the police or, more usually, by the Home Office. In 1993 about 1,300 former asylum-seekers were deported. And some people 'disappear', joining a substantial number of other people living in Britain without the correct documentation. Demographers estimate that there are between 300,000 and 500,000 people living in Britain without the correct immigration documentation, including many children and young people.

Police Registration

Asylum-seekers, people with ELR and refugees may be required to register with the police if they are from non-Commonwealth countries and over the age of 16. A person should go to the Refugee Council or the Alien's Registration Office, 10 Lamb's Conduit Street, London WC1 if he or she lives in the Metropolitan Police Area, or to the main local police station if they live outside London. A person needs to take two passport sized photographs, a passport or other documents of identification, and a

APPLYING FOR ASYLUM

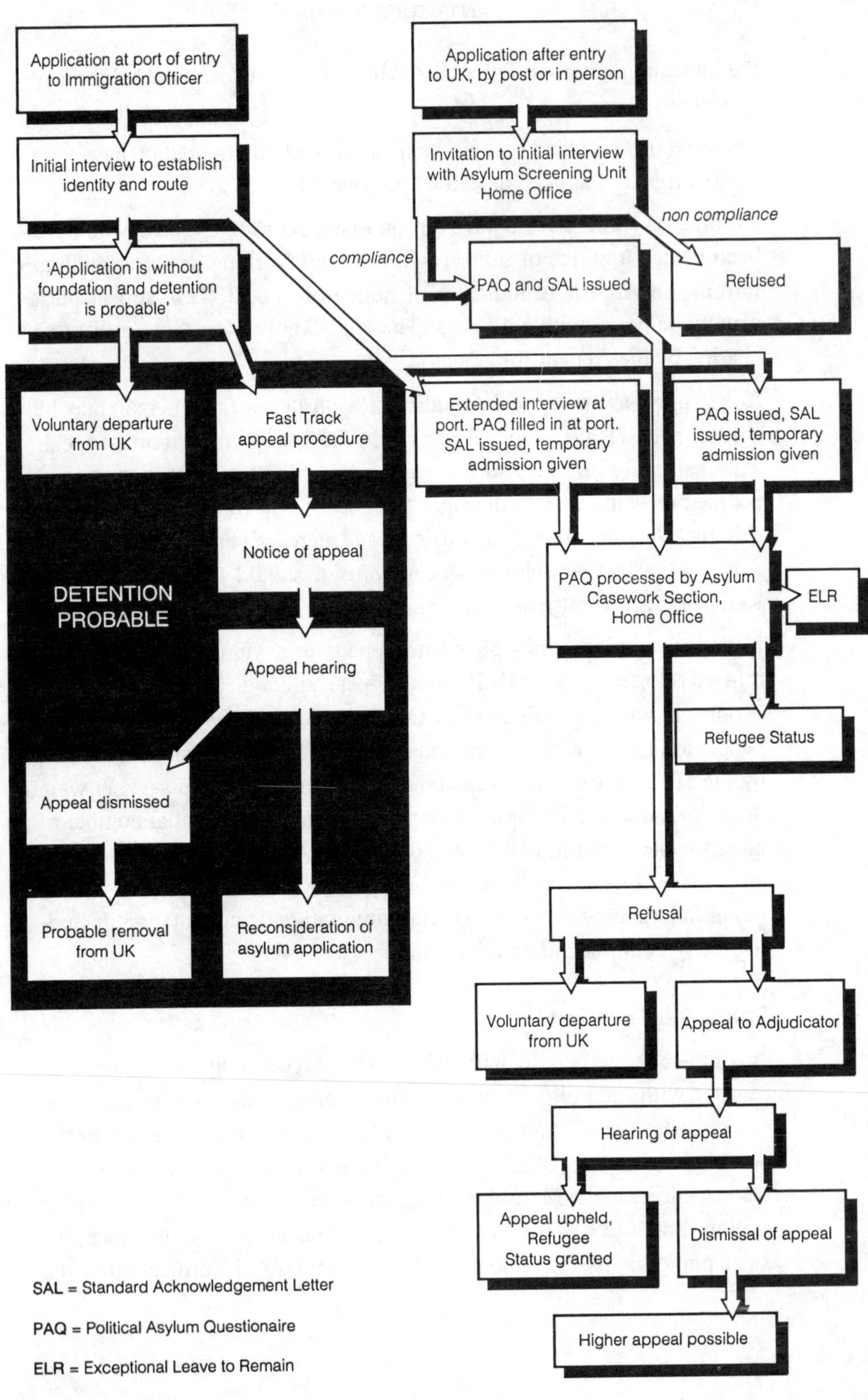

fee (currently £30). A Police Registration Certificate is then issued. The Refugee Council will refund this fee for those receiving income support.

Any changes in address, employment, marital status or other circumstances should be notified to the police. A person needs to inform the police in advance if he or she plans to be away from home for more than two months. Police registration lasts for as long as a person's leave to remain lasts.

When a person has the right of permanent residence in Britain, police registration is no longer needed.

☐ The Rights of Asylum-Seekers and Refugees

A person's immigration status may affect their rights in Britain, including educational rights. The following tables summarise a person's rights according to their immigration status.

	ASYLUM SEEKER	EXCEPTIONAL LEAVE TO REMAIN	REFUGEE STATUS
Rights To Stay	Until a decision is reached on the asylum application	Initially a person is given one year's ELR. This is renewed at intervals usually one, three and three years. After seven years a person with ELR can apply for permanent residence in Britain. It may take a long time for permanent residence to be granted. After one year of permanent residence a person may apply for British citizenship, providing other criteria are met.	A refugee is initially given four years leave to remain in Britain. After four years he or she can apply for permanent residence. After one year of permanent residence a refugee may apply for British citizenship, providing other criteria are met.
Overseas Travel	An asylum-seeker may not leave the UK until his or her case is determined.	People with ELR and refugee status are free to travel providing they have the correct documentation.	
Travel Documents		People with ELR are expected to maintain the validity of their own passports. If this is impossible the Home Office will sometimes issue a British travel document, providing the person can show that he or she made every attempt to renew their own passport.	People with refugee status are not permitted to travel on their national passports. Instead if a person wishes to travel he or she must apply for a UN Convention Travel Document (CTD). Giving the protection of UNHCR it offers the right to travel world-wide, apart from the refugee's country of origin. Holders of a CTD must comply with immigration and visa requirements of the countries to which they want to travel. A person wanting a CTD should apply to the Travel Document Section, Home Office, Lunar House, Wellesley Road, Croydon, enclosing the required fee, two passport sized photographs, any passport and a person's police registration certificate. There is usually a long wait before documents are issued.
Healthcare	Asylum-seekers, people with ELR and full refugees status are entitled to the same healthcare provision as other UK residents. Their entitlements are outlined in Health Circular (82) 15, circulated by the Department of Health.		

	ASYLUM SEEKER	EXCEPTIONAL LEAVE TO REMAIN	REFUGEE STATUS
Work	Asylum-seekers are initially not allowed to work or to participate in Government training schemes. After six months asylum-seekers may request permission to work from the Home Office. It then issues a form called GEN25 which states that person has permission to work.	People with ELR or refugee status have the same rights to work as any other British resident.	
Welfare Benefits	Asylum-seekers are entitled to a reduced rate of welfare benefits, currently 90 per cent of the adult personal allowance of income support, plus full child allowances and any applicable premium. Asylum-seekers are also entitled to Housing Benefit and loans from the Social Fund. A IS96 or GEN32 identification letter, or a Standard Acknowledgement Letter (SAL) is used to prove the asylum-seeker's status. But many Benefits Agency offices have adopted the practice of not paying benefit until a SAL is produced. This should be challenged. Asylum-seekers do not have to visit an Unemployment Benefits Office in order to 'sign on'. The rules concerning welfare benefits, particularly for young people, are very complicated. Asylum-seekers should also be briefed on the type of questions that the Benefits Agency might ask, as these can appear intrusive. Further information can be obtained from the Refugee Adviser's Handbook, or from specialist agencies listed in Part Three of this book.	People with ELR and refugee status can claim benefits in the normal way, under normal regulations. They are required to 'sign on' at a Unemployment Benefits Office.	

	ASYLUM SEEKER	EXCEPTIONAL LEAVE TO REMAIN	REFUGEE STATUS
Housing	Under the 1985 Housing Act local authorities have an obligation to house certain people who are deemed to be in priority need, and who are not intentionally homeless. A person is in priority need if he or she, or a member of his or her family has children under 16, or under 19 in full time education, or is pregnant, or is the victim of an emergency such as a fire, or is vulnerable due to old age, disability, illness or risks to that person's well-being. For asylum-seekers, however, the duties under the 1985 Housing Act have been modified. Local authorities no longer have a duty to provide accommodation where an asylum-seeker 'has, or has available any accommodation, however temporary, which it would be reasonable for him to occupy'. In future local authorities may refuse to deal with asylum-seekers until they are literally living on the streets. For asylum-seekers housed under the provisions of the 1985 Housing Act local authorities may now only provide temporary accommodation. When an asylum-seeker receives a positive decision on an asylum application, whether it is ELR or refugee status, the person has to submit a new application for housing.	There are no housing restrictions for people with ELR or refugee status.	
Education For Under 16s	Parents are obliged to send their children to school in Britain. The right to free education is irrespective of immigration status. The right to education for children with refugee status or ELR, and asylum-seekers under 16 is outlined in DES Circular 11/88 Annex B 'The Admission to County and Voluntary Schools of Children from Overseas'.		

	ASYLUM SEEKER	EXCEPTIONAL LEAVE TO REMAIN	REFUGEE STATUS
The Education of 16-18 Year-Old Students in the School Sector	Education is free for school students between the ages of 16 and 18 years, irrespective of immigration status. But between 16 and 18 students are only accepted into a school at the discretion of the head teacher and LEA.		
Fees in Further and Higher Education	An asylum-seeker is initially classified as an overseas student for fees (and awards). This means asylum-seekers may have to find considerable sums of money to pay for fees for full time courses. At the time of writing there is only one rate for fees for part time courses; no distinction is made between overseas and home students. Many asylum-seekers, therefore, enrol on part-time courses. A college is able to define what it means by part-time or full-time, but a part-time course cannot be more than 21 hours per week, excluding meal breaks and private study. The Department for Education may soon change part-time fee policy, introducing an overseas students rate. But colleges also have some discretion in fee policy. Some London colleges have waived the overseas student rate for asylum-seekers studying on basic ESL courses. After three years ordinary residence in UK an asylum-seeker becomes a home student. Residency starts on the date a person applies for political asylum. Other rules on residency are complex, but to be a home student an asylum-seeker must have been in the UK during the three years immediately preceding the course (1st September for a course starting in October, Ist January for a course stating in the spring term and 1st April for a course starting in the summer term).	People with ELR are also treated as home students for the purposes of applying for tuition fees at all levels of education.	Refugees are treated as home students for the purposes of applying for tuition fees at all levels of education.

	ASYLUM SEEKER	EXCEPTIONAL LEAVE TO REMAIN	REFUGEE STATUS
Grants for Further and Higher Education	An asylum-seeker has to fulfil three years ordinary residence in the UK before he or she is entitled to apply for a mandatory grant.	People with ELR must fulfil three years ordinary residency in the UK before they qualify for a mandatory maintenance grant. Eligibility for discretionary awards is determined by individual LEAs.	If accepted on a designated course a refugee is entitled to a mandatory maintenance grant. If a refugee is already studying before refugee status is granted he or she can apply to an LEA for a mandatory grant for subsequent terms. Refugees may also apply for discretionary awards. Some LEAs, however, require refugees to have lived in an area for a certain time before giving a discretionary award. A refugee also has the right to claim income support and study on a full-time ESL course for up to nine months, providing he or she starts the course within 12 months of arriving in the UK.

☐ Closing the Door in Britain

All western European countries have slowly stopped primary immigration. In Britain the first major restrictions placed on post-war immigration came with the passage of the 1962 Commonwealth Immigrants Act which introduced a work-voucher scheme for potential Commonwealth immigrants. Over the next twenty years further legislative barriers made primary immigration more and more difficult. Measures such as the 1971 Immigration Act and the 1981 British Nationality Act attracted wide criticism as discriminating against the Britain's black and ethnic minority communities. The Conservative Party now has a manifesto commitment to ending all primary immigration to Britain.

Until 1985 asylum-seekers and refugees faced few restrictions. But since then they have been increasingly viewed as another group of primary immigrants, and hence people to be kept out. Legislative and policy measures have been enacted to effect this aim. At the same time asylum-seekers have been attacked in the media and by politicians. Asylum-seekers are being labelled as 'bogus' before they have the chance to put their case.

This has undoubtedly contributed to increased racism and xenophobia, including violent attacks on refugees. Throughout Europe extreme right-wing parties have scapegoated refugees, using them as a way of gaining support. The attentions of the far right have often been prompted by a hostile media.

But the response to racism has not been to punish the offenders, but to blame the victims. Many politicians, too, are using the rise of racism as a means of justifying restrictive asylum policy. Good race relations, it is argued, depend on keeping down refugee numbers. New legislation is then introduced.

The British Government has developed a four-pronged approach in changing asylum policy, namely:

- barriers that prevent asylum-seekers arriving in Britain
- deterrent measures that make settlement in Britain more difficult
- a tightening of the criteria by which the Immigration and Nationality Department judges an asylum application, hence a greater chance that an asylum-seeker will be refused refugee status
- a democratic deficit in immigration and asylum practices, with greater importance being put on Immigration Rules, and on secretive attempts at the European harmonisation of asylum practices.

Barriers

The simplest way of keeping asylum-seekers out of any country is to impose a visa requirement for nationals of that country. For an endangered person this can present a formidable obstacle. To obtain a visa a valid passport is needed, but a passport may have to be sought from a government, often the very authority from which a person fears persecution. Even if an endangered person has a valid passport, obtaining a visa can be fraught with problems. The journey to the embassy may be perilous, and the visit may be interpreted as evidence of dissent. The customary wait for the issue of a visa may be dangerous in itself. A visa may also be refused.

Britain has repeatedly imposed visa requirements when refugee claims from a particular country have increased: on Sri Lankans in 1985, on Ghanaians in 1986, on Turkish nationals in 1989 on Ugandans in 1991 and on citizens of Bosnia-Hercegovina, Serbia, Macedonia and Montenegro in 1992.

As a result an endangered person must either try and board an aircraft without passport and visa, or obtain forged travel documents. In Bangkok, Madras, Ankara, Nairobi and other cities 'travel agents' extort money from desperate refugees, in return for tickets and forged travel documents. At the time of writing hundreds of young Tamil men are marooned in slum hotels in Bangkok waiting for their families to find money for forged documents.

Visa requirements have been coupled with the passage of the 1987 Immigration (Carriers' Liability) Act. This legislation fines airlines and other carriers £2,000 per passenger transported without the correct travel documents. It has resulted in airline staff taking over the responsibility for immigration control, without training or scrutiny.

Entry to UK can also be barred at the port. The crudest method of doing this is summary ejection. Potential asylum-seekers are excluded at the port of entry before they can make their asylum application. This contravenes international and national legislation, but such illegal expulsions happen. In 1989 over 100 Turkish Kurds were returned to Turkey before they could make asylum applications. Other cases never come to light.

The new 'fast track procedures', introduced in the 1993 Asylum and Immigration (Appeals) Act also mean that certain asylum-seekers are barred from entering Britain. Asylum-seekers whose cases are judged at a port of entry to be 'without foundation' can be refused and detained. Their rights of appeal are limited, and such a group may be removed from Britain within eight days of arrival. The main reason that asylum-seekers' applications are judged to be without foundation is that they have come from or travelled through a 'safe' third country. Asylum-seekers who change planes as transit passengers now find themselves being returned to their last port of call.

Deterrents

The British Government has also introduced legislative and policy changes which refugee agencies consider to be a deliberate attempt to deter potential asylum-seekers. The Refugee Council believes that the use of detention, the restriction of rights to welfare benefits, housing and education are deliberate deterrents targeted at asylum-seekers.

As described on page 16, asylum-seekers are liable to detention, in immigration detention centres, prisons and in police cells. Since the passage of the 1993 Asylum and Immigration (Appeals) Act the number of detainees has doubled. Certain nationalities — at the moment Zaireans and Ghanaians — appear to be more at risk of detention.

Some detainees may have been imprisoned in their home countries. For such a group detention is a time of great anxiety. People suffer flashbacks, reminding them of their original imprisonment. The fear of return is great.

The unnecessary trauma caused by detention has been highlighted by Stephen Tumin, HM Inspector of Prisons. There have been four suicides since 1990. Self-harm and hunger strikes are regular occurrences.

Asylum-seekers face income support restrictions: they may only claim 90 per cent of the personal allowances of income support. This discriminatory measure causes great hardship for many newly-arrived people. Asylum-seekers' rights to public housing have also been limited by the 1993 Asylum and Immigration (Appeals) Act. Asylum-seekers and people with ELR also have reduced rights to further and higher education.

Deterrent measures do not prevent desperate people from fleeing — the European Commission has recently described deterrent measures as unworkable (*Communication on Asylum and Immigration*, February 1994). But deterrent measures do make the lives of asylum-seekers already in the UK much more difficult. They prevent them from rebuilding their lives and integrating into British society.

The Tightening of Substantive Criteria

To be deemed a refugee a person has to prove that he or she 'has a well-founded fear of being persecuted for reasons of race, religion, nationality, membership of a particular social group or political opinion' (1951 UN Convention Relating to the Status of Refugees). But there are no internationally agreed standards for deciding who falls within the UN definition. Instead individual governments choose their own criteria. This varies from country to country, and depends on policies made by politicians. A country's criteria for determining asylum may also be secret.

Since the mid-1980s the criteria for gaining full refugee status has tightened across western Europe. Proportionally fewer asylum-seekers are now granted full refugee status, and many more are refused. In 1982 59 per cent of asylum-seekers received full refugee status. During the last half of 1993, only 5 per cent of asylum-seekers received full refugee status.

Categories of decisions, by percentage, 1982-1993

Year	Refugee Status	ELR	Refusal
1982	59	12	31
1983	40	32	28
1984	33	39	28
1985	24	57	19
1986	14	68	18
1987	13	64	23
1988	25	60	15
1989	31	59	10
1990	26	63	11
1991	9	40	51
1992	3	44	53
1993	7	48	46
1993 second half of year	5	18	77

Source: Home Office

☐ The 1993 Asylum and Immigration (Appeals) Act: What It Means for Asylum-Seekers

The Asylum and Immigration (Appeals) Act received Royal Assent on 1 July 1993, and became fully operational on 26 July 1993. Already the Act's provisions have resulted in a greater number of people being rejected on 'safe third country grounds' usually at the port of entry, an increased use of detention, and an increased number of asylum-seekers being refused public housing.

References are made to

The Act's Sections
The Act's Schedules
The Asylum Act Procedure Rules
The Immigration Rules

Section One and **Section Two** of the Asylum and Immigration (Appeals) Act incorporates the 1951 UN Convention and 1967 Protocol Relating to the Status of Refugees into primary legislation. This is welcomed by lawyers as it means that the application of asylum legislation can be challenged in the courts in the light of the Convention.

Section Three requires that all asylum-seekers be fingerprinted, including children. No lower age limit has been specified. Failure to provide fingerprints may lead to refusal of asylum. Fingerprint records will be destroyed within one month of a grant of permanent residence in Britain.

Section Four and **Section Five** limit an asylum-seeker's access to public housing. Previous to July 1993 asylum-seekers had the same rights as other people to local authority permanent accommodation if they were deemed to be homeless and in 'priority need' categories as defined by the 1985 Housing Act. Those in priority need are pregnant women, families with children under 16 or under 19 in full time education, and those who are vulnerable because of age, illness or disability. The Asylum and Immigration (Appeals) Act modifies this legislation and reduces local authority responsibilities to homeless asylum-seekers.

Local authorities are obliged to make enquiries about an applicant's immigration status if they have reason to believe he or she is an asylum-seeker.

Asylum-seekers will now not be accepted as homeless if they have any accommodation available, however temporary, which is judged reasonable for them to occupy.

Asylum-seekers accepted as homeless may only be given temporary accommodation.

Once a positive decision on the asylum application is made, the refugee must begin a new homelessness application.

Sections Four and Five of the Asylum and Immigration (Appeals) Act have profound implications for the well-being of children. Asylum-seekers and their families are now more likely to be housed in temporary accommodation, will spend greater periods of time in temporary accommodation, and are more likely to end up in sub-standard private rented housing. Children growing up in bed and breakfast hotels — the usual form of temporary local authority accommodation — are geographically mobile, find it difficult to do homework and may have specific health problems caused by over-crowding.

Local authorities need not discriminate, but Sections Four and Five of the Asylum and Immigration (Appeals) Act gives them the option to do so. In times when public housing is in short supply it is an option that may well be taken.

Section Six is targeted at those who entered Britain with a student's visa, a visitor's visa or other forms of leave to remain. If that person applies for asylum and is refused, his/her existing leave to remain (on the previous visa) may be curtailed. That person may be detained pending deportation. This section also extends powers to detain asylum-seekers who made their claim 'in country'.

Section Seven and **Section Eight** extend and change the appeal system. All asylum-seekers are now given the right of appeal against refusal of their asylum application, or variation of their leave to remain. The appellant has the right to a full oral hearing, in the first instance to a Special Adjudicator. An appeal against the Special Adjudicator's decision may be made to an Immigration Appeals Tribunal on a point of law. The asylum-seeker will also be able to appeal to a Court of Appeal against a decision by the Immigration Appeal Tribunal.

The Asylum (Appeals) Procedure Rules state the time limits on lodging an application for appeal, and time limits for receiving a decision. For those refused, and given the decision in person the time limit is two days. Most people who are given notice in person are detainees. Those given postal notification of a refusal have ten days in which to lodge notice of appeal.

The appeal hearing will normally be completed within 42 days, and the written determination issued within another five days.

These time limits make it very difficult for asylum-seekers to find legal representation, an interpreter if needed, and to prepare their cases. The Asylum (Appeals) Procedure rules give the strictest time limit to detainees, whose access to advice is the most problematic.

One class of asylum-seeker has no rights of appeal against the Special Adjudicator's decision — these are cases judged to be 'without foundation' because they do not 'raise any issue as to the UK's obligations under the UN Convention' or are 'frivolous' or 'vexatious'. This group are likely to be detained, given notice in person and have only two days in which to find legal representation. Their appeal has to be heard within five days of notice of appeal.

Section Nine and **Section Ten** remove the present right of appeal against the refusal of a visa or prior entry clearance. Before July 1993 those who were refused leave to enter at a British Consulate had the right of appeal. In 1991 some 1,495 out of 8,010 appeals were successful. These two sections discriminate against Britain's ethnic minority communities including refugees, who are more likely to have relatives overseas who might wish to visit the UK.

Section Eleven extends the 1987 Immigration (Carriers' Liability) Act to cover transit passengers. It requires those who wish to pass through Britain *en route* to another country to hold a valid visa for entry to that country.

Changes in the **Immigration Rules** announced in July 1993 are likely to increase an asylum-seeker's chances of being refused. Immigration Rules are statutory instruments attached to immigration law. They decide in practice whether and how a person can enter or stay in the UK. The 1971 Immigration Act gave the Home Secretary the power to make and change Immigration Rules without needing to change the law. Changes are simply presented to Parliament, which may or may not debate them. Parliament cannot amend Immigration Rules, but can only accept or reject them.

Under the new changes in the Immigration Rules an asylum application may be refused and that person removed without examining the substance of the asylum application:

> if the asylum-seeker arrived from a safe third country in which the applicant has had the opportunity to make contact there with that country's authorities to seek protection'
>
> and if the asylum applicant is part of a group whose claims are not related to the criteria for refugee status under the terms of the UN Convention.

Under the Immigration Rules an asylum application may be refused if the asylum-seeker:

> has failed to make a prompt and full disclosure of material facts
>
> has failed to apply forthwith on arrival
>
> has made 'false representations'
>
> has destroyed, damaged or disposed of passports or travel documents
>
> has engaged in activities in the UK after application inconsistent with his previous beliefs and behaviour, and calculated to create or enhance his claims for refugee status
>
> if the applicant could have moved to a part of his or her country in which he does not fear persecution, to which it would be reasonable to expect him or her to go.

The changes in the Immigration Rules present a series of traps into which asylum-seekers could fall. Asylum-seekers might not understand all the 'material factors'. Many asylum-seekers can only escape persecution by using false documents, and are often advised to destroy them. No-one knows on what basis the Home Office will make judgements about the safety of other parts of an asylum-seeker's country. The net result of the Immigration Rule changes is that a greater proportion of asylum-seekers will be refused.

Those monitoring the Asylum and Immigration (Appeals) Act have noted a sharp increase in the proportions of asylum-seekers being detained, an increase in those refused local authority accommodation, and an increase in the proportions of asylum-seekers refused refugee status or ELR.

☐ Fortress Europe

Within Europe the steady rise in the number of people seeking asylum, coupled with the impending abolition of the EU's internal borders, has prompted a vigorous political debate on refugee policy. A harmonised approach is emerging. But there are concerns that the harmonisation of policy is reducing the rights of asylum-seekers and refugees, and preventing desperate people from finding sanctuary in Europe.

Individual EU member states are changing national legislation, with countries copying one another's restrictive practices. The process of harmonisation is being speeded up by the workings of two groups: the Schengen Group and the Steering Group on Immigration and Asylum (formerly the Ad Hoc Group on Immigration).

The Schengen Group comprises ministers and civil servants from all EU countries apart from Britain, Denmark and Ireland. The Steering Group on Immigration and Asylum represents all twelve EU member states. But neither of these groups are European Community institutions. Instead they are secretive fora, and not subject to parliamentary scrutiny. Both groups represent an attempt to by-pass the European Parliament's democratic processes. They are part of the 'third pillar' of the European Union.

The Schengen Group has signed a treaty known as the Schengen Agreement. When implemented in 1994 the Schengen Agreement will provide for:

the increased policing of external borders

harmonisation of national visa policies

harmonisation of carrier sanctions

rules by which asylum-seekers will have one chance of applying for asylum in Schengen state

a uniform Schengen visa

a computerised database called the Schengen Information System holding information on criminals, asylum-seekers and visitors to Schengen states.

The Steering Group on Immigration and Asylum has an agenda which is very similar to the Schengen Group. It currently has five working parties on migration, asylum, visas, external frontiers and forged documents.

The Steering Group on Immigration and Asylum and has signed one treaty — the 1990 Dublin Convention — and is working on further treaties and policy agreements. These are described below.

1. The Dublin Convention. This determines which EU state is responsible for hearing an asylum application. Like the Schengen Agreement it means that an asylum-seeker can only have his or her case heard in one EU member state.
2. The Treaty on the Crossing of External Borders. This has been drafted but not signed. It is likely that this treaty will result in tighter security on the EU's external borders, a common visa policy, and a common carrier's sanctions system. It may also result in the introduction of a shared security database.
3. A harmonised system of dealing with asylum cases judged to be unfounded. It is likely that most EU countries will introduce fast track procedures for dealing with such cases. Most asylum-seekers who have travelled through safe third countries will be rejected. The Steering Group on Immigration and Asylum is currently trying to define what is meant by a 'safe third country'.

4. Harmonisation of the substantive criteria of asylum. EU member states will attempt to harmonise what they interpret as 'a well founded fear of being persecuted'.
5. The development of asylum and immigration agreements with non-EU states such as Canada, Austria, Sweden, Poland and the Czech Republic, thus extending 'fortress Europe'.
6. The Centre for Information, Discussion and Exchange on Asylum (CIREA). This is organisation is part of the Steering Group on Immigration and Asylum. It holds human rights data on refugees' countries of origin. It is intended that this information will be used to judge asylum applications.
7. The Centre for Information, Discussion and Exchange on the Crossing of Borders and Immigration (CIREFI). This organisation is also part of the Steering Group on Immigration and Asylum. It will hold data on asylum-seekers and visitors to the EU.

European Community or European Union Policy?

The European Union is founded on three pillars: the European Community institutions, common foreign and security policy and common justice and home affairs policy.

The central core pillar comprises of what is now known as the European Community (EC). The European Commission and the European Parliament are EC institutions. The term European Community correctly describes actions undertaken within this pillar.

The central pillar of the European Community is flanked by the pillar of common foreign and security policy, and the pillar on co-operation in the fields of justice and home affairs. These two pillars exist outside the formal framework of the European Community. Actions taken are, therefore, not subject to European Community law. In summary these two pillars provide for intergovernmental co-operation.

In the past asylum policy has been determined by intergovernmental co-operation. Under the terms of the treaty of Maastricht asylum policy will continue to be an intergovernmental matter. It will become part of the third pillar of the European Union. There are, however, provisions within the treaty of Maastricht (Article K9), which allow for asylum policy to be transferred to the European Community. This would make for greater judicial and parliamentary supervision and democracy. But the current trend is to resist democracy; it is easier to determine asylum policy in secret.

Most refugee and human rights agencies believe that European governments and the Steering Group on Immigration and Asylum are cutting a broad swathe through the humanitarian principals of the 1951 UN Convention Relating to the Status of Refugees. Genuine asylum-seekers are being prevented from reaching safety. Europe is host to just seven per cent of the world's refugees. If affluent nations cannot share responsibility for victims of conflict and human rights abuse, one cannot expect the world's poorest nations to continue to provide sanctuary to refugees.

PART TWO
Refugees in Schools

Chapter Three

Towards an Education Policy for Refugee Students

☐ A Legacy of Policies

In March 1994 there were an estimated 21,500 refugee children in Greater London schools and a further 2,000 in schools outside the capital (Refugee Council, 1994). The largest communities were Somalis, Sri Lankan Tamils, Zaireans and Turkish Kurds. But Britain has no written central government policy for the settlement of these refugees. Only three local authorities have a refugee policy covering issues such as housing, education and social services. Most refugee students have arrived at a time of great change within the education system, when there is no overall consensus on supporting students from ethnic minority groups. A legacy of past beliefs is influencing present policy.

This chapter outlines Britain's historical responses to refugees within the education system. It examines other social and political factors which can influence a refugee student's educational achievement and to which schools and LEAs must respond and, finally, it sets out a positive educational framework for supporting refugee students.

Assimilation

Today's Zairean and Kurdish students are the latest in a long line of migrants and refugees to have entered British schools. Britain has had a refugee presence for over 700 years, since Armenians fled from the Ottoman Empire and settled here. During the latter part of the 17th century over 100,000 French Huguenot refugees sought sanctuary in southern England. Between 1880 and 1914 some 200,000 Jewish refugees from eastern Europe fled to Britain. Although separated by 200 years, the educational response to Huguenots and eastern European Jews was very similar: from 1680 until 1970 the policies adopted towards refugees and migrants were assimilationalist. Teachers aimed to make 'little Englishmen' out of refugees and migrants as quickly as possible. The Jewish Free School, first established in London's East End, had the stated aim of rapidly integrating Jewish students into British society. Students were discouraged from speaking Yiddish. Teachers concentrated on basic English literacy.

Such policies continued until the late 1960s. The educational response to children from eastern Europe and, indeed, from the Indian subcontinent, was to provide resources to teach English as a second language. The 1966 Local Government Act provided a special fund — Section 11 — targeted at groups whose language and culture was significantly different from the rest of the community (and initially only New Commonwealth immigrants). Over 80 per cent of Section 11 funding is still used to fund ESL projects.

Multiculturalism

In the mid-1960s assimilationist policies became increasingly unpopular. Racial prejudice made the assimilation of visible minorities an impossibility, even had the new arrivals considered rapid assimilation desirable. Migrants from the Indian subcontinent and, later, Ugandan Asian refugees fully intended to maintain their languages and cultures in Britain. Research revealed that bilingual children performed better in schools where there was bilingual teaching and/or bilingual resources. Students preferred schools and teachers who valued their home culture. The assimilist model gave way to multiculturalism.

Multicultural education aimed to celebrate linguistic and cultural diversity. There were two distinct goals: to improve provision for children from ethnic minority groups and to prepare children from the majority community for life in a multi-ethnic society (Swann, 1985). Schools began to use bilingual resources and to celebrate Muslim, Jewish and Hindu festivals as well as Christmas. Advisory teachers in multicultural education were appointed. The Swann Report (1985) marks a point at which multicultural education policies had maximum impact, and describes many good practices in multicultural education. Nevertheless it drew much criticism, most of all for identifying racism in society and schools as a major determinant of students' attainment.

Anti-racism

From the mid-1970s multiculturalist education policies began to be censured as no more than a liberal response to a deep-rooted problem in British society, namely racism. Multicultural education did little to counter the underachievement of some students, particularly African-Caribbean boys, nor did it acknowledge the many manifestations of racism in British society. Schools and LEAs began to develop policies which aimed to confront racism and promote equality of opportunity. Such policies covered the following issues:

The curriculum: Does it reflect the experiences and needs of minority groups? Is it a truly multicultural curriculum or does it represent minority groups in a stereotyped manner?

School resources: Do they show positive representations of all sectors of society?

Racist incidents: How do schools deal with racist incidents, both inside the school and outside?

Streaming and setting: Are all minority groups equally represented in all streams and sets?

Discipline: Are some groups more likely to be excluded from school?

Labelling: What assumptions are made about students from different groups? Do schools label them? What expectations do teachers have of them?

Teachers from ethnic minority groups: How are they recruited? Do they have equal promotion prospects?

A large number of LEAs and schools paid lip-service to anti-racist education but only a small number of schools had good policies which were implemented, monitored — and worked.

Anti-racist education was controversial, soon becoming associated with socialism rather than good educational practice. Within schools it generated a good deal of hostility, as teachers were asked to examine their own attitudes and assumptions. And because anti-racist education challenged many of the values of the establishment it began to attract the attention of the New Right.

Dismantling Anti-Racism and Multiculturalism

At the very time that the greatest numbers of refugee students were being admitted to British schools (1989-1992), central government was engaged in making sweeping changes in the education system and challenging many of the progressive education policies introduced in the previous 25 years. Not only equal opportunities policies but child centred education are being challenged by a government intent on going 'back to basics'.

The educational changes brought in by the 1988 Education Reform Act have put huge demands on teachers' time and energy. The pressure renders many schools unable to respond fully to the needs of refugee students: they do not have the time to develop imaginative policies to support them. This factor, more even than cuts in public expenditure or ideological challenges, means that refugee students' educational needs may not be met.

Successive Conservative governments have also diminished the power of local government. The 1988 Education Reform Act changed the way in which schools administered their budgets. Under the Local Management of Schools (LMS), headteachers and governors have much more control over their monies. The Education Reform Act also brought in grant-maintained status (GMS), whereby schools opting out of LEA control receive their money from central government. They can choose whether to buy into LEA services such as ESL support, teachers' centres and multicultural education teams. Many on the right of the Conservative party envisaged a system where all schools would opt out. LEAs would wither and die, and along with them all the multicultural and anti-racist advisers. At time of writing however, the drying up of cash incentives to opt out has halted what was in any event a generally small shift to GMS.

Cuts in public expenditure have reduced the power of local government to generate progressive policies. When an LEA makes budget cuts the first to go are advisory teachers and teachers' centres, as they are perceived as a luxury. ESL teachers are next to go, as many LEAs do not perceive them as being part of the mainstream, statutory service and have to contibute more towards their salaries than the 25% originally required by the 1966 Local Government Act.

Central government has also challenged the multicultural consensus, prompted by lobbying from the New Right. Politicians and academics such as Roger Scruton have been adept at using the media to castigate anti-racist education.

The National Curriculum prescribes much of what is taught in school and is arguably more Eurocentric than the previous curricula of schools. It places greater stress on assimilation and on a single 'British' culture and allows less scope for teaching about the achievements of African and Asian peoples. Minority languages such as Hindi, Panjabi and Farsi are no longer classified as 'modern foreign languages' to be taught as part of the National Curriculum but can only be offered as a second foreign language.

The New Right has also lobbied for the dismantling of teacher education institutions, which they see as the power-base of progressive ideas. Greater emphasis has been put on classroom-based training and much less on theory. There is therefore less time to read and reflect upon anti-racist policies or to develop new ideas and resources.

Good multicultural and anti-racist education still survives in certain schools, often carried forward by older teachers. But as a progressive and evolving philosophy anti-racist education has been dealt a severe blow. Most refugee children have arrived in Britain at a time when there is an attack on the very policies intended to support them. If refugee students are to be supported in the long term it is essential that those committed to anti-racist and multicultural education sharpen their response to the changes of the last ten years.

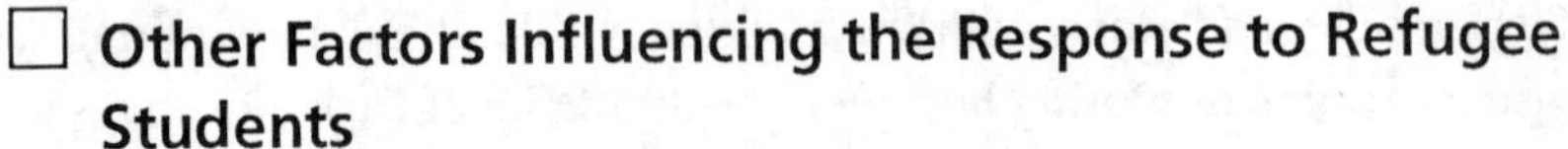

Other Factors Influencing the Response to Refugee Students

A Diversity of Needs

Refugee students are a heterogeneous group so have no single educational need. They come from many different countries and, within those countries, come from different ethnic groups and have different class origins. Refugee children have different educational backgrounds; some may not have attended school at all and others might even have attended English medium schools in their home countries.

Children and their families will have different experiences of persecution, and of flight to Britain. This will affect how they come to terms with loss and trauma. Furthermore, refugees have many different experiences in their life in Britain. Students have a diversity of needs which can be very difficult to meet. LEAs and schools, therefore, need flexible policies to be able to respond to the needs of their refugee students.

Demography

Of the 23,500 refugee children in British schools, some 85 per cent are estimated to be living in Greater London. More refugees live in the inner London boroughs, but most outer London LEAs have an average of 400 children. In many parts of London and outside there are likely to be small numbers of refugee children in each school. They may or may not be visible and if there are only a few, their needs might be treated by the school as of low priority.

Implications of the Government's Refugee Policy

The numerous recent legislative and policy changes targeted at asylum-seekers and refugees are described in detail in Chapter Two. Many of these changes place great stress on asylum-seekers and refugees, and make it more difficult for them to integrate into British society. In particular social security and housing restrictions place great stress on refugee children.

Asylum-seekers are entitled to only 90 per cent of the personal allowances of income support. They are prevented from seeking employment during their first six months in Britain. As a result, many newly arrived asylum-seekers are having to cope on a very low income, without household basics. Children from poor families suffer more stress and are less likely to be effective learners. Schools must develop policies to support children living in poverty.

The 1993 Asylum and (Immigration Appeals) Act has also restricted asylum-seekers' access to public housing. Asylum-seekers and their families are now more likely to spend protracted periods in temporary accommodation such as bed and breakfast hotels, and are rendered more geographically mobile. Children in temporary accommodation are more likely to underachieve at school and to have an interrupted education. Schools have yet to develop policies to support homeless children but education is essential to their future.

Checklist of Common Problems Experienced by Refugee Students

The problems encountered by refugee students are very diverse and cannot always be generalised. Some problems do, however, occur more frequently. Among the issues reported to the Refugee Council are:

- problems securing a school place
- schools which do not accept documentation given by a family
- problems settling into a new school
- educational problems caused by bad housing
- withdrawn behaviour
- aggressive behaviour
- lack of concentration
- bullying, often with a racist motive
- refugee children feeling that they are dismissively labelled by teachers
- lack of ESL support, particularly for Stage Three and Four Language learners.

The legislative and policy changes introduced in the past ten years have been accompanied by a media campaign of vilification of refugees. Articles have appeared in some right-wing newspapers accusing refugees of being economic migrants wishing to exploit the welfare system in Britain. Such pejorative articles appear to increase hostility to refugees (MORI, 1991). Local authorities, who reflect much of public opinion, may be less likely to invest scarce resources in projects to support unpopular groups such as refugees.

☐ Establishing a Positive Educational Framework

There are undoubtedly many factors which are causing refugee students to underachieve in schools. But there are also many examples of good educational provision. The Refugee Council services a working group called the All London Steering Group on Refugee Education, made up of teachers, advisers, inspectors and education officers. The group has been meeting for three years to exchange information about refugee issues and good educational practice and to lobby for resources for refugee students in schools. The Refugee Council and the All London Steering Group encourage specific practices to be implemented by central government, local government and schools. They are as follows:

1. Just asylum policies which live up to Britain's commitment to the 1951 UN Convention and 1967 Protocol Relating to the Status of Refugees.
2. Adequate funding from central government to meet the settlement and educational needs of refugee children and families. Funding is particularly needed for public sector housing and ESL support.
3. Central and local government policies for the settlement of refugees, encompassing housing policy, social services, healthcare, education and funding for non-governmental organisations. Local authorities should be encouraged to form cross-departmental working groups to ensure that the needs of refugees are met.
4. School policies for supporting refugee students which draw on past experiences of working with children from ethnic minority groups, promoting anti-racist and multicultural education, and working with homeless children.

5. In-service training for teachers and support staff on refugees and their educational needs.
6. Induction practice which makes new schools welcoming for refugee students.
7. Good pastoral care and counselling for refugee students who may have suffered traumatic experiences in their home countries and stressful events in Britain.
8. Good quality ESL provision in schools.
9. Schools that teach about human rights and the refugee experience, thus preparing all students for life in a multi-ethnic democracy.
10. School and LEA policies which enable refugee children to maintain and develop their first language. Such policies should include the funding and support of refugee community supplementary schools. Where large communities live in one area, schools and LEAs could

Eritrean refugee children in Sweden were interviewed about what they found liked about their school. They cited.

- Teachers who made some adjustment to their teaching methods, recognising that refugee children's past experiences were of a more formal education system.
- Teachers with clear and high expectations.
- Teachers who asked them about themselves.
- Teachers who made an effort to include refugee children's experiences in the curriculum.
- Teachers who took racism seriously.
- Schools which invited in members of refugee community organisations.
- Teachers who came to special cultural occasions held by refugee communities.

(Melzak and Warner (1992) *Integrating Refugee Children into Schools.*)

employ peripatetic teachers of refugee languages and enable students to study their mother tongue during school hours.

11. Schools should engage in positive home/school liaison and should improve links with local community organisations.

Some of these ideas are explored or illustrated in the case studies and the subsequent chapters in this book.

☐ Case Study

Anson Primary School, Brent

Anson Primary School in the London Borough of Brent has a newly-opened nursery unit attached. In 1993 there were some 54 refugee students in the school, mostly from Iran, Iraq, Somalia and Afghanistan. Some 34 different home languages are spoken by the children attending Anson Primary School and refugee students make up about 20 per cent of the total roll.

Two factors have contributed to the high proportion of refugee students. For one thing, the school is perceived as being supportive to refugee children and information about the school is passed by word of mouth — so some refugee children are travelling long distances to attend the school. Secondly, there is much private rented and bed and breakfast accommodation near the school and many children attending the school, not all of them refugees, are living in temporary accommodation. In 1992 some 154 children entered the school (excluding those starting their first year) and some 156 children were taken off roll.

The numbers of refugee children began to increase in 1989. Staff at the school noticed that many refugee parents sat in the school playground. They invited the parents into the school and learned more about their experiences, needs and aspirations. Some parents then offered their services as classroom assistants, particularly as story-tellers.

Anson School became concerned about what was happening in the school playground. Before 1991 it consisted of a large area of tarmac, often the arena for boisterous games. Some children felt very insecure in the playground and hated breaktime. It was decided that it should be redesigned and the school applied for funding. An urban aid grant of some

£84,000 was secured and the playground was redesigned so that children had many small places where they could play and sit.

At the same time, the school appointed a play worker whom they paid out of local sources of funding. Her job was to use play to help new students settle into class. Working from 8.15am to 17.15pm, she had a chance to talk to all the pupils while working in small groups. During class time she took small groups out of class and played games with them. At lunchtime she organised indoor games and arts and crafts with children who wished to stay inside and from 15.20pm she ran an after school club, for which parents were charged £1 per hour.

The play worker's project has been evaluated by the Department of Education, University of Aberdeen, and found to be effective. In particular, refugee children settle down more rapidly. They also learned to play again, a skill which can be lost during persecution and flight. Unfortunately funding for the playworker's post has now ceased and she is now employed only part-time as a welfare assistant and playworker.

Children who arrive mid-term are assigned a befriender, another child who takes them around the school during the first few days. Children receive a map of the school. The rest of the class is also told about where new refugee pupils come from. The school also tries to meet parents and introduce them to other families when they come to collect their children. There is a written induction policy and all staff have received in-service training about refugee children.

Betty Davies, the head teacher, has recently been appointed as a Primary Inspector with responsibility for Travellers and refugees. She works with the Travellers and Displaced Persons Team, a unit which supports refugee children in schools and provides in-service training and a newsletter for teachers in Brent.

Anson School has one of the highest proportions of refugee and homeless students of any primary school in Britain. In most other schools resources, and the number of refugee students, would not permit the employment of a playworker to help newly arrived children settle into a new environment. But schools and LEAs could consider employing peripatetic playworkers, shared between a consortium of schools. And many more schools could look at the design of their playgrounds and ensure that there are quiet places that children can be in during breaktime.

□ Case Study

Hampstead School

Hampstead School is a comprehensive school in North London. About half its students are bilingual, and nearly one in ten is a refugee. Many of the refugee students are from Eritrea and Somalia, and among them are 15 unaccompanied refugee children. Until 1989 the school had not considered the special needs of refugee students. Then a Somali student at this school became seriously ill, and teachers were later told that her illness was caused by stress and malnutrition. As a result of this the school began to re-examine how it supported refugee children. Through the hard work of a small group of teachers, Hampstead School has formulated a broad-based policy to support refugee students.

The Tavistock Clinic, an organisation that offers individual and family therapy within the national health service, was invited to work in the school. Two child psychotherapists visited Hampstead School, and formulated a programme to support refugee students. All teachers in the school have received some in-service training on refugee issues, and how to support traumatised refugee children. The Tavistock Clinic facilitates group counselling sessions, which run in the school. One group is exclusively for girls, other groups are organised for students of different ages. The group counselling was initially reserved for refugee students, but today group counselling is available to any student who is finding it difficult to cope.

Any refugee student who cannot cope with group counselling is offered individual counselling at the Tavistock Clinic. A child psychotherapist also visits Hampstead School every month, to meet with teachers who have concerns about individual students. The teachers can then discuss with the psychotherapist these worries and can formulate strategies to support such students.

The school also makes use of the services of an advisory teacher employed by Camden LEA. She visits the school every week to see refugee students who have particular social or educational needs. If a child's family have problems with housing, for example, she will try and sort this out.

Hampstead School has also pioneered other ways to support refugee students. Since many of the refugees have just arrived in Britain, Hampstead School has established a fund called The Children of the Storm to enable refugee children to buy clothes and other essentials. Sixth form students have been involved in raising money for the new charity, and the level of awareness about the needs of refugee students is very high among Hampstead's sixth form.

The induction programme for new student has been modified. The school employs three ESL teachers, who provide support to refugee students in the classroom. Pressure on these teachers in intense, and imminent educational cuts mean that extra resources for ESL teaching are unlikely. There are after-school English classes, and also a homework club for students who live in bed and breakfast hotels. Through subjects such as history, geography and English, all of Hampstead's students are taught about refugees, who they are and why they have come to Britain. Hampstead's curriculum also tackles issues such as human rights, racism, bullying and bereavement. Recently the school has formed a link with a school in Eritrea, and awareness has been raised about one of the countries of origin of refugee students through the link.

Hampstead School's broad-based approach to supporting refugee students is bearing fruit in the form of examination achievements. But the input from the Tavistock Clinic, albeit at no charge to the school, has been expensive. Resources would probably not permit such an input in other schools. But the model of providing group counselling could be replicated, as there are many schools in London where members of staff have validated counselling qualifications.

☐ Case Study

Waltham Forest LEA

Seven London LEAs are employing teachers whose specific job is to support refugee students. These posts are funded from a variety of sources, including central budgets and Section 210 of the 1988 Education Reform Act.

Waltham Forest is one LEA that employs 'refugee support teachers'. There are about 500 refugee children in Waltham Forest schools. The largest groups are Tamils, Somalis, Turkish Kurds and Zaireans. Two refugee support teachers are funded from the LEA's central budget. They are based at a teacher's centre and work alongside ESL support teachers funded by Section 11.

Waltham Forest is one of the few local authorities in Britain which has a refugee policy. This was formulated by a cross-departmental working group, including representatives from the education department. It identifies the work of the two refugee support teachers as being a priority.

The support teachers work in partnership with parents and mainstream teachers. They visit school by invitation and

— work with teaches to identify a child's needs

— give direct support to individual students and to classes

— suggest curriculum materials

— recommend strategies and resources for current and future needs

— visit families at home

— liaise with community organisations; provide in-service training for teachers and other staff

— make follow-up visits to monitor the progress of refugee children.

The work of the two teachers seems to be successful; refugee community organisations speak highly of them. Other LEAs are employing 'refugee support teachers' with a similar brief, and it is a model of good practice which is worth replicating.

Chapter Four

Welcoming newly arrived Refugees into Schools

All students who arrive after the start of the year need special induction procedures. Induction is designed to help them settle into a new school and become effective learners as quickly as possible. It aims to make the first crucial weeks in a new school a happy experience.

A good induction policy is particularly important for refugee children for several reasons. Firstly, almost all refugee children arrive in school mid-term. Secondly, they often come from countries where the education system is very different and schools may be differently organised. The style of teaching is usually more formal, laboratory practicals for example might be unknown. The range of subjects taught inthe home country might be different. Drama and learning through play might be quite new and not be perceived as educational. And, lastly, refugee children may have had their school life interrupted, because of war or unrest in their home countries.

Investing time in developing good induction policy is almost certainly cost effective, anticipating and preventing problems later. The following checklist is helpful for schools to examine their induction policy.

1. Do children and their parents have to attend interviews with the LEA before a child is admitted to a school and if so are interpreters provided?
2. Does your school use trained interpreters, if needed, when interviewing new students and their parents? How easy is it to obtain interpreters? Does the local authority have an interpreting and translating unit? If not could you lobby for one?
3. Who conducts the first interview with child and parents? Is the interviewer aware and sensitive to refugees' past experiences? Has he or she received any in-service training about refugee children? Is it always the same teacher who conducts the interviews?
4. Are parents shown around the school when their children are admitted? Do you explain to them about the subjects their child will study? Do you discuss possible differences in learning methods between the UK and the family's home country?
5. Does your school or local authority have literature prepared for parents, explaining about the British education system? Is it translated into the appropriate languages? If not, could such material be developed?
6. Do parents receive a welcome booklet explaining about the school's particular requirements and is it available in the relevant language? Is other key information similarly available?
7. Are parents informed of their rights to free school meals or uniform grants?
8. Do students receive any welcome materials such as a map of the local area, plan of the school, name of their class teacher and timetable. Is this material accessible to students who may speak little or no English?
9. Is the tutor group informed that they will be receiving a new arrival?
10. Is there a befriending system for newly arrived students in their first days? Are befrienders briefed for the job — making sure the new student knows where the toilets are, what to do about lunch, where to go for different lessons, and making sure they are introduced to the teachers and prompting them about instructions.

11. Are all the teachers concerned informed about a new students, via staff meetings or a noticeboard?
12. Are new students interviewed to assess their past educational experiences and future needs and interviewed also by an ESL teacher? How are each child's past experiences and current needs recorded?
13. Is the student's progress reassessed after a designated period of time, for example one month?
14. Can students who are not coping be withdrawn for small group tuition?

The final point, that of withdrawal of students, is controversial. During the 1960s and 1970s many bilingual children were withdrawn for English lesson in language centres or special classes within their school. Bilingual children missed important parts of the curriculum because of this practice, and also the opportunity to converse with classmates. The policy of withdrawal was later actively discouraged by most teachers committed to anti-racist education.

There may be some circumstances, however, where withdrawal to a small tutor group on the school site can be beneficial for newly-arrived refugee children. A minority are so traumatised and disorientated by recent experiences that they may be unable to cope in class. The Refugee Council believes that for such children withdrawal may be appropriate during the first few weeks in a new school, as part of an induction procedure.

☐ Case Study

George Orwell School

George Orwell School is a mixed comprehensive school in the London Borough of Islington. About 35 per cent of its students are refugees, mostly from Turkish Kurdistan and Somalia. All staff in the school have taken the issue of supporting refugees very seriously, and have developed very positive practices.

In the early 1980s George Orwell School acquired a bad reputation among local parents and was criticised for poor results and discipline. The numbers of students enrolled at the school fell, and at one time the school was threatened with closure. In 1990 a new head teacher was appointed. At the same time the numbers of refugee students increased dramatically (as a result of its previous reputation there were many school spaces unfilled). Caroline Lodge, the new head teacher, had a long standing commitment to pastoral care. Together with other staff she worked to make a welcoming environment in the school, and developed policies to help refugee children. Today George Orwell School is a very different place, and in 1993 obtained good examination results.

A central plank of George Orwell School's philosophy is that refugee children need to feel welcome in a new school. A great deal of emphasis is placed on supporting a newly arrive refugee student. George Orwell School

- ensures that all parents receive information about their entitlements to free meals, transport and clothing grants and other services
- gives all new students a yellow introduction card which says 'my name is ....., my class teacher is .....'
- provides all teachers with information about newcomers including their country of origin and first language
- has a 'buddying' scheme whereby new students are befriended by another member of their tutor group (a speaker of the same language if possible)
- has developed special induction work in each subject. This intends to support speedy language acquisition
- monitors the progress of each student
- runs peer group counselling
- has good contacts with other agencies including social services, housing departments, immigration lawyers and refugee support groups
- uses interpreters to ensure that all parents know about school events and parents' evenings
- ensures that refugee issues are examined in the school curriculum;
- gives all teaches training about the needs of refugee children

— examines issues such as bereavement and loss in the pastoral curriculum

— has produced an exhibition and video about refugees.

The school recognises that its refugee policy is evolving. More work has to be done to improve the transition to further education or the workplace for refugee children. In 1993 the school secured some additional funding for a refugee project. This was used to improve induction procedures, to provide training, and to make an exhibition and video about refugee children. The latter was made by a group of children working with a video producer. It is moving testimony the strength and resilience of refugee children in George Orwell School.

Chapter Five

Support for English as a Second Language

Rachel Warner, Minority Rights Group

Refugee children arrive in Britain speaking — and sometimes reading and writing — a great many different languages. It is important for teachers to remember that refugee children are competent speakers of a language, or possibly two or more. Their skills in their first language should be valued and encouraged. Bilingualism should be viewed as an asset rather than a problem. Research has also shown that bilingual children are more likely to make good progress in schools which value a child's home language and culture.

Some refugee children may have learnt English in their home countries, others will be beginners. Almost all refugee children will require help in developing their speaking, reading and writing skills.

☐ Funding for Language Support

Since the late 1980s the funding of ESL teaching has become a political issue, with many teachers and education officers claiming that central government funding is not sufficient to meet the needs of newly arrived asylum-seekers. A survey carried out by the Refugee Council in 1991 showed that expenditure on ESL provision in London schools had not increased in that financial year in proportion to the increased number of refugee children arriving in London LEAs. In some London LEAs funding for ESL actually decreased in real terms.

Funding for ESL can come from several different sources. These are discussed below.

1. Section 11 of the 1966 Local Government Act/Single Regeneration Budget

Section 11 is a fund by which central government can make grants to certain local authorities, and in some cases non-governmental organisations, to enable them to make special provision for teaching English as a second language and to support black and ethnic minority communities in the short term. It applies only to England and Wales. Section 11 funding has never been activated in Scotland, as local authorities and the Scottish Office argue that the needs of ethnic minority communities in Scotland can best be met by the appropriate delivery of mainstream local authority services. The 1966 Local Government Act does not apply to Northern Ireland.

Section 11 funding has always been a controversial source of funding, with educationalists holding different views about its long term benefits. Some argued that the motives behind Section 11 were assimilist; others believed that it marginalised ESL teaching because it was a special fund coming from the Home Office, not the Department for Education. But in the current economic climate Section 11 has provided the main source of funding for ESL: some 89 per cent of Section 11 is spent in education, mostly funding ESL teaching posts. Over 10,000 teachers are currently funded by Section 11.

From 1966 until 1993 this funding was only available for projects targeted at people from the Commonwealth. Since most refugees are from countries outside the Commonwealth this meant that most refugees — an estimated 70 per cent — could not directly benefit from Section 11 funded projects. This was felt to be unjust, and also impractical at a school and LEA level. In 1993 a Private Member's Bill extended that target group to include 'ethnic minority communities whose language and customs differ from those of the rest of the community'. From 1994 the Home Office will accept funding bids for LEA projects targeted at asylum-seekers and refugees. But just when the Home Office is extending the target groups it is cutting the Section 11 budget and making major changes in its administration. A fund of £130.8 million in 1993/94 is to be cut to £110.7 million in 1994/95. In the financial year 1993/94 Section 11 funding paid for 75 per cent of LEA project salary costs. In 1994/95 this will be reduced to 57 per cent of salary costs, with LEAs having to find the remainder, often a substantial amount.

In 1995/96 there will be major administrative changes to Section 11. Some 55 per cent of Section 11 funding will be transferred from the Home Office to the Department of the Environment to be incorporated into a new Single Regeneration Budget, to fund urban regeneration programmes. The Single Regeneration Budget will also include monies from numerous other urban funds such as City Challenge and Housing Action Trusts, and will total £1.2 billion. It will be administered in ten regional offices.

The remaining 45 per cent of Section 11 funding will continue to be administered by the Home Office. This part of the fund will go to the shire counties not covered by the Single Regeneration Budget.

There are two concerns surrounding the Single Regeneration Budget. Firstly there is very little funding available for new projects. Secondly ESL projects are going to have to compete with large scale construction, transport and other high profile projects. It is feared that refugee education might not be seen as a priority alongside large, costly, urban regeneration programmes.

Teaching trade unions and organisations representing ethnic minority communities have launched a vigorous campaign to defend Section 11. But unless there is a change in policy by the Home Office, it is likely that LEAs will be unable to sustain many Section 11 projects. Up to 4,000 ESL teachers and other staff will be made redundant, expertise will be lost, children's educational attainments will be severely restricted and the impact on ethnic minority communities will be devastating.

Examples of Section 11 Work

Section 11 staff work mainly in education but also in housing departments, social services departments, business advisory units and for non-governmental organisations. Since 1990 a small proportion of Section 11 funding, known as the 'Ethnic Minority Grant', has been channelled to Training and Enterprise Councils (TECs). The TECs then distribute this money to non-governmental organisations, for employment related projects. Section 11 projects usually last for three years but a few run for five.

The following brief list offers a glimpse of the wide range of valuable work undertaken under Section 11:

providing English language support and other services in schools and colleges

planning and leading in-service training sessions for teachers and lecturers, and formulating school policies on anti-racist and multicultural education

organising home/school liaison schemes, visiting students and their families in their homes, setting up and running parent's rooms and bases, assisting with parent's evenings and providing special displays

working in schools and colleges to improve pastoral care and developing procedures to deal with bullying and racial harassment

providing careers guidance in schools and colleges, and for community organisations

providing advice and information on business and enterprise schemes

providing information and advice on housing matters, and working to prevent racial harassment on local authority housing estates

providing translation and interpreting services.

2. Local Education Authority Funded Special Projects

Before 1994 refugees from outside the Commonwealth had not been able to benefit from projects funded by Section 11. To overcome this disparity, some LEAs set up projects to support non-Commonwealth students in schools. One example is Ealing LEA's Support Team for International Children. There are currently about 2,000 refugee children in Ealing schools, mostly from non-Commonwealth countries. Ealing LEA has funded a project aimed at supporting these children. Seven peripatetic teachers are employed by the Support Team for International Children. A Somali refugee is herself one such teacher. The teachers visit schools and assist individual children. They also provide in-service training for teachers and operate an educational network for members of refugee communities. The latter is a platform for refugees to meet and discuss current educational issues.

After April 1994 such LEA funded projects are likely to be much more closely integrated with Section 11 funded projects. In Scotland and Northern Ireland all LEA-wide ESL projects are funded by local government.

3. Special Central Government Funds Aimed at Asylum-Seekers and Refugees

Section 210 of the 1988 Education Reform Act provides a small cash-limited fund for the education of refugees and displaced people who are resident in camps and reception centres. This section also provides funding for projects targeted at Travellers and circus children. Section 210 replaced the old 'no area pool fund', aimed at adults and children not permanently resident in one LEA. About twelve LEAs in England and Wales have been beneficiaries of Section 210 funding for refugee projects.

The fund is administered by LEAs, who have to submit detailed project proposals to the Department for Education well in advance of the start of the year for which funding is sought. A mid-October deadline for LEA applications for projects to start the following financial year has so far been demanded.

There are two major problems associated with Section 210 funding. Firstly, only a tiny proportion of Britain's refugees are living in reception centres and can therefore qualify for this funding. The Refugee Council believes that Section 210 funding should be extended to cover asylum-seekers and refugees who are living in local authority funded temporary accommodation: the majority of refugee children are currently being housed in such accommodation. This group is as geographically mobile as those initially housed in reception centres; they, like them, often move between LEAs. Another disadvantage is that refugees arriving after the mid-October deadline are not eligible for funding until at least a year after their arrival. There is a clear need to lobby for more flexibility in funding deadlines.

The Department of the Environment has also made available to local authorities a source of funding to aid the settlement of refugees from former Yugoslavia who arrived between April 1992 and 7th November 1992.

4. School Budgets

LMS allows for a percentage of a school's budget to be allocated to meet the needs of ethnic minority students, if required. But as most refugees are living in inner cities, there are presently many competing demands on this budget line. Most London LEAs state that LMS formula funding does not meet the needs of refugee children, and therefore continue to co-finance Section 11 and other special projects.

The Refugee Council is concerned that Grant Maintained Schools who have not purchased LEA language support services, may not prioritise ESL when allocating their budgets. Bilingual children might not receive the language support they need or they might be discouraged from enrolling at the school.

☐ How Students Are Given Language Support

Schools and LEAs organise their English language support for bilingual students, including refugees, in a variety of ways. ESL support can be given by:

withdrawing the child to a language centre, either full-time or part-time (as is still done in parts of Britain)

withdrawing the child to special classes within the school for some lessons every week

giving the bilingual child ESL support within the classroom.

In the past many bilingual students spent their first months in Britain learning English in language centres. They remained in the language centre until deemed to have learnt enough English to join mainstream education in schools. Today withdrawal of bilingual students is much more likely to take place within the school, where pupils will spend a certain number of lessons per week with an ESL teacher, who is either a permanent member of the school's staff or a peripatetic teacher.

There has been much debate over the withdrawal of bilingual students from lessons, particularly to language centres. The practice of withdrawing students may be a cheaper and superficially more convenient manner of providing language support and much good work has been done in language centres and withdrawal groups. But it has been shown that children learn English most effectively by working among English speaking students and taking part in activities with them. The language of the normal mainstream classroom provides the best context for language learning, because the bilingual students are learning English for a purpose — to learn the subject being taught — not English for its own sake. Group activities in a classroom involve discussion, so pupils learn by listening to other pupils and relating discussion to what they see happening. Many group activities also involve repetition, which is also helpful. A big motivation for learning English is wanting to join in the activities of their peers, both inside and outside lessons (Cummins, 1984; Siraj-Blatchford, 1994; Wiles, 1985).

If bilingual students are withdrawn from the mainstream, whether into language centres or withdrawal groups, all these incentives to learn English are removed. Additionally the only model of correct English the bilingual student will hear would be the teacher's, because all the other students will have limited English. Students will not experience the 'social learning' of English which happens in the playground. Most importantly, bilingual students will not have the same full access to the curriculum as other students. The content of lessons in a language centre can be far removed from the school, and this will not help a bilingual student integrate into the school.

Developing the English of bilingual pupils should be seen as the responsibility of all teachers but once bilingual students are withdrawn from the mainstream it is easy for teachers to view ESL as the sole responsibility of the specialist teacher. One of the many advantages of ESL teachers working in collaboration with classroom teachers is that the mainstream teacher will be encouraged to develop skills in English language support.

Clearly, establishing ESL support within the mainstream classroom is the most satisfactory way of providing language support to bilingual students. But there may be occasions when it is appropriate for bilingual students, particularly in secondary schools, to be withdrawn for a few lessons a week for a limited period of time. It is hoped that in the current economic climate schools will retain sufficient flexibility in teacher allocation to allow for this.

If students are to be withdrawn from some lessons, this should always be discussed with the students and with appropriate subject teachers. Older bilingual students may be withdrawn for the following reasons:

- if they are total beginners, particularly if they need help with very basic literacy in English;
- if students request help with particular GCSE assignments;
- if Stage Two and Stage Three language learners are having specific problems with, for example, certain tense forms, they may be withdrawn for a few lessons to concentrate on particular problems;
- to enable a student who appears to be traumatised and possibly withdrawn or aggressive to develop a trusting relationship with an adult, and even to discuss and write about some of the events that have led to their becoming a refugee.

Partnership Teaching

In an ideal situation an ESL teacher is seen as an equal partner with the class teacher, participating in planning lessons and developing materials with the class teacher, and introducing topics to the whole class. Such partnership teaching has been found to be effective but can be costly in terms of staff time.

The other way of supporting bilingual students in the mainstream is for an ESL teacher to go into lessons and work solely with bilingual students on particular tasks. This may be appropriate if, for example, students are working on GCSE assignments but the danger is that the ESL teacher may seem to be marginalised, particularly if she is not a permanent member of staff. By association, the bilingual students might seem to be marginalised too. It can also fuel resentment if native speakers feel that bilingual students are getting more help with work than they are. Mainstream teachers should always introduce ESL support teachers to the whole class and explain why the new teacher is present in the lesson.

☐ How Teachers Can Help Bilingual Students in the Classroom

As part of the induction interview an ESL teacher should find out what languages newly arrived bilinguals speak, whether they are literate in their home language and the level of education achieved before coming to Britain (see Chapter Four). The ESL teacher should assess the English language acquisition stage of the new student. All this information should be made available to all the subject teachers concerned.

☐ Helping a Beginner

To help beginners to feel welcome in a class and to start learning English, the following procedures may be helpful:

Make sure you know how to pronounce the student's name properly, and try to greet him or her every lesson.

Make sure the student knows your name: introduce yourself and write down your name for the student.

Sit the student next to a sympathetic member of the class, preferably one who speaks the same language and can translate.

Try to encourage the student to contribute to the lesson by using his or her mother tongue.

Do not worry if the beginner says very little at first, as plenty of listening time is important when starting to learn a new language. It helps the student to 'tune in' to the sounds and intonation of the new language. But obviously just listening all the time is frustrating for the student.

Try to teach beginners some useful phrases such as:

Yes
No
Miss/Sir
Thank you
Please can I have .....
I don't understand
I've finished
Hello
Goodbye

Encourage students to help give out equipment, and collect books, so they have to make contact with other students. But don't treat them as the class dogsbody!

English Language Acquisition Stages

Stage One: Beginner Bilingual
Students may remain silent in the classroom or use a little English if encouraged to do so. They have minimal or no literacy in English. If involved in learning activities in groups they need considerable support, or they need to be able to use their mother tongue.

Stage Two: Developing Bilingual
These students can participate in all learning activities but it will be very evident in speaking and in writing that the students' first language is not English. They will be able to express themselves orally in English quite successfully but if they are to make progress they will need considerable support in writing English and with reading.

Stage Three: Developing Bilingual
These students have sufficient English language skills to enable them to be successfully involved in all activities. Their oral and written English is developing well but their written English will tend to lack complexity and will show evidence of structures and errors associated with this level of language acquisition.

Stage Four: Fluently Bilingual
These students are totally fluent in English. They write as native speakers.

Encourage pupils to learn the names of equipment, symbols or terms essential for your subject. Use pictures and labels. Students can make their own 'dictionaries' for key words for your subject. There are also some commercially published dual language lists of key words for different subject areas, which can be used in the classroom (see Further Resources).

Ask students for the mother tongue equivalents of English terms.

Short vocabulary lists can be provided for each lesson.

If students are literate in their first language, try to obtain bilingual dictionaries and encourage students to use them. Students may have their own dictionaries at home which they should be encouraged to bring in.

It may be appropriate for students to write in their mother tongue at first.

If students are literate in their mother tongue, a teacher can use books in the mother tongue for initial reading lessons. It may be possible to obtain books in the mother tongue for particular subject areas. Using mother tongue materials in this way will not impede the learning of English. Students are far more likely to feel confident about using English and not worrying about making mistakes if they feel their mother tongue is valued.

Collaborative learning activities are very helpful for learning English. But working in groups with other students will be a new experience for many refugee children, as most have come from countries where the educational system is more formal than in Britain. Other students in a group need to be supportive too.

Visual cues are extremely helpful, for example videos, slides, pictures, diagrams, flash cards and illustrated glossaries.

Reading material can be made easier by discussing it and relating it to the student's own experiences. If reading material is recorded on cassette, students can listen and read simultaneously.

It is important to maintain students' confidence in learning a new language, and help them feel they can complete written work, however simple. Beginners will initially need to copy, and they may need practice with handwriting. The following types of simple tasks are appropriate for beginners:

copying labels on to pictures or diagrams
copying simple sentences under pictures
matching pictures to names
filling in missing words in text, but with the missing words supplied.

Beginners should always be given homework if their classmates members receive it, even though it needs to be very simple.

☐ Helping Second Stage Learners

Second Stage learners can engage in all the learning activities in a classroom, and their understanding of conversation and oral instruction is generally good. But this group of students require considerable support with written work and reading.

Their understanding of text will be helped by visual clues, for example watching the video of a novel before studying it as a class reader. Class or group discussions of texts would also be helpful, as would role play and audio cassettes to listen to before the lesson. Teachers can prepare simple summaries of the main points of books, texts or lessons.

Written tasks for second stage learners need to be structured. The following type of tasks may be helpful:

Sequencing—where students have to put statements in the right order before writing them out. This can be done as a pair or group activity.

Ticking charts and filling in tables, which can then be used as a basis for writing sentences.

Deciding whether statements are true or false.

Providing structured questions. If questions are designed carefully, the answers can add up to a piece of continuous writing when put together. This helps students who otherwise find continuous writing difficult.

Teachers should provide models of the type of writing they want to see, for example the correct layout of a letter or the results of a scientific experiment. That maths is highly dependent on the use and understanding of English should not be forgotten. Certain maths schemes, such as SMILE, require a good understanding of English and need adaptation if they are to be used successfully with beginners and Second Stage learners.

☐ Helping Third Stage Learners

This group of students can cope with the demands of the curriculum and will be able to produce extended pieces of writing, albeit with some errors. Unfortunately the language needs of Third Stage learners are neglected in many schools and, as a consequence, their skills are not extended beyond this stage.

It is important for teachers to remember that the English language skills of Third Stage learners are still developing. They still need help with reading and writing and in extending their vocabulary. Written work will benefit from the provision of models and plans. When written work is marked it is helpful to explain grammatical mistakes to students. It is also important to watch out for words that students are not using: a piece of writing might be competent but use only a limited range of tenses and vocabulary. Can students be shown alternative expressions and extra tenses? Do they need to know how to use reported speech and the passive voice?

☐ Case Study

Lunchtime Link

Lunchtime Link is a scheme developed by Community Service Volunteers for use in schools with large numbers of bilingual students. Groups of sixth form students receive some training, then help a small group of bilingual students with their English. The students commit themselves to giving up one lunch time every week.

The volunteers do not give formal English lessons. Instead they use a variety of specially chosen games that help bilingual students improve their vocabulary, spelling and conversational skills. Scrabble and Boggle are among the games that are used. Two teachers are responsible for co-ordinating the project. They provide the training and organise such matters as the use of rooms and storage cupboards. But after a few trial sessions the sixth form students run the sessions by themselves

Further details about Lunchtime Link can be obtained from Community Service Volunteers.

☐ English Language Qualifications

Bilingual students have to face numerous formal and informal assessments of their communication skills, particularly when applying for jobs or progressing on to further and higher education. For those wishing to enter higher education a qualification in English is usually a requirement. Most institutes expect students to have obtained GCSE English or an equivalent qualification.

GCSE English is the most widely recognised qualification in English. It is, however, sometimes difficult for a bilingual student to achieve the standard demanded because the examination is designed to assess native speakers. Furthermore, it assumes familiarity with cultural references.

A pass in the Joint Matriculation Board Test in English Overseas is accepted as the equivalent of GCSE English Grade C by many educational institutes. It is mainly aimed at those studying science 'A' Levels and is restricted to people who have been resident in Britain for less than ten years. Further details about this test can be obtained from the Northern Examining Association's Joint Matriculation Board.

The Associated Examining Board runs a test in English for Educational Purposes, aimed at a broad spectrum of students. It is recognised by some educational institutes as the equivalent of GCSE grade C. Further details about this course can be obtained from the Southern Examining Group's Associated Examining Board.

The Cambridge Examination Syndicate administers three different English as a foreign language qualifications geared towards the needs of non-residents. One of these examinations — the Cambridge Certificate of Proficiency — is accepted by many educational institutions as the equivalent of GCSE grade C. The Cambridge First Certificate in English and the Cambridge Lower Certificate are not acceptable entry qualifications for higher education.

Chapter Six

Mother Tongue Maintenance

Britain has a rich linguistic heritage and refugees' languages are part of it. Surveys in Greater London — the most ethnically diverse part of Britain — indicate that almost 200 languages are spoken by school students.

Since the late 19th century and the entry of Jewish refugees from eastern Europe, there has been educational debate about the use and maintenance of a refugee child's mother tongue. At first education policy aimed to integrate refugee children as quickly as possible into 'British' society. Children were taught to speak, read and write the English language but little attention was given to home language or culture or to the experiences of children from ethnic minority groups within the school system. Some educationists believed that bilingualism actually hindered a child's progress in learning English.

In the late 1960s opinion began to change. Assimilist policies were seen as unworkable and unpopular because they ignored Britain's cultural and linguistic diversity and ignored widespread prejudice within British society. Schools and LEAs began to move towards multicultural education policies. Such policies aimed to encourage and celebrate linguistic diversity, among other goals.

The benefits of bilingualism began to be recognised by educationalists. Bilingual children need to build on linguistic and conceptual skills acquired in the early years. Bilingual children who have been taught their mother tongue as well as English may also find it easier to acquire subsequent languages. Fluency in the mother tongue enables bilingual children to communicate with parents and other members of the community. A person's sense of identity is closely linked to language; mother tongue teaching and positive language policies help children from minority groups promote their own identity through their language.

Refugee children have further need to maintain their mother tongue. Many refugee families aspire to return to their home countries and will obviously need to be fluent in its language.

In the 1970s and 1980s LEAs encouraged schools to have policies to enable bilingual children to value and maintain their mother tongues. They supported bilingual teaching and mother tongue teaching. They gave mainstream teachers in-service training on language issues and bilingualism, and funded some supplementary schools. The Swann Report (1985) articulated many of these positive policies.

☐ Bilingual Education and Mother Tongue Teaching

In an ideal world bilingual students should have the opportunity — if they want it — of developing their mother tongue in mainstream education. Nursery and infants schools can employ teachers and classroom assistants on either a permanent or peripatetic basis who speak the child's first language. In primary and secondary schools a pupil's first language can be used as a medium of instruction alongside English, so that the child may be taught for a set part of the school day in, for example, Somali and for the rest of the time in English. But providing such bilingual education has huge resource implications for schools and LEAs. At present only a handful of British schools are offering this service.

A community language such as Somali can also be taught as a modern language, in both primary and secondary schools — mother tongue teaching. In the past several refugee communities helped develop GCSE examinations in their respective community languages. A-Level Tamil, GCSE Farsi, GCSE Turkish, GCSE Vietnamese and GCSE Cantonese were taught by peripatetic teachers in some schools in London. But such initiatives have been dealt a double blow, by cuts to LEAs budgets and by the introduction of the National Curriculum. The latter has defined what constitutes 'modern foreign languages': all EC languages plus Japanese, Chinese (Mandarin) and Chinese (Cantonese), Russian and Arabic. The languages of the Indian sub-continent and Vietnamese are not on this list and may be squeezed out of the timetable in inner-city schools. Farsi has recently been lost as a GCSE subject.

There are also practical constraints to providing bilingual education and mother tongue teaching. Refugee communities are often small and widely dispersed; if there are only a few refugees speaking a particular language in a school, it will be much more difficult to make provision for bilingual education and mother tongue teaching. The Refugee Council believes, however, that LEAs could examine ways of sharing resources across LEA boundaries. Two local authorities could employ a teacher of Vietnamese or Somali, for example, and students from these local authorities could travel to a central location to study the language.

Outside school hours some adult and further education institutes are offering mother tongue classes in refugee community languages. Some of these courses are aimed at children and families. In London, for example, mother tongue courses are being offered in Kurdish, Turkish, Arabic, Chinese (Cantonese) and Tigrinya. Many refugee communities run supplementary schools which teach children's mother tongues.

☐ Supporting the Mother Tongue in Primary and Secondary Schools

In most British schools it is not possible to teach the refugee child's mother tongue. But there is still a great deal teachers can do which support and value a student's mother tongue. This support may not greatly extend the student's skills in their language, but the psychological significance of it should not be underestimated. Students are unlikely to learn English successfully if they feel their capability in their mother tongue is not valued and that they are being asked to abandon their first language in favour of English.

The following approaches have been found helpful in schools:

Ask students about their first language(s)! Students should feel that their teachers are genuinely interested in their languages.

As part of the initial assessment of bilingual students they can be asked about their mother tongue, whether they are literate, and if they speak other languages. If students are literate in their first language, they can be asked to produce a piece of writing. Even without being able to read what students write, a teacher can learn a good deal about students from the way they approach the task, the speed and confidence with which they write, and their handwriting. Obviously if you can get the piece translated you will learn more.

As well as samples of work in English, student's writing in their first language can be put in their profile folders.

ESL and English teachers can ask students to write about themselves in English and their mother tongues. These testimonies can be typed on a word processor: many school computer departments now have programmes in a range of scripts. The Minority Rights Group's Voices project (page 83 and 84) provides a useful framework for testimonies.

Teachers should try to increase their knowledge of the language competences of their students so they can show sensitivity and not, for example, ask students to write if they are not literate in their mother tongue. Teachers should also try to find out as much as possible about supplementary schools run by refugee communities. Students who do not attend these supplementary schools should be encouraged to attend.

Schools should include mother tongue and dual language books in class and school libraries and encourage bilingual students to read them. Refugee community organisations, language centres and ESL teams should be able to tell teachers where they can obtain appropriate books. Schools should also purchase mother tongue/English dictionaries for students.

Schools can run language awareness courses for all students, and bilingual students can contribute to them. Younger children can do surveys about the languages spoken in their class or school, presenting the results in the form of bar graphs and charts. They can make displays showing different scripts and schools can put up signs and posters in different community languages.

The Minority Rights Group's *Voices* Project

The Minority Rights Group has collected and published a series of dual language testimonies written by refugee children in London schools — *Voices from Eritrea*, *Voices from Somalia* and *Voices from Kurdistan*. The latter book contains testimonies written in Kurdish (Sorani), Kurdish (Kurmanji) and English.

The Minority Rights Group worked with refugee students and ESL teachers to collect the testimonies. After the accounts were typed all students had the chance to change their testimonies. The testimonies were then published in the form of these three books.

For the refugee students who wrote and produced these accounts it has hugely increased their confidence. The *Voices* series is now being used with newly-arrived refugee children. They can read the accounts in their mother tongue and English. Many refugee children who have used the books have been heartened by reading about others who were in the same position as they themselves were; there is no doubt that *Voices* has been a great psychological boost to refugee children in many schools and a valuable teaching aid. The testimonies in the *Voices* series also raise awareness among teachers and all students about refugees from Somalia, Eritrea and Kurdistan and can be a resource for teaching about such issues as migration.

ESL teachers in schools can undertake their own Voices projects, helping refugee students to prepare their own testimonies, and producing them on desk-top publishing software. There is software available in many different scripts, and schools and community groups often have access to it.

From *Voices from Somalia*
Mohammed Warsame, 13 years old
Hackney Downs School, London

'Waxaan ku koray oo aan degganaa ilaa intaan imanayey Ingland Jeniwary 1990. Waxaan degannaa miyiga Burco oo aanu guri weyn ku lahayn. Dugsi maan gelin — waxaan rarci jiray xoolahayaga. Shaqaadayduna taasay ahayd. Waxaan kici jiray subixii sideeda.

Waxaan qabto waxaa ugu horreyn jiray inaan xoolaha si aanay u baxsan. Waxaan kale oo lisi jiray riyaha iyo geela. Hooyaday iyo walaakay ayaa iyana i caawin jiray. Caanaha ayaanu cabi jiray oo subag, burcad iyo ciirba ka sameysan jiray. Waxaabahan waxaan ka helaa imminka dukaamada waaweyn sida Seynsburi iyo Tesko. Hooyaday waxay u iib geyn jirtay subagga iyo caanaha Ceerigabo. Markaa ayey noo keeni jirtay khudrad iyo wixii kale ee aanaan haysan ama sameysan karin. Maalin walba shaqo joogto ah ayey ahayd xoolo raac, guri sameyn oodis. Aad bay u hawl badnayd laakin waqtigu markiiba wuu ku dhaafayey.'

'I grew up in Bur'o in Somalia, and lived there until I came to England in January 1990. I lived in the country in a big house. I didn't go to school — I looked after the animals we kept. I looked after camels and sheep and goats all day — that was my job. I would get up at about eight o'clock in the morning. My first task was to water and feed the animals. All day I would sit out in the hills watching the animals, making sure they did not wander off. I would also milk the goats, camels and sheep. My mother and brother also helped with the milking. Our family used the milk for drinking and we made butter and cheese and yoghurt too. I can get some of these things here in Hackney from Sainsbury's and Tesco's. My mum would sell the milk and cheese in the market in Erigavo. Then she would buy fruit and vegetables and anything else we could not grow or make ourselves. It was the same every day — everyone was very busy working in the house or with the animals or fixing fences or repairing the buildings. The work was hard but time passed quickly.'

☐ Refugee Supplementary Schools

Every Saturday morning over 10,000 children can be found learning their mother tongue in classrooms and living rooms throughout Britain. They are students in supplementary schools run by refugee communities. Despite the enthusiasm shown by the students and the importance attached to them by the refugees themselves, the work of these schools is largely unrecognised by LEAs, and they are consequently starved of resources.

The supplementary school movement has a long history in Britain. The earliest voluntary classes were started by Jewish refugees from eastern Europe. After the Second World War Polish and Ukrainian refugee communities organised supplementary schools. Today there are about 60 Polish schools in Britain, accommodating 5,000 students. In the 1960s immigrants from the New Commonwealth began to set up supplementary schools, teaching South Asian languages, English, religious studies and Arabic.

In the 1970s refugees from the poorer countries of Africa and Asia started arriving in Britain. New communities were formed and new schools started. Today refugees from eastern Europe, Latin America, Eritrea, Ethiopia, Sudan, Somalia, Afghanistan, Armenia, Assyria, Iran, Iraq, Kurdistan, Sri Lanka and Vietnam all run supplementary schools. The focus of activity is mother tongue teaching, but the curriculum is much wider. Supplementary schools also teach their students the geography and history of their homeland, give religious education, provide adult education and organise sport and leisure activities. They also enable young refugees to meet friends who are going through similar experiences.

The Swann Report (1985) acknowledged the work of supplementary schools and made a series of recommendations about how LEAs could support that work. But few of these recommendations have been adopted; indeed the 1990s have seen a reduction in LEA and school support for supplementary schools. Fewer supplementary schools now receive LEA funding and fewer have access to free premises. And access to suitable premises is an ongoing problem for supplementary schools.

Mainstream schools have greater financial autonomy since the implementation of the 1988 Education Reform Act — a change known as Local Management of Schools (LMS). One outcome is that mainstream schools are less willing to give community organisations the free use of school premises in the evenings and at weekends. In London several supplementary schools have been forced to use alternative and less satisfactory premises and several have ceased to operate because they lost the free use of school premises.

There are other problems too. Textbooks and other teaching resources are often in short supply. Few of the volunteer teachers have received training.

The Refugee Council would like to see schools and LEAs offer the use of free premises to supplementary schools. LEA teacher advisers could run training courses for the volunteer teachers. Individual schools could develop closer links with neighbouring supplementary schools. Mainstream teachers and their students could visit supplementary schools, and projects and displays could be developed about the work of supplementary schools.

☐ Case Study: The Iranian Community Centre's Supplementary School

The Iranian Community Centre (ICC) set up its first Farsi class in 1984. A small number of children living in Ealing attended. As the numbers increased, funding was secured from the former Inner London Education Authority. Today the ICC runs its classes in a school in Islington.

Over 70 children now attend the school. It offers Farsi at three levels and also ESL for children, ESL for adults, dance, music and drama. The Farsi teachers use a range of teaching aids; through play and games children widen their vocabulary.

ICC has no problem recruiting volunteer teachers from the Iranian community. But they do have problems maintaining a regular commitment from some teachers, particularly in the latter part of the school year.

Parents work in close partnership with the supplementary school teachers. They help in class and in the library. While their children learn Farsi, parents can take part in ESL classes. There is an active parent's association.

The ICC used to order teaching material from Iran but this has now become impossible. New Farsi books are being published in other countries, but there is no money to buy them. A shortage of funds means that ICC cannot afford to print its own materials.

After the abolition of the Inner London Education Authority in 1990, three London LEAs gave funding to the ICC to run the school. But these grants were not renewed and the operation of the school was threatened. Today the ICC receives funding from the BBC Children in Need. This does not meet all the school's costs and parents are asked to contribute.

Chapter Seven

The Emotional Needs of Refugee Children

Refugee children will have experienced a multiplicity of different stressful events. They might overcome and cope with some or all of these experiences. Like adults, most children cope with the multiple stresses of being a refugee; some, however, remain psychologically vulnerable and a few manifest disturbed behaviour. This chapter examines the factors that influence a refugee child's psychological well-being and suggests ways in which schools can give refugee children emotional support.

☐ A Refugee Child's Experience

Refugee children undergo many different events in their journey to Britain and in rebuilding their lives in this country. These events can be summarised as a culmination of **loss, trauma** and **change.**

Loss

Refugee children may have lost:

parents, other key carers, brothers and sisters and extended family
friends
their home
material belongings
favourite toys

familiar surroundings
familiar ways of doing things
their parents' attention and support in a new country.

Trauma

Refugee children may have experienced or witnessed:

high intensity war, bombing or shelling
the destruction of their homes
the violent death of family or friends
the injury of family of friends
getting separated from family
being injured
the arrest of members of their family or friends
being arrested, detained or tortured
being forced to join armies or militias
being raped
grave shortages of food, water or other necessities
the fear of discovery or arrest
hostility in their new homeland
material deprivation in their new homes
being with people who do not understand or know about the violent events they have experienced.

Change

Refugee children may experience:

major cultural changes such as learning a new language and a different set of cultural norms
going to a very different type of school
changes in standard of living and status in society
seeing their parents as vulnerable people
other emotional changes in their parents such as being more protective or authoritarian.

When working with refugee children it is important not to make assumptions about their experiences or to label refugee children as being 'different' or 'traumatised'. All children's experiences of loss, trauma and change are different. And each child reacts differently to these experiences.

☐ Adverse and Protective Factors

After a traumatic experience such as bereavement it is normal to manifest strong emotional reactions, but with time these usually lessen. Children's reactions to such events are very variable both in the short term and the long. Many factors influence a child's psychological well-being. The duration and intensity of trauma, the child's age, the child's personality and character, the quality of childcare and the child's experiences in a new country all affect how they will come to terms with being a refugee. Some things make it more likely that problems will arise. Other factors protect a child against long term psychological distress.

The adverse factors that make it more likely that a child will suffer long-term psychological stress include:

- Traumatic events which are overwhelmingly intense or last for a long time. Repeated exposure to stressors, both acute and chronic, greatly decrease a child's ability to cope.
- Experiencing inconsistent childcare; a child may have lost parents and have a difficult relationship with new carers. Other children may have lost their parents' attention.
- Seeing exile as being inexplicable and not being able to understand the changes in their lives. Younger children are more vulnerable, since they can less easily understand events such as death.
- Encountering difficulties in finding housing, or having problems at school.
- Being isolated from other people from the home country.
- Having low self-esteem and little to look forward to.
- Not being able to talk about traumatic events for fear of disclosing secrets or for other reasons.
- Having other problems unrelated to the refugee experience which may make it difficult to cope in a new country, for example a learning disability.

There are also protective factors that make it less likely that a child will suffer long term psychological stress, including

- Having parents who can give their children full attention and good quality childcare.

- Having access to other people who can give friendship and support, particularly members of their own community.
- Having some understanding of the reasons for exile. Obviously younger children may have an incomplete understanding of such stressful experiences so may be more vulnerable. But children who are able to integrate traumatic experience into their belief system are less likely to suffer long-term distress.
- Having access to permanent housing, a certain immigration status, and enjoying a reasonable standard of living in a new country.
- Being able to maintain some links with their homeland.
- Being happy in a new school and able to achieve things at school, feeling optimistic about the future and that they are making progress are important protective factors.
- Related to the above is the matter of self-esteem; children who have good self-esteem are more likely to overcome traumatic events.
- Being able to talk about stressful events and in this way gain mastery over them.

☐ How Children Show Stress

Some refugee children will settle into their new schools. Others may be disorientated or unhappy at first but eventually learn effectively. A minority of refugee children manifest disturbed behaviour. It is important for teachers to be observant and to know when children are unhappy or very distressed. Only then can appropriate support be given. Teachers can understand how children are responding to traumatic events by asking them about how they feel and observing how they behave and get on with others. The presence of some of the following behaviour may indicate that a child is very distressed (Richman, 1993):

- Losing interest and energy or being very withdrawn — a child may sit around all day and show little interest in surroundings.
- Being aggressive or feeling very angry. Children can manifest aggressive behaviour for a number of reasons. Some children copy the violence they have seen around them. Young children may be unable to put their feelings into words and use violence as an outlet. Trau-

matic experiences can make children feel tense and irritable and they may lose their temper easily.

- Lacking concentration and feeling restless. Children who are worried or unhappy often find it difficult to concentrate on their work. They might day-dream or become very withdrawn, or they might be very restless.
- Feeling very irritable.
- Repetitive thoughts about traumatic events. Young children act out stressful events or problems, in their thoughts and in their play and drawings. Playing out events helps the young child to develop understanding of these events and gain control over difficult emotions. When a child plays out a violent or traumatic event time and time again it indicates that the child is not getting over the experience. Children may have repetitive thoughts about a traumatic event or may keep drawing the same violent scene.
- Physical symptoms such as poor appetite, eating too much, breathing difficulties, pains and dizziness.
- Losing recently acquired skills and faculties, for example keeping dry at night.
- Nightmares and disturbed sleep.
- Crying and feeling overwhelming sadness.
- Being very nervous or fearful of certain things such as loud noises.
- Being unable to form relationships with other children. A child may be too sad and withdrawn to want to play, or perhaps unable to trust other children. A newly arrived refugee child might also not understand what other children are doing. Refugee children may become isolated, rejected by other children because they are perceived to be different or possibly because of disturbed behaviour.
- Having difficulties in relating to adults because they do not trust them. Sometimes refugee children try to keep away from adults because they fear loss. They might be reluctant to show affection to a significant adult least she or he disappears.

☐ What Schools Can Do To Help Refugee Children

Providing emotional support for refugee children is an integral part of any school's refugee policy. It cannot be considered in isolation from things like providing a welcoming environment, good home/school liaison and ESL support. A school which meets refugee children's academic and social needs is one where they feel happy. Conversely, no amount of counselling will enable children to feel happy if they are encountering racism at school or are not making educational progress.

Teachers can do a great deal to provide emotional support for refugee children. They need to have the support of colleagues and senior management. Resources, principally time, have to be allocated for working with emotionally traumatised children. Teachers who provide counselling to refugee children need the skills and confidence to deal with painful issues such as death, torture and rape: death is the ultimate taboo in British society and it can be extremely difficult to communicate with a child who has seen family murdered.

Schools can consider the practices set out below.

Training

In-service training should aim to increase teachers' knowledge about refugee children's background and to develop their listening and communication skills. Naomi Richman has written an excellent training manual, *Communicating with Children* (1993). Intended for people working with children who are encountering difficult circumstances, it contains useful information and training exercises. It looks at issues such a being a good listener, creating trust and starting a conversation. *Communicating With Children* can be used for school-based in-service training.

Specialist organisations such as the Medical Foundation for the Care of Victims of Torture offer in-service training. Some teachers may also want to consider attending validated counselling courses.

Talking to Children

One of the most important things a teacher can do is to talk to distressed children, listen to what they say and take their communication seriously. To do this effectively teachers have to make a regular time to be free and have some degree of privacy. A room or an office can be designated for this purpose at breaktime or after school.

Counselling

A small number of refugee children will need more intervention. Some schools offer individual or group counselling to children who have suffered abuse or stressful experiences. Such counselling is usually facilitated by teachers who have obtained counselling qualifications or by other professionals.

Working With Parents

If a child experiences difficulties at school it is essential to develop good communications with parents and other key carers at the earliest opportunity, using an interpreter if needed. Sometimes parents' and children's problems are closely interlinked.

Strategies for Individual Children

Where a particular child gives cause for concern it is important to observe that child's behaviour over a period of time. Teachers should avoid jumping to immediate conclusions or labelling the child and should try to find out about the child's background and the reasons for the behaviour. Children can be asked why they are feeling sad or angry and teachers can think about a strategy to support them.

Knowing When to Refer a Child

Sometimes a child manifests disturbed behaviour for a protracted period of time and does not respond to support strategies. Schools may rapidly exhaust all options. They should consider referring the child to another agency with expertise in working with traumatised children. It is worth finding out as much as you can about relevant agencies. Is there anyone in the school psychological service who has expertise on working with refugee children? (The quality and type of service offered by child guidance clinics and schools' psychological services are highly variable, and not all professionals have experience of working with children from different cultural and linguistic backgrounds). There may be other specialist services in your locality which could be of use.

Autobiography and Creative Writing

Children can be encouraged to write about themselves, their home country and present circumstances. They can make a scrapbook or picture book about themselves. Such autobiographical techniques are frequently used with refugee children as a way of helping them to develop understanding of complex events and feelings. Younger children can use paints and crayons to draw pictures about themselves and work with an adult to write captions for their drawings.

Play and Drama

Schools can use games and drama with small groups of children, to explore issue such as fear and trust or to help newly arrived children to settle in.

Providing Safe Places

Starting a new school can be a very frightening experience for refugee children. British schools are large and noisy. Refugee children can feel lost, especially if they do not speak much English when they first arrive and have few friends. Although children might be able to cope during lesson time, breaktime can be overwhelming. It is important that schools have safe areas such as a room or a quiet space where children can sit if they do not feel like participating in playground activities.

The Pastoral Curriculum

Bereavement will affect everyone at some time in their lives and learning about loss, death and bereavement is important for all students. Some schools have developed excellent resources about bereavement for use in religious education or personal and social education but not all schools tackle the issues. Where there are refugee children in a school it is essential the pastoral curriculum be used to examine bereavement and loss. That way refugee children will not be made to feel different and can realise that other children too might suffer similar experiences.

☐ Learning from Others

There are many imaginative mental health programmes working with refugee children in different parts of the world. Two British initiatives — at Hampstead School and George Orwell School — are described in Chapter Three and Four. Schools can exchange ideas about good practice and teachers in Britain can also learn much from those in other countries. Here is an example of a project with Mozambican refugees in Zambia.

Ukwimi Refugee Settlement

Ukwimi Refugee Settlement in eastern Zambia was by 1991 home to 22,000 Mozambican refugees. Most of the refugees were subsistence farmers, with a few professionals among them. Ukwimi Refugee Settlement is located in a very isolated part of eastern Zambia, where refugees are allowed to cultivate land which has been allocated to them.

The refugees had been caught in the civil war between the Mozambican Government and Renamo guerrillas. Research carried out by the International Catholic Child Bureau indicated that a large number of refugees had lost immediate family, witnessed violence or had been used as forced labour by Renamo.

The International Catholic Child Bureau was asked to implement a programme to support war-traumatised refugee children. Mothers of pre-school children were given training to help them understand the importance of play. The school teachers in the settlement were brought together for a series of training sessions and asked in the first session, to identify the children about whom they were concerned. The teachers were then taught to understand the concept of stress and to recognise when children are showing stress-related behaviour.

After this the teachers spent two days on a course entitled 'an introduction to counselling'. This course identified the differences between teacher and counsellor but it also enabled the teachers to gain experience of counselling. After the course the teachers were all visited by the trainers and given further support in their schools. The course was not evaluated but after six months the teachers were asked to report back on the work they had done in their schools. Although this programme was implemented in a poor country, something similar could equally well be run in Britain.

Chapter Eight

Unaccompanied Refugee Children

Children who arrive alone in Britain are the most vulnerable group of refugee children, because they lack the support of a family. Family separation or loss, moreover, never occurs in isolation — an unaccompanied refugee child will have experienced other traumatic events such as war.

Every year between 250 and 500 unaccompanied refugee children — accurate statistics are not available — arrive in Britain. Children may flee on their own for a variety of reasons. Their parents may have been killed or imprisoned. They may have become separated from parents during war. Many parents arrange for their children to travel to another country because they believe their lives are in danger, because of war perhaps, or being associated with a persecuted political or minority group. In at least 25 countries children under 16 make up significant percentages of national armies, guerrilla groups or both. Parents may send a child away to prevent forced recruitment; for this reason more male unaccompanied children reach Europe than do girls.

In the last four years unaccompanied children have arrived in Britain from Ethiopia, Eritrea, Uganda, Sri Lanka, Somalia, Angola and former Yugoslavia. Most unaccompanied children arriving in Britain have been sent to this country by their parents, although contact with parents is often fractured. Some unaccompanied children come to Britain with family friends, others are brought by an agent. Many are handed over without warning to a community organisation, or simply abandoned. A significant number of refugee children arrive in the care of older siblings — usually just a few years senior. Although technically not unaccompanied, these children have very similar needs to unaccompanied refugee children.

British asylum law currently makes no distinction between adult and child refugee — unaccompanied children follow a very similar procedure in applying for political asylum. New Immigration Rules, however, are meant to acknowledge an unaccompanied child's vulnerability. Immigration officers are meant to pay attention to a child's welfare. A child should be interviewed about the substance of his or her claim in the presence of a guardian, advocate or legal adviser. It is a complex and difficult process. A panel of advisers has now been appointed to guide young refugees through the asylum process. This panel is co-ordinated by the Refugee Council. It aims to work for better treatment of unaccompanied refugee children and address some of the concerns raised by childcare professionals.

☐ Concerns

- The asylum procedure is hugely complex and children may find it difficult to find out about their rights and entitlements. Local authorities, who have legal responsibility for caring for unaccompanied children, might have little expertise in asylum law. In the past some local authorities have failed to make asylum claims on behalf of children in their care.
- Many local authorities lack the financial resources, skills and knowledge to meet the needs of refugee children. As a consequence many children receive unsuitable and inadequate care. Research has shown that it takes local authorities longer to respond the the needs of unaccompanied refugee children. Some refugee children are cared for in unsuitable residential arrangements, sometimes with emotionally and behaviourally disturbed children. About 25 per cent of unaccompanied refugee children have no contact with people from their own

community. Some refugee children have been allocated local authority accommodation but not provided with any additional support.

- Generally, refugee children being cared for by older siblings receive little extra support.
- Once they leave care, many unaccompanied refugee children receive little further support and guidance.

Many refugee organisations believe that the needs of unaccompanied refugee children, as outlined by the 1989 Children Act, are not being met. The Children Act is a positive piece of legislation, and it is worth reflecting on its obligations as they affect refugee children.

The Children Act brings together all legislation pertaining to the welfare of children. Areas covered in the Children Act include:

- — definitions of parental responsibility
- — definitions of 'children in need'
- — legal procedures for protecting children
- — amendments to adoption and fostering law
- — the obligations of local authorities to provide care for children in need or on remand
- — secure accommodation for children
- — the regulation of child care and residential care services.

There are also regulations and guidelines to support the Children Act. These are not primary legislation but can be used for judicial review. Local authorities also have their own guidelines and procedure.

Under the Children Act, local authorities have a duty to ensure the welfare of 'children in need' up to the age of 16. Local authorities may also provide services for 16 and 17 year olds if they are assessed as being in need. According to the Children Act a child is defined to be in need if 'he is unlikely to achieve or maintain, or have the opportunity of achieving or maintaining, a reasonable standard of health or development without the provision for him of services by the local authority; his health or development is likely to be significantly impaired, or further impaired, without the provision of such services; or he is disabled.'

Unaccompanied refugee children may be either 'accommodated' or looked after by a local authority. Most usually an unaccompanied refugee child is 'accommodated', meaning the local authority only provides support and does not have parental responsibility for the child. A local authority will only assume full parental responsibility and take out a full care order if a child is 'at risk'. This normally means at risk from abuse or neglect.

The Panel of Advisers for Unaccompanied Refugee Children

The Home Office has funded an pilot advocacy service for unaccompanied refugee children. The service is administered by the Refugee Council and funding initially lasts until April 1995. If it is successful there are hopes that funding for the project will be renewed.

Some 30 advisers have been recruited and trained. They come from a wide range of ethnic groups. Children will be paired with advisers according to factors such as ethnic background and gender. The children's advisers will:

— befriend the young person

— guide them through the asylum process

— give advice

— help them to stake a claim to statutory rights

and

— offer some kind of cultural link.

Unfortunately, the panel of advisers have no statutory power to ensure that children have their care needs met. The advisers have a difficult role to play: if the get into too much conflict with local authorities the authorities will no longer refer children to them.

Children ask for support from the panel of advisers. They may also be referred by social workers, lawyers, community groups, teachers and other professionals. Of course, if children are referred to the panel of advisers, their consent should first be obtained. The relevant social services department should also be informed.

In providing support for children in need a local authority has to provide services which are appropriate to a child's race, culture, religious background and linguistic group. These obligations are of clear relevance to unaccompanied refugee children. The Children Act also stresses the need for children to be kept informed about decisions affecting them. It stresses the need for effective partnership between statutory and voluntary organisations.

☐ Care Options

Adoption

As many unaccompanied refugee children have parents who are still alive, adoption is not usually an appropriate option.

Fostering

Some unaccompanied refugee children have been fostered after they arrive in Britain. Ideally, foster families should come from similar ethnic and linguistic groups and receive proper support from the local authority. Unfortunately, many refugee families do not feel settled enough to put themselves forward as foster families and there is a shortage of foster families from refugee communities. The local authorities, in turn, lack the expertise to enable them to recruit foster parents from refugee communities. Research has shown that where refugee children are placed with non-refugee families there is a high breakdown rate. Clearly more work has to be done by local authorities to encourage refugee families to foster children.

Informal Care Arrangements

Many refugee children who arrive in Britain without their parents are cared for by other relatives and family friends. These arrangements are often successful but not always.

Residential Care

About 50 per cent of unaccompanied refugee children are cared for in residential homes, which might be run by a local authority, voluntary agencies (voluntary children's homes) or privately. Some local authorities and organisations, such as the Refugee Council, have homes specifically for refugee children. In such homes children have a great deal of contact with members of their own community and also the support of other children who have undergone similar experiences. But the majority of unaccompanied children live in non-specialist homes and up to half of them may have little contact with members of their own community. This is an area of serious concern.

Supported Local Authority Accommodation

Some unaccompanied refugee children who have attained sufficient maturity are provided with their own housing but supported by a social worker. In Australia and Canada unaccompanied refugee children often share housing and support workers, but this option is rarely used in Britain.

Finding the right option can be difficult. As there are usually very small numbers of unaccompanied refugee children in a given local authority, their needs may be invisible. It is essential that local authorities keep data about unaccompanied children. Where there are a small number of children in one area, the local authority should consider co-operating with others in making childcare arrangements. Refugee community organisations must be involved in discussions about childcare.

□ The Teacher's Role

Many unaccompanied refugee children are eager to learn and often develop trusting relationships with their teachers. In turn, teachers and lecturers are often the first outsiders to know when care arrangements are going wrong. A child might be experiencing difficulties with the people that are caring for them, or a foster placement could have broken down. A child may have no contact with other refugees or an unaccompanied young person may be living in a bed and breakfast hotel, hostel or flat and be unsupported.

It is essential that teachers working with unaccompanied refugee children understand their experiences and needs, and be informed about referral agencies. There should be at least one teacher in every school who has received in-service training on unaccompanied refugee children. Schools must ensure that they develop good links with social service departments and refugee organisations.

Unaccompanied refugee children do not have access to the advice and support that parents can give. They may find it more difficult to get up in the morning, complete homework and generally organise their time. Parents give advice — on suitable careers for example. The school has to step in and offer advice and must also ensure that children are helped to acquire skills such as cooking and keeping a household budget, to enable them to survive in the adult world. It is important that schools give unaccompanied children extra support, guidance and encouragement. Where a child has few contacts with others from their culture, schools can play a positive role by encouraging such contacts.

If a child is encountering major problems, schools have a duty to investigate and to work with other agencies to ensure that the child receives appropriate care. This will require time and patience and might involve teachers stepping outside their role.

Chapter Nine

Education for Human Rights

☐ Why Teach About Refugees?

There are about 19 million refugees in the world today plus a further 25 million internally displaced people. The numbers of refugees has doubled in a decade; it is a world on the move as never before. The movement of refugees is likely to be among the major political and moral issues of the 21st century. These are issues about which the citizens of tomorrow require information.

Work about refugees helps school children to find out more about current issues such as the conflict in the Balkans. It creates opportunities to explore concepts such as human rights, justice, fear, safety, and experiences such as leaving home and being a newcomer. It can be a way of encouraging children to develop attitudes such as empathy for other people and a commitment to justice and should prepare all students for life in a multicultural democracy. And work about refugees is one means by which concepts and skills demanded in the National Curriculum may be taught.

When developing curricular activities about refugees it is important to be very clear about the aims of such work. Moreover, the work must be located within the context of an anti-racist curriculum. It is no good using multicultural resources if the school does not challenge racist name-calling among students.

Below is a list of ideas for work about refugees.

☐ Early Years

Teachers can use books that tell refugees' stories.

Folk stories from refugees' countries of origin can be used or schools might invite a refugee story-teller to visit.

Teachers should use resources that depict refugees (and other minority groups) doing everyday things like shopping and cooking.

Find appropriate resources and examples from a wide range of cultures: dual language books should be purchased and black dolls should be used alongside white dolls. But it is important to look at resources critically. The Working Group Against Racism in Children's Resources (1990) has developed a useful guide for the selection of resources for young children. Teachers might prefer to develop their own checklist — the important thing is to ensure that resources do not perpetuate bias or stereotypes.

Involve refugee parents in the nursery group, for example inviting parents to cook for the group.

Nurseries should celebrate Muslim, Jewish and Hindu festivals as well as Christmas and Easter.

Make sure that the nursery values bilingualism. Children should be encouraged to use their home language during games. There should be labels and signs in a relevant languages. Children can learn songs in different languages.

The early years are an important time for learning the social skills and values needed in adult life. The early years curriculum should enable children to explore values such as sharing and respect.

☐ The Human Rights Curriculum in the Primary School

Many of the suggestions for work with under fives will also apply in primary schools. Here, teachers have more opportunities to undertake cross-curricular projects on themes such as home, children in other countries and moving house. Such work can very easily incorporate a refugee theme.

The National Curriculum's recommendations can be exploited, as the following examples illustrate:

History

Key Stage One recommends that children study changes in the way of life of British people since the Second World War. This should examine patterns of immigration. Children can read testimonies and look at artefacts and documents.

Key Stage Two recommends that children study a core unit on the Tudor and Stuart times. This should involve work on the contribution of Huguenot refugees. Two further study units can involve a refugee perspective. *Victorian Britain* allows for a study of Jewish immigration. *Britain Since 1930* looks at the impact of the Second World War and social changes, and specifies a study of displacement and immigration.

English

Children can develop the skills specified in the National Curriculum while learning about refugees. The literature studied can include accounts at all levels that deal with social injustice, for example, *Friederich*, and with refugee experiences, as in *When Hitler Stole Pink Rabbit.* Primary school children can:

listen to stories and poems about refugees;
listen to refugee story tellers;
read stories about refugees;
compose their own stories about having to flee from their homes;
describe things they have seen on the television concerning refugees;
make a wall display about refugees;
use a cassette recorder to make a radio programme about refugees;
have children make a survey of the many languages spoken in their locality.

Geography

Working within the National Curriculum, children can trace the journeys of refugees on maps. Children can make a world map to show the origins of children in their school. It is also recommended that children study migration patterns at Key Stage Two.

Art

Children can look at the paintings and artwork of different cultures. There are a number of refugee artists living in Britain who could be invited to visit the school.

☐ The Human Rights Curriculum in the Secondary School

History

Key Stage Three offers a core study unit on the making of the United Kingdom 1500 to 1750 and students can look at the contribution of Huguenot refugees to British life. Key Stage Three also recommends the study of a core unit entitled 'the Era of the Second World War'. Students have to look at the human effects of the Second World War, such as the Nazi Holocaust and the flight of refugees. This core unit looks at the immediate aftermath of the war and the formation of the United Nations and the drafting of the Universal Declaration of Human Rights.

Teachers have the opportunity to develop their own supplementary study units, and students must study a past non-European (sic) society, for example indigenous civilisations of central America.

At **Key Stage Four** students study economic, social and cultural changes in Britain, Europe and the world from 1900 to 1970. This involves an examination of migration and work on international conflict and co-operation from 1945 to 1970. Students will have to examine the role of the United Nations and some of the causes of conflicts in particular regions. Students should also complete a supplementary study unit on the 20th century history of a non-British region of the world, for example Russia and the Soviet Union, the Indian sub- continent, Africa South of the Sahara or the Middle East.

English

Within the English curriculum, students can:

read the testimonies of refugees;

conduct interviews with adult refugees;

compile news reports and write editorial columns;

produce a news broadcast about refugees;
examine the ways in which different newspapers cover refugee issues;
present personal opinions about refugees to other people;
devise a public information campaign about refugees.
Texts can again explore social injustice, for example *Talking in Whispers* and the experience of being a refugee, such as *A Shield of Coolest Air.*

Geography

Students can develop map skills by using maps of different parts of the world. They can examine the reasons for migration and its impact particular areas.

Social Studies

There is a great deal of scope for learning about refugees in this subject. Examination syllabi oblige all students to study race issues and discrimination.

Religious Education

All the major religions feature stories of flight: Jesus's escape from Herod, the Exodus of the Jews from Egypt and the return to the Land of Israel, exile in Babylon, Mohammed's journey to Mecca. Teachers can also deal with contemporary moral issues such as human rights or the way we welcome newcomers.

Craft, Design and Technology

Students can explore possible projects such as providing low-cost shelter for refugees or water and sanitation in refugee camps.

Food Technology

Students can cook the foods of a number of different countries. They can learn about nutritional issues such as those faced by refugees in camps.

Art

Many great artists have been refugees at some time in their lives: Klee, Kandinsky, Ernst and Kokoschka are just a few examples. A class could do a project about the work of artists who escaped the Nazis. Students could produce creative work on themes of fear, escape and safety. Schools can work with refugee artists.

Science

Students can examine the impact of large migrations, for example the issues raised by the flight of two million Rwandan refugees .

Physical Education

Children can play some games of different countries, for instance Kabbadi (known as Thattukili by Tamil speakers), a game played throughout the Indian sub-continent, can be played in PE lessons.

☐ Schools with Refugee Students

More and more British schools have refugee students, particularly those in Greater London. Teachers will obviously have to be sensitive to the feelings of refugee children when initiating class projects on refugees.

Refugee children may have experienced great trauma in their home countries or during their escape. They may have seen members of their own family killed, injured or arrested. Such horrific events cannot easily be discussed in the classroom. Refugee children might not want to talk about their home country or family circumstances because they are worried about family left at home or feel that it might jeopardise their chances of staying in Britain. They might not want to talk about their experiences because they do not want to feel different from other children, or are embarrassed about the popular images of their home country. Some Somali, Eritrean and Ethiopian children have felt unable to admit that they were from these countries because the only image their teachers and fellow pupils had of these countries was of famine and disease.

There are, however, ways of making refugee children feel secure while at the same time increasing knowledge about their home countries. Displays about life in students' countries of origin are one way. Some schools have invited members of refugee communities to tell folk stories or cook traditional dishes. Such work assumes greater importance at a time when hostility to refugees is on the increase. The most important aim of any school project on refugees is to develop empathy towards those who have had to flee. The ultimate message is that refugees are ordinary people who have experienced extraordinary events. In the words of a refugee and a survivor of a Nazi concentration camp:

> *'Dear Teacher,*
>
> *I am the survivor of a concentration camp. My eyes saw what no man should witness: gas chambers built by learned engineers, children poisoned by educated physicians, infants killed by trained nurses, women and babies shot and wounded by high school graduates. So I am suspicious of education. My request is help your students become human. Your efforts must never produce learned monsters, skilled psychopaths, educated Eichmanns. Reading, writing and arithmetic are important only if they serve to make our children more human.'*

(Discovered on the noticeboard of a headteacher's study in Bradford).

Chapter Ten

Early Years Provision

Certain social factors mean that the refugee population in Britain has a greater need for childcare provision than do people who are not refugees. It is a largely unmet need. This chapter examines existing provision and make suggestions for positive practice.

At least 70 per cent of refugee children under five come from homes where little or no English is spoken. These children need social contact with others whose first language is English and this should be provided in a nursery. The age profile of refugee communities in Britain is younger than the general population. In 1992, 75 per cent of asylum applicants were under 35 years of age. There are proportionally more refugee children under five than among the population as a whole.

Similarly, a greater proportion of refugees with young children are in further or higher education than in the population as a whole. Many newly-arrived refugees are attending English classes or obtaining new qualifications to enable them to compete in the British job market. Unpublished research conducted by the Refugee Council in 1989 indicates that certain groups of refugee parents are more likely to work unsocial hours than the general population. The need for childcare is, therefore, greater but the ability to pay for it is less: average refugee earnings are lower than in the general population.

Childcare provision varies from area to area. All local authority social service departments run day nurseries for children judged to be needy; recommendation for attendance usually comes from a social worker. But the geographic mobility of many needy refugee families ensures that social service departments rarely engage in long term support of such families. The most deprived refugee children, housed in temporary accommodation, are the ones least likely to be admitted to social services nurseries.

Most LEAs provide nursery schools and nursery classes attached to primary schools but there are a few LEAs which provide no nursery provision. Even in those which have extensive nursery provision the demand for places vastly exceeds availability. Again, it is the most needy refugee children who, by virtue of their geographic mobility, are likely to be the losers.

Social service and LEA nurseries are staffed by qualified care workers. In most parts of Britain nursery teachers will have had some training on equal opportunities issues.

Some parents rely on private nurseries, for which a fee has to be paid. The costs of private nursery provision are beyond the reach of most refugee parents. Some further and higher education institutes organise creches for young children to enable parents to study, and usually charge a small fee. This type of provision is important for refugee women and should be expanded.

Alternatively, parents can take their young children to playgroups, usually for a few hours each weekday. Playgroups usually charge a small fee for attendance and the children are supervised by play leaders. Some refugee community organisations have organised playgroups. This type of provision is of great importance to refugee women, who may need time to study or to sort out housing, welfare benefits and other issues.

Refugee community organisations and other groups run mother and toddler clubs. These run for a few hours every day and create opportunities for women to meet other mothers. There is a chance to talk to other women while the children play and this is important for a women who are otherwise isolated.

But for most children under the age of three childminding is the most common form of childcare available. Parents may use a friend or relative or a registered childminder. Although many childminders provide an excellent service, few have receive training on equal opportunities issues.

□ Challenges for the Future

Refugee parents need affordable childcare and expansion of nursery places and playgroups is clearly needed. Refugee children, moreover, require early years provision which challenges racism and values their home cultures.

Research carried out by David Milner (1975) and A. G. Davey (1983) indicate that by the age of three children distinguish between different skin colours and attach different social values to them. Most young children develop ideas about race which are in line with adult prejudices (Milner, 1983). If children are to progress into the adult world with positive views about people from different ethnic and cultural backgrounds, anti-racist education has to start with nursery teachers and childminders. The responsibility for developing anti-racist early years provision lies with training institutes, LEAs and social services departments who registered childminders. In order to meet the needs of young refugee children the following issues should be considered.

More nursery nurses and teachers from refugee communities should be recruited. People from minority ethnic groups are still underrepresented on National Nursery Nurse Examination Board courses. The Commission for Racial Equality's *From Cradle to School* (1989) describes positive recruitment practice. College prospectuses must be distributed to community organisations and courses should be advertised in the ethnic minority press. Entrance tests should be examined for cultural bias. Colleges could be encouraged to provide access courses similar to the course run by the Daycare Trust.

More refugee childminders should be recruited by social services departments. Like all childminders, they should be given support and training: attitudes to issues like physical punishment of children differ among cultures and it is important that potential childminders receive information about legal requirements in Britain, particularly the Children Act (1989).

Social service departments should give training and support to all childminders to ensure that they are aware of good equal opportunities practices. For example they can be encouraged to buy toys, picture books and other resources reflecting cultural diversity. The National Childminding Association and the Preschool Playgroups Association should be required to disseminate information about refugee children.

Information about childcare provision in specific areas must be made available in appropriate community languages and should be distributed to community organisations and displayed in bed and breakfast hotels. Local authorities should research childcare needs and provision within local areas and should be encouraged to give more support to refugee community initiatives such as the Armenian Community Playgroup (see p.119).

Support for bilingual children, the development of a curriculum for racial equality and the promotion of positive links with the home are all components of good early years provision and are described elsewhere in this book.

Case Study — The Daycare Trust's First Base Project

The Daycare Trust is a non-governmental organisation working to promote positive childcare practices. It has recently organised a training course in childcare for refugee women from Somalia and Eritrea. Some 55 women have completed the course and funding is being sought to repeat it.

The First Base Project aimed to provide the basic skills that would enable refugee women to complete further training. It was spread over ten weeks and included a placement in a nursery. The areas covered in the course included child development, nutrition and hygiene, first aid, play and learning skills, equal opportunities practice, counselling and listening skills. Participants were given ESL support and all fees and travel expenses were paid. At the end of the course the participants received a certificate validating completion of the programme.

Case Study — The Armenian Community Playgroup

London's Armenian community numbers about 12,000 people, living mostly in Ealing and adjacent boroughs. A focus for community activity is the Centre for Armenian Information and Advice (CAIA). In 1987 a group of young Armenian parents identified a need for a playgroup for Armenian under fives. With the aid of a small grant from the London Borough of Ealing, a summer holiday scheme was set up in 1987. Some 35 children attended and it was judged to be a great success. The CAIA then decided to establish a permanent playgroup. The group now meets for five days a week, charging a small attendance fee for each session.

The playgroup has faced many challenges. The first was finding volunteer play leaders from within the Armenian community. Most parents did not realise that a successful playgroup needs continual support and active participation. But the CAIA has encouraged some parents to take a validated course and become qualified play leaders. Access to premises has been a major difficulty and the playgroup has had to move several times. The CAIA feels that all refugee community playgroups or mother and toddler schemes should have secure tenancy agreements.

Funding has come from a variety of sources including local authority grants and donations from Armenian trust funds. Consignments of children's books and teaching materials have been sent from the United States. With better funding, more teaching resources could be obtained from the United States and Armenia.

Chapter Eleven

Working with 16-19 Year Olds

Adolescence is a difficult time for all of us. We are undergoing physical and emotional changes and having to make decisions that will affect the rest of our lives. Having to cope with life in a new and unfamiliar country can add immense extra strains at an already trying time. Accordingly, refugees aged 16-19 have special educational and social needs, namely:

access to appropriate courses in colleges of further education;

pastoral support in colleges of further education;

careers advice which takes into account their particular needs; and

access to youth work.

☐ Colleges of Further Education

Young refugees who arrive in Britain after the age of 16 usually attend colleges of further education or tertiary colleges if they choose to continue with their education. In order to meet their needs colleges must examine their fee policy. Many young asylum-seekers have had very interrupted education, and the courses offered must take this into account. Colleges can, for example, offer access courses for those hoping to go on to further study. ESL support should be available where needed and all tutors must receive training about working with bilingual students.

Colleges should examine the way they give pastoral support. Many young refugees are lonely and isolated. Colleges of further education can be impersonal places, particularly for those studying on part-time courses. Refugees might have experienced traumatic events in their home countries and uncertainty over family left behind, over immigration status and housing can cause great stress. Student counsellors should be aware of the particular needs of young refugees. Colleges should ensure that they are welcoming places and possibly organise social events for students who are isolated.

☐ Careers Advice for Young Refugees

At 16, with the end of compulsory education, five possible options are open to young refugees. They can remain at school, enrol at a sixth form or tertiary college, enrol at a college of further education, enter a Youth Training Scheme or seek to obtain a job. At 18 similar decisions have to be made; for any young person the many possible choices can be confusing. A career adviser's role is to help young people make informed decisions about their future employment and education paths and to help them progress into further and higher education, training or into employment. With any young person, the careers adviser has to assess needs, advise and teach skills such as interview techniques. With young refugees a careers adviser has to be aware of additional factors before giving advice, namely:

immigration status affects access to further and higher education;

refugees often lack information about the British job market and the further and higher educational system;

the experience of becoming a refugee and living in exile may affect a person's confidence and future aspirations.

Asylum-seekers are classified as overseas students during their first three years in Britain. This means that an asylum-seeker is liable to pay an overseas student's fee for a full-time course in further or higher education (although some further education colleges waive this ruling for asylum-seekers). This is much more expensive than a home student's fee. Overseas students are not entitled to maintenance grants. After three years of 'ordinary residency' asylum-seekers become home students. Young people who are asylum-seekers may have their future options limited because they lack the finance to progress to further or higher education. Careers advisers need to be aware of this issue and shape their advice accordingly.

Young people granted 'exceptional leave to remain' in Britain are home students as regards fees. But they need three years' ordinary residence before they can qualify for a maintenance grant, which further limits their careers options.

Cultural factors influence choice of career. In refugees' countries of origin the method of job hunting is very different to Britain. People may rely on word of mouth or government notice boards rather than newspaper advertisements. Recruitment and selection procedures may be different. This influences how young refugees might go about looking for a job. Careers advisers may need to give young refugees additional support in searching and applying for work.

The status of different jobs varies from country to country. For example in Sri Lanka teaching is a high status job. In Poland the teaching profession is afforded much lower status. These perceptions affect the career aspirations of young refugees. Furthermore, people need knowledge of the types of job available in Britain if they are to job-hunt successfully but many refugees are wrongly or inadequately informed about the British job-market, as the research shows (Marshall, 1991). Many refugees believe that mining and heavy industry employ large numbers of people, when in fact more people are employed in tertiary industries such as banking, finance, retailing, education and the health service. Careers advisers working with young refugees must not assume that they have accurate knowledge the British job market and must be prepared to correct misconceptions.

Many young refugees aspire to return home at the earliest opportunity. This too will influence their career choices, attracting them to jobs or courses that are relevant to their home country. Other young refugees will feel that they are living in between two countries and will be unwilling to commit themselves to long courses in Britain.

Finance for Education

Rules on fees and awards are complex. Those advising young refugees should consult the *Refugee Education Handbook* (World University Service, 1994). Asylum-seekers, those with ELR and refugee status attend school free of charge up to the age of 16. Refugees and people with ELR may continue to attend schools or colleges of further education free of charge up to the age of 19. Asylum-seekers aged 16-19 may continue to attend school without paying a fee. Asylum-seekers may be obliged to pay a tuition fee at some colleges of further education depending on the policy of the college.

As stated above refugees are accorded home student status from the date they are granted leave to remain in Britain. Tuition fees for full time courses for home students are much lower than those for overseas students. Additionally a home student will qualify for a mandatory award if studying on a 'designated course'. The award will cover tuition fees and provide a maintenance grant. Designated courses include:

a first degree
an HND course
a diploma in higher education; and
initial teacher training.

An up-to-date list of designated courses is available from the awards section of the relevant LEA. If someone with refugee status wishes to study on a non-designated course or non-advanced course they are treated a a home student and can apply for a discretionary grant to cover accommodation and other expenses. Most LEAs require a person applying for a discretionary grant to have lived in the locality for a specified period of time. At the time of writing the giving of discretionary awards has been severely curtailed.

People with exceptional leave to remain are treated as home students for the purposes of paying tuition fees, but they must fulfil three years ordinary residence before qualifying for a mandatory maintenance grant. Those applying for non-designated courses will have to fulfil the requirements of the LEA, usually residence in the locality for three years. Young people recently granted ELR usually require some financial savings if they are to study full time.

Asylum-seekers are classified as overseas students during their first three years of residence in Britain. Most newly-arrived asylum-seekers do not have the financial resources to engage in full time education. Instead they may study on part-time courses where there is at present no fee differential between home and overseas students (this may change in 1994). Many asylum-seekers who study part time may also be entitled to claim income support.

Rules on Studying and Income Support

Income Support is administered by the Benefits Agency (BA) for the Department of Social Security (DSS). The DSS does not consider itself responsible for financing education, which is seen as the responsibility of the Department for Education. However, Income Support regulations allow claimants (including refugees) to study under certain circumstances.

The Income Support entitlements of people in education can be broadly classified under three headings:

16 to 18 year-olds in relevant education
those defined as 'students'
those in part-time education.

16 to 18 year-olds

The DSS is restrictive about which 16 to 18 year-olds can claim while in 'relevant education'. Relevant education is defined by the DSS as non-advanced further education courses (up to and including A level) of more than 12 hours per week (IS (Gen) Regs 13)

Some 16 to 18 year-olds can obtain income support while in relevant education and will not be required to sign on (IS (Gen) Regs 13). Among those who may be able to get these benefits are certain categories of refugees: they may be able to study and receive income support if they have 'no parents nor any person acting in the place of parents'. If a young person's parents are not able to enter Britain because of immigration laws that person will also be able to claim income support while studying.

Those who have refugee status and have started an English language course of more than 15 hours per week, within 12 months of arriving in the UK, are allowed to claim income support. This concession lasts for a maximum of nine months.

18 and 19 year-olds can be in relevant education and claim income support if they satisfy conditions under the '21-hour rule'. These are listed below. The claimant may have to give up the course, however, if suitable employment becomes available.

The 21-hour rule

A person can claim income support and study at any level under the 21-hour rule provided that:

a) S/he is signing on and available for work; and

b) is prepared to give up the course if suitable work becomes available; and

c) the course is less than 21 hours per week, excluding lunch hours and private study; and

d) s/he has been unemployed or sick or on a YTS for at least three months continuously before the start of a course, and is in receipt of income support, unemployment or sickness benefit; or

e) in the last six months before the beginning of the course the person was unemployed or sick and in receipt of the above benefits for a total of three months altogether; or

f) the person was on a YTS for a total of three months, and in between these periods was working full-time or earning too much to qualify for benefits. (IA(Gen)Regs9(1)(c),(2)

☐ Access to Youth Work

Many newly-arrived young asylum-seekers spend their first months or years in Britain in temporary housing, often in a bed and breakfast hotel. They may live there with their families or, if unaccompanied, by themselves. Bed and breakfast hotels are invariably overcrowded so young people will find it difficult to study, especially if they have to share a room. Leisure opportunities are also restricted so youth clubs and summer holiday projects are particularly necessary.

Many young refugees have anxieties about their sexual or cultural identity. Their opinions may be in conflict with their parents'. The process of acceptance into British society may pressure young refugees into breaking away from their cultural roots. Some young refugees are happily able to live in a bicultural environment — behaving like a British person when with British friends and adopting the cultural norms of their homeland when with compatriots. But others find themselves on the fringes of two cultures, not fully accepted by either. This will affect their self-esteem and sense of identity.

Questions about identity can be tackled by meeting with other young people who have similar experiences and youth clubs provide a place where young people can meet with others in a similar situation.

Positive youth work with refugees requires special skills. A refugee population is geographically mobile and may not be familiar with youth work as a concept. Extra effort has to be made to publicise youth clubs. This requires good links with refugee community groups and also the schools which young refugees attend. Youth workers must be sensitive to the needs of refugees and familiar with working in a multicultural environment. Ideally, youth services should employ some refugees.

Sadly, there are very few positive examples of good youth work practice with refugees. A few refugee community organisations run youth clubs and summer holiday projects. A few tertiary colleges in London have youth work projects targeted at young refugees. But funding for youth work has become increasingly difficult to obtain and youth work carried out by LEAs has suffered large budgetary cuts in recent years. It is a trend that must be reversed if the social needs of young refugees are to be met.

Chapter Twelve

Making Links

A school is not an island but merely one institution in a society made up of businesses, governmental and non-governmental organisations and families. Every working day the school makes contact with other organisations and individuals. Some of the most successful schools are the ones which have strong links with parents, the caring professions and other groups. This chapter looks at some of the links a school must establish if it is to offer real support to refugee students.

☐ Home/School Liaison

In recent years there has been a great deal of rhetoric stressing the importance of parental choice and parental involvement in education. But despite the directions of the 1988 Education Reform Act, refugee parents have very little contact with their child's school. What contact they do have may only occur when particular problems arise, for example when a child is in trouble. In most British schools more could be done to improve the link with the homes of refugee pupils.

It is worth considering some of the reasons why schools are not successful in making positive links with refugee parents. Refugee parents who are newly-arrived may be unfamiliar with the workings of the British education system. They may have come from countries where there is very little parental participation in education and where events such as parents' evenings are unknown.

Past experiences may make refugee parents suspicious of authority and wary of contact with schools. The uncertain position refugee parents find themselves in may make them nervous of challenging institutions. Language is another factor preventing parental participation; over 70 per cent of adult refugees arrive in Britain speaking little or no English. Positive home/school liaison policies must take these issues into account. Siraj-Blatchford (1993) describes the type of ethos that schools should aim for to encourage good links with parents from minority ethnic groups. Her recommendations can be used as a basis for good practice. Siraj-Blatchford suggests that schools should:

> make all parents feel that they are wanted and have a positive role to play
>
> show parents that they can always make their feelings and opinions known to staff, and that these will be dealt with respectfully and seriously
>
> demonstrate that parents' linguistic, cultural and religious backgrounds are valued
>
> show that the school is part of the community it serves.

☐ Ideas for Action

Every school should have a teacher responsible for home/school liaison. That teacher should be aware of refugee issues.

Essential information should be translated.

Schools and LEAs should work together to prepare welcome booklets for new families to explain about the education system and the school. This material should be translated into relevant community languages.

Parents should be made to feel welcome when they first come to a school. They should be shown around and introduced to staff and other parents. Schools can organise social events such as a coffee morning for parents who are new to the locality.

Parents should be invited to help in the school's activities.

More effort could be made to recruit educational welfare officers and teachers with a home/school liaison brief from refugee communities. Where smaller numbers of refugees are found within one local authority educational welfare officers can be shared with another local authority.

☐ Making Links with Refugee Community Groups

There are over 200 refugee community organisations in Britain. These self-help groups work with particular communities. They offer long term support and enable refugees to gain control over their own lives.

Refugee community organisations vary in size and in the activities they perform. Some have paid staff, others depend on the energy of volunteers. Some community organisations represent certain ethnic, political or religious groups from one particular country. Schools must be sensitive to these differences and be aware that newly-arrived refugees may well be wary of community groups and individuals from their home country.

Among the services that refugee community groups offer are:

advice on immigration law, welfare rights and housing

ESL classes, employment training and careers advice

supplementary schools for refugee children

senior citizen's clubs

women's groups

cultural events and outings

the production of newsletters and information

campaigning on issues affecting refugees ırom that community.

It is important that schools develop good links with refugee community organisations in their locality. If a school wishes to improve the participation of refugee parents in its activities, community groups can be approached and asked to give some encouragement . Refugee community groups can sometimes be called upon to provide interpreters or to mediate where a serious problem has arisen. Refugee community groups can be invited to send members to speak to students or to participate in activities such as cooking, storytelling and other cultural projects.

□ Links With Other Professionals

Refugee children often have a multiplicity of social needs, requiring schools to approach other service providers such as social service departments or homeless person's units. Perhaps the greatest need for good communications with other professions arises from the particular healthcare needs of refugee children. These are described below.

Access to Healthcare

Refugees have unequal access to healthcare and related social services. There are three reasons for this. Firstly, newly arrived refugees may not know how the British healthcare system works. As healthcare is usually organised differently in the country of origin, a family may not know how to register with a GP or that they have to make appointments, or know about the range of services available. Secondly, housing conditions in Greater London have made refugees a very geographically mobile population and this prevents continuity of healthcare. Lastly, refugees are more likely to be refused registration with a GP than other sectors of the population (Refugee Council, 1994). In cost-conscious times someone who does not speak fluent English may be perceived as being more expensive to treat. All these factors mean that teachers and the school medical service should not assume that a refugee family is registered with a GP.

Geographic mobility may mean that refugee children miss the school entrance medical examination (usually carried out in a child's second term at school) and immunisations, because they do not stay long enough at one school. The LEA, as a purchaser of healthcare, should be encouraged to look at its contract with the school medical service and ensure that refugee children receive a school entrance medical examination soon after they arrive at a new school.

Health Issues Specific to Refugees

Most refugees in Britain have come from poor countries which are experiencing conflict. The primary healthcare system in these countries may be overburdened or have broken down. People may not have been immunised. Some groups of refugees may also have travelled through refugee camps where there is inadequate sanitation and insufficient clean water. These past experiences mean that asylum-seekers may arrive in Britain suffering from communicable diseases, particularly tuberculosis, gastro-intestinal infections and parasites and malaria. The school medical service must be informed that a child has arrived from a particular country. Refugee children may have suffered from war injuries (about 20 per cent of Somalis fleeing northern towns during 1988 will have suffered war injuries). These might not have been treated. A small minority of young refugees may have been tortured in their home countries and bear the physical scars of torture.

Malnutrition is a condition experienced by some newly-arrived asylum-seekers, particularly those who have spent time in refugee camps. Refugees living in bed and breakfast hotels in Britain may also suffer from malnutrition, as they might not have proper cooking facilities and have to rely on take-away meals. Additionally, it is debatable whether asylum-seekers who have to survive on 90 per cent of income support can afford a balanced diet. The school medical service must be made aware of these issues and the schools themselves must ensure that school meals meet nutritional guidelines and that refugee children do not miss out on health education. Some schools provide breakfast for children, or have home-work clubs for homeless children where they also receive food. Food technology departments in schools must ensure that young refugees receive health education and information about a balanced diet, particularly if they are unaccompanied.

Refugees may also be at risk of certain diseases and conditions because of their ethnic origin. The commonest of such conditions are two blood disorders: sickle cell disease or trait and beta thalassaemia or trait. These are both haemoglobinopathies, affecting the haemoglobin in the red blood cells. Haemoglobin is a protein contained in the red blood cells, whose function is to transport oxygen around the body. Someone who has insufficient haemoglobin or haemoglobin of the wrong sort suffers from anaemia.

People inherit genes from their parents that determine the form of their haemoglobin . Most people inherit the HbA gene from both parents and this renders them HbAA. Unfortunately there are some abnormal forms of haemoglobin such as sickle haemoglobin (HbS) and beta thalassaemia haemoglobin. The gene for sickle haemoglobin occurs among people from Africa and of African-Caribbean origin. The gene for beta thalassaemia occurs in the eastern Mediterranean, Turkey, Kurdistan, Iran, parts of India, southern China, Vietnam and West Africa. In Cyprus, one person in seven has beta thalassaemia trait; the frequency of the gene does differ from region to region. In the past, people with sickle cell trait or beta thalassaemia trait were more likely to survive malaria. This advantage explains why the gene has survived.

Children who inherit HbA from one parent and HbS from the other will have sickle cell trait — HbAS. Normally they have few symptoms. But if they inherit the sickle gene from each parent (HbSS) they will have sickle cell anaemia and will often feel tired and become breathless after exercise. They may be more prone to infections but will be able to lead a normal life for much of the time. The condition can suddenly worsen, however and cause very severe pains. This is termed a crisis and is caused by the irregularly shaped red blood cells blocking blood vessels. A crisis can be prompted by such occurences as dehydration or strenuous exercise and teachers need to know how to create a crisis-free life for young people with sickle cell anaemia. Those affected by sickle cell anaemia should avoid heavy exercise. Affected children should always stay warm and must not be allowed to become dehydrated. A child with sickle cell anaemia should not be compelled to go outside at breaktime in winter, and a sensitive school should provide a legitimate reason to stay indoors, such as making the child a library monitor.

Those who carry a single copy of the beta thalassaemia gene are themselves healthy. Children born to parents who both carry the beta thalassaemia gene have a 25 per cent chance of suffering from thalassaemia major. Children with thalassaemia major are normal at birth but gradually become increasingly anaemic. In the past most children with thalassaemia major died in their first decade. Today children are treated with regular blood transfusions and injections of a drug called Desferal which removes excess iron from the body.

Female genital mutilation is a major health concern among certain refugee communities in Britain. It is a controversial issue, generating strong feelings among refugees and among healthcare professionals. If those at risk are to be supported, it is essential that the relevant caring professions have good links with each other.

Female genital mutilation is practised in many African countries, as well as in Yemen and Oman, and in their refugee and migrant diaspora. It is carried out by Muslims, Christians, Jews and animists and many believe that it is justified by religious teaching. It has, however, no basis in any religious creed. It some countries female genital mutilation is part of a girl's rites of passage into adulthood. In some societies, too, an uncircumcised woman is viewed as shameful and unclean. Female genital mutilation is also used by families as a means of controlling girls' sexuality, and to deter them from marrying outside their ethnic group.

Female genital mutilation takes three forms: circumcision, excision and infibulation. Circumcision involves cutting the hood of the clitoris, whilst excision involves the removal of the clitoris and all or part of the labia minora. The most severe form of genital mutilation is infibulation. This involves the removal of the clitoris, labia minora and part or all of the labia majora. The two sides of the vulva are then stitched together and eventually scar tissue forms. A small opening is left for the passage of urine and blood.

Most women in Somalia, eastern Ethiopia and northern Sudan are infibulated, usually at between five and ten years old. Female genital mutilation has been banned in Eritrea and no longer affects Eritrean refugees in Britain. Female circumcision is practised among certain ethnic groups in southern Sudan, eastern Uganda and northern Zaire and in many parts of west Africa. Within particular countries female genital mutilation may affect some ethnic groups but be unheard of in other parts of the same country.

In Britain the issue of female genital mutilation mostly affects the Somali, Sudanese and Yemeni communities. Although illegal, the operation still takes place in Britain, amid great secrecy. Alternatively, parents take their daughters to Africa or the Middle East during the summer vacation. There are immediate risks to the girl's health, as well as long-term complications. An infibulated woman may suffer from chronic bladder and uterine infections. At marriage, the husband will cut some of the scar tissue, to enable the marriage to be consummated. Sexual intercourse is likely to be painful for an infibulated woman. Complications during childbirth are unavoidable: in Somalia a pregnant woman has her scar cut open and is then re-infibulated following every delivery. Labour is longer and there is an increased risk of infection, maternal and child death and perinatal brain damage.

There has been little research into the psychological consequences of female genital mutilation but there is no doubt that the practice is traumatic and has overwhelming psychological effects on the girl. That a woman's body has been violated, her central organ of sexual pleasure removed and sexual intercourse made painful is likely to have major psychological effects. The Foundation for Women's Health and Development (FORWARD), a London-based organisation, has set up a helpline for circumcised women. FORWARD has responded to many cases of young, articulate girls and women who are suffering distress as a result of female genital mutilation.

In African and European countries today, however, there are promising initiatives among women's groups and from governments, aimed at ending the practice of female genital mutilation. In Eritrea the practice has been banned for several years. In Somalia the Somali Women's Democratic Organisation has called for legislation, to be backed up with an educational campaign. The Somali Government appointed an official commission on infibulation, banned the operation in hospitals and funded an educational campaign. But the achievements and organisational base of the campaign ended as Somalia plunged into chaos in 1991.

In Britain, legislation prohibiting female genital mutilation came into force in 1985, with the passage of the Prohibition of Female Circumcision Act. Female genital mutilation has been incorporated into child protection legislation by local authorities, and there have been close to 40 cases where action has been taken to protect girls at risk. But intervention is often difficult, and social workers face the dilemma of whether intervention will permanently divide a girl from her family.

FORWARD, the Sudanese Women's Group and the London Black Women's Health Action Group are among the organisations working to eradicate the practice. Among the Somali and Sudanese communities there are an increasing number of individuals and organisations willing to speak out against the practice, often in the face of hostility. They view female genital mutilation as a form of child abuse and an infringement of human rights. But educational campaigns among communities that practice female genital mutilation are underfunded, badly co-ordinated and do not reach all members of relevant communities (Minority Rights Group, 1992).

Teachers need to know about female genital mutilation. Girls who have been infibulated are extremely unwilling to take part in physical education. They may be absent frequently, as menstruation can be very painful. It will also take an infibulated girl a long time to pass urine: in schools where children have little privacy this can lead to questions, teasing and enormous embarrassment.

Many operations take place during the summer vacation, whether in Britain or a Middle Eastern or African country. It is often the teacher who is the first person outside the family to know that a child is intending to travel abroad. If the teacher believes that a girl is at risk he or she should inform the head teacher or another member of staff with senior pastoral responsibility. Advice can be sought from agencies such as FORWARD. A meeting with the girl's family should be arranged in order the explain the school's concerns. It should be clearly stated to the family that the practice is illegal in Britain. It is inevitable that this meeting will be difficult. If the outcome of the meeting is unsatisfactory, a child protection officer in the local social services department should be informed.

Mental Health

Refugee adults and children have specific mental health needs related to persecution and exile. These have been examined in Chapter Seven. It is imperative that good links should be forged with the schools psychological service and child guidance clinics.

Interpreting and Translation

As about 65 per cent of adult refugees arrive in Britain speaking little or no English it is essential that key information concerning the child's health is translated for parents.

Sex Education and Cultural Issues

The 1993 Education Act makes sex education a compulsory subject is all secondary schools. Governors of secondary schools are responsible for developing school policy on sex education, involving parents in the process. Human reproduction has to be taught via the science curriculum but schools now have freedom to decide how they will teach the broader issues of sex education. Parents can withdraw their children from sex education classes. Primary schools are now being encouraged to teach sex education, and school governors have responsibility for deciding if and how it will appear on the curriculum. Attitudes towards sexuality differ among ethnic and religious groups; religious and ethnic diversity create many challenges for those developing positive sex education policies. The following issues should be addressed by those working in a multicultural environment.

Assumptions
Teachers and youth workers often make assumptions about the attitudes that people from different religious and ethnic backgrounds have to issues such as sex and HIV/AIDS. But any minority ethnic group will have as wide a range of opinions as the majority group. Religious groups also approach issues of sexuality in different ways, for example there is no Islamic consensus on homosexuality. Among many 'progressive' teachers there is the belief that religion offers only negative perspectives on matters of sexuality. This attitude can affect the self-esteem of young people brought up in a religious tradition. Teachers and youth workers must not perpetuate stereotypes and must take into account the wide range of opinions within minority groups.

A Student-Centred Approach
The best way of finding out the wide range of opinions within a particular community is to listen to young people and identify issues that concern them. Sex education must address the concerns and needs of young people. In achieving this end it may be necessary to distinguish between the young person's needs and the concerns of those who speak on their behalf: parents, community leaders and those with particular political agendas. It may be necessary to acknowledge inter-generational conflict and internal power play.

Gender
There may be girls from all cultural backgrounds who will not speak openly in mixed groups about issues concerning sexuality. It is essential that young women are able to spend time in single sex groups. Sex education should explore issues such as gender roles in a relationship. But, again, it is important that teachers do not make

assumptions about the role of women and men in specific cultures. In every refugee community there are many personal differences in the positions adopted by men and women and in ideas about masculinity and femininity.

HIV/AIDS

HIV and AIDS is an issue affecting every young person in Britain. But refugee communities present special problems in terms of HIV prevention work and service delivery. Some refugees have fled from countries where the rate of heterosexual HIV infection is greater than in Britain. HIV education in Britain has, however, mainly been directed at the gay community and intravenous drug users. There is an assumption that HIV/AIDS is a 'gay disease'. Clearly this must be challenged but without stigmatising refugees who come from West and Central African countries. The needs of families affected by HIV and AIDS in London are closely linked with race and refugee issues but highlighting this can draw accusations of racism. As a result women and children in refugee communities are not getting the support they need. As well as developing school-based sex education programmes, LEAs and health authorities should be meeting with and supporting community groups active in HIV prevention. There are several successful HIV/AIDS initiatives, for instance, among the Zairean and Ugandan communities.

Refugee children may be directly affected by HIV/AIDS. One or both parents may be affected and children may experience multiple bereavements. Barnado's Positive Options is presently supporting children and families affected by HIV/AIDS, helping them plan for the future.

By March 1994 some 669 children in the UK had AIDS or were HIV positive (Public Health Laboratory). Among them were some refugee children who had aquired the condition through mother to child transmission. It is unlikely that the UK will see a decrease in the numbers of children affected by HIV and AIDS so schools should develop policy to support these children.

PART THREE

Refugee Groups in Britain

☐ Refugees from Afghanistan

Over 3,000 Afghan refugees have fled to Britain since 1979.

Afghanistan has a population of 16 million. The capital is Kabul.

Ethnic Groups

Afghanistan is a multi-ethnic society, and there is an emerging ethnic dimension to the conflict. The largest group are the Pushtuns (Pathans), comprising about 50 per cent of the population. They live in eastern and southern Afghanistan (and also in Pakistan). Also living in southern Afghanistan are the Baluchis.

Three major ethnic groups live in northern Afghanistan: the Turkmen, Uzbeks and Tadzhiks. Central Afghanistan is peopled by Hazara, Aimaq and Nuristani people.

Central control of power has always been weak in Afghanistan. Afghans owe their first loyalty to their family, and then to the clan and ethnic group to which they belong.

Languages

Pushto and Persian (Dari) are the two official languages.

Pushto is spoken by about 60 per cent of the population, mostly in southern and eastern Afghanistan. It is the first language of the Pushtuns. Pushto is also spoken in the North West Frontier Province of Pakistan, although a different dialect is used there.

Pushto is an Indo-European language, most closely related to Persian. It is written from right to left in the Perso-Arabic script, with a number of additional letters to accommodate sounds not found in Persian or Arabic.

Persian is spoken by about 30 per cent of the population, mostly in western Afghanistan. In Afghanistan the Persian language is usually called Dari. It is written from right to left in the Perso-Arabic script.

Tadzhik is spoken in north west Afghanistan, on the border with Tadzhikistan. Most linguists consider Tadzhik to be a dialect of Persian. In the Republic of Tadzhikistan this language is written in the Cyrillic script, but in Afghanistan it is still written using the Perso-Arabic script.

Hazara and Aimaq, spoken in central Afghanistan, are also considered dialects of Persian.

Uzbek is spoken by over one million people in Afghanistan. It is also the national language of Uzbekistan. It belongs to the Altaic language family. It was originally written in Perso-Arabic script, but the Soviet Union Uzbek was later written in the Cyrillic script. In Afghanistan Uzbek still uses Perso-Arabic letters.

Turkmen is spoken by about 500,000 people in north west Afghanistan. It is also the national language of Turkmeniya. It is an Altaic language, closely related to Turkish. In Turkmeniya it is written using the Cyrillic script, but in Afghanistan it use Perso-Arabic letters.

Uzbek, Persian and Pushto have an extensive literature, in the form of poetry and some modern novels.

Names

The naming system differs between ethnic groups. But most Afghans have two or three names: a first name, followed by the father's first name, and then sometimes a family or descriptive name. The first names used are usually Islamic names. The descriptive name can relate to a person's characteristics, or from where he or she comes.

In western Europe this descriptive name is often used as a family name. Thus a woman will take her husband's descriptive name when she marries. Otherwise a woman will keep her two names after marriage.

Religion

Almost all Afghans are Muslims. The majority are Sunni Muslims, although about 10 per cent are Shi'a Muslims. Most Shi'a are Hazara, from central Afghanistan. One of the elements in the present conflict is that the Hazara wish to claim a larger share of power in Afghanistan.

Shi'a Muslims are those who believe that Ali and his descendants are the leaders and successors to Mohammed. Ali was the Prophet Mohammed's cousin and husband of his daughter Fatima. Sunni Muslims believe that the Prophet Mohammed had no successors. Ali was killed at Kerbala (now in Iraq), and this is a major place of pilgrimage for Shi'a.

About 12 per cent of the world's Muslims are Shi'a, the rest being Sunni, or belonging to other smaller sects. Sunni and Shi'a Muslims worship at different mosques. The day of Ashura, marking the death of Husain (the prophet's grandson and another Shi'a leader), is an important Shi'a festival, marked by processions.

Education System

State education in Afghanistan has been severely disrupted because of fighting, and many middle class parents have made private arrangements. No schools are currently operating in Kabul. There are schools operating in towns such as Herat and in some rural areas, funded by USAID and Arab organisations.

Primary education starts at six or seven and lasts for six to eight years. The medium of instruction is either Pushto or Dari, depending on the part of the country. English is taught as a second language in the latter part of primary education. Arabic may be taught in some schools.

There is an entrance examination for admission to secondary education. It is not compulsory. Secondary schooling can last for six years, and there is an opportunity to specialise in technical subjects.

Boys and girls study different subjects. Since 1990 there has been gender segregation in all schools.

Most children in rural areas drop out of school, if they attend at all. The literacy rate is 12 per cent for men and 3 per cent for women.

Economy

Afghanistan is a mountainous country. Its economy is agricultural and the main crops are wheat, fruit, vegetables and livestock. Little has changed in the countryside during the last 500 years.

The rural and urban economy has been disrupted by war and Afghanistan is one of the world's poorest countries.

A Chronology of Events

The country which is now Afghanistan has been colonised by many different empires in the last 2,000 years. From 1767 to 1973 Afghanistan was ruled by a succession of tribal leaders and kings. Governments ruled from Kabul, although central control has never been strong.

In 1883 Afghanistan's present borders were drawn. At this time Afghanistan was a neutral country between two powerful empires: the British and Russian Empires.

1919

A new government comes to power in Afghanistan and attempts a programme of modernisation. It attempts to abolish the veil for women. This so angers many traditional leaders that no government dares try further reforms until the 1950s.

1933

King Zaher Shah comes to the throne. He introduces a new constitution and land reforms. Political parties are legalised.

1973

King Zaher Shah is deposed. Mohammed Daud, the King's cousin and former Prime Minister installs himself as president. His new government initially includes members of all political parties but as time passes opposition is suppressed. Some opposition politicians flee the country.

1978

Mohammed Daud is killed in a coup. The People's Democratic Party of Afghanistan (PDPA) comes to power. This party follows a communist ideology, and draws most support from urban areas. The new government starts an ambitious programme of reforms, targeted at the poor. There are major land reforms, and a literacy campaign in launched. Although the reforms sound good they are hastily and insensitively carried out. Many people oppose the reforms, and some use violence to stop their being implemented.

At the same time the PDPA becomes divided by bitter arguments. Those who oppose the PDPA are arrested, killed or have to leave the country. Between 1977 and 1980 over 200,000 people flee.

1979

Afghanistan's President is killed by members of a PDPA faction. Hafizullah Amin becomes the new president, and human rights violations worsen. Armed resistance to the PDPA grows stronger; these fighters are known as *mujahideen.* By the end of 1979 the PDPA appears to be losing control. On 27 December 1979 Soviet troops enter Afghanistan.

1980-82

After the Soviet invasion the *mujahideen* grow more organised. They are supplied with arms by the USA, Saudi Arabia, France and Britain. Fighting worsens, and by 1982 3,300,000 refugees have fled to Pakistan, and 2,850,000 to Iran. Nearly 5,000,000 Afghans are internally displaced. Life for refugees is very hard, with many basics in short supply.

1986

The *mujahideen* control much of the countryside, while the Afghan government controls urban areas. Fighting is worst in rural areas, and nearly 30 per cent of Afghan villages are destroyed.

1989

Soviet troops withdraw from Afghanistan. The Afghan government, led by President Najibullah, is expected to fall within weeks. But it survives, partly because the *mujahideen* are not united in their opposition. Fighting continues, especially around Kabul, Kandahar and Jalalabad. Western Afghanistan begins to enjoy some peace.

1992-94

The Government of Najibullah falls in April 1992. But the *mujahideen* are not united and cannot form a replacement government that enjoys the support of the majority. Rabbani eventually becomes president but has no power.

Fighting breaks out between different factions. It is concentrated in Kabul and other parts of eastern Afghanistan. By 1993 there is intense fighting between four factions in Kabul. The population drops from 2,000,000 to about 500,000. There are no public services and the city is on the brink of famine.

The *mujahideen* are divided along ethnic, religious, ideological and personal lines. Refugees continue to return from Iran. But the return of refugees from Pakistan is halted by fighting.

Afghan Refugees in Britain

About 3,000 Afghan refugees have fled to Britain. Most are living in Greater London, and are concentrated in the London Boroughs of Barnet, Brent, Camden, Ealing, Hounslow and Westminster.

Some refugees arrived in 1973 after the coup d'etat. Others arrived in 1977-1980 as human rights violations worsened in urban areas. The numbers of Afghans arriving in Britain has increased since 1992.

The refugees express many different political opinions. Some are observant Muslims, others are not. Almost all Afghan refugees are from urban areas. Most worked as professionals or merchants in Afghanistan. Many are highly qualified.

There are several active community organisations The Society of Afghan Residents in UK offers advice, ESL for adults, cultural activities, a youth club, a supplementary school teaching Dari and Pushto, employment training and job search, a women's group and an embroidery project.

☐ Refugees from Angola

About 10,000 Angolan refugees have arrived in Britain, most of them since 1989. Angola has a population of 11 million, of which 27 per cent live in urban areas. The capital is Luanda.

Ethnic Groups

There are three main ethnic groups in Angola and many smaller minorities. The largest ethnic group are the Ovimbundu, comprising about 37 per cent of the population. They speak Umbundu as their first language. Ovimbundu live in all parts of Angola but are concentrated in the central highlands. Jonas Savimbi, UNITA leader, belongs to this group.

The Kimbundu comprise 26 per cent of the population. Their traditional homeland is around Luanda, and in the northern and central regions. They speak Kimbundu as their first language.

The Kikongo are the other large group, mostly living in northern Angola and in Cabinda (as well as Zaire). The Kikongo comprise about 15 per cent of the population and speak Kikongo as their first language.

Languages

The official language of Angola is Portuguese. The most important African language is Mbundu. Mbundu comprises two dialects: Umbundu, spoken by the Ovimbundu of central Angola, and Kimbundu, spoken by the Kimbundu of northern Angola. Some linguists argue that Umbundu and Kimbundu are separate languages rather than dialects.

Kikongo is spoken by about one million people living in northern Angola. Chokwe is spoken by about one million people in north east Angola. All Angolan languages are closely related. They are Bantu languages, belonging to the Niger-Congo language family.

Names

Most Angolans usually use the European naming system. They have a first name, followed by a family name. Many Angolans have Portuguese first names, and many have Portuguese family names.

Religion

Between 80 and 90 per cent of the population hold traditional beliefs but in urban areas the majority of people are Roman Catholic. There are also smaller numbers of Methodists, Baptists and people belonging to African churches.

Education System

Schooling starts at six or seven and lasts for eight years. *Ensino de Base* (primary education) is divided into three cycles or levels. The first level lasts for four years, the second for two years and the third for two years. At the end of the third level students must pass a national examination to go on to *Ensino Medio* (secondary education).

Ensino Medio is a four year vocational course, finishing with the Secondary School Leaving Certificate. Students who complete secondary education may go on to university, but only after working for the state for two to five years. There are also some two or three year pre-university courses, and this offers an alternative route to higher education. The Secondary School Leaving Certificate it comparable to a GCSE examination (British Council, 1991).

The medium of instruction in all schools is Portuguese. The literacy rate for men is 49 per cent, and for women 33 per cent with the lowest rates being in rural areas. The state education system has been severely disrupted by war.

Economy

Angola is basically an agrarian economy and an estimated 71 per cent of the labour force work as farmers. The main crops are maize, sugar cane, palms, coffee, cotton, sisal and vegetables. Angola is a fertile country but the civil war has disrupted farming. Fighting has been concentrated in the central highlands which are the main food producing area. Angola has had to import food since the mid 1980s, and there has been famine in 1989-90 and 1993-94.

Angola has many natural resources and is potentially one of the richest countries in Africa. There are extensive oil reserves in Cabinda, and 90 per cent of the country's export earnings come from crude oil and petroleum products. There are also many mineral reserves such as iron ore, copper, gold, diamonds, uranium, phosphate, lead and zinc.

The war has totally disrupted the economy. Domestic commerce is at a standstill and in many areas the only functioning economy is the barter system.

A Chronology of Events

Before the 13th century Angola was inhabited by Khoi San people. Waves of peoples speaking Bantu languages then moved south into Angola, displacing the Khoi San. The first Europeans arrived in Angola in 1482 when Diego Cao, a Portuguese explorer, reached the mouth of the River Congo. This marked the start of colonisation which was first carried out by trade missions, and then by military expeditions.

For over 300 years Portuguese colonisers made a great deal of money out of the slave trade. The Portuguese offered some Angolan ethnic groups money for the capture of slaves. As a result there was much internal conflict in Angola between those who were and were not recipients of Portuguese money. War and slavery reduced the population of Angola from 18 million in 1450 to about eight million people in 1850. The slaves were transported to North America, Brazil, Sao Tome and Portugal. Nearly 50 per cent perished during the journey.

1850

The Portuguese control the coast of Angola, while the interior is controlled by Angolan traders and local lords. Slavery is still legal.

1884

The Berlin Conference grants Angola to the Portuguese. The boundaries are set in 1891.

1895-1921

A series of military campaigns gives Portugal control of the interior. Portuguese are encouraged to settle in Angola to strengthen their presence. Some Angolans are given a missionary education, and then get jobs in commerce and government. They are known as the *assimilados* — assimilated Angolans.

1945-1960

Portuguese migration to Angola triples, the numbers of settlers reaches 350,000. Many of the Portuguese migrants are unable to read and write. The poorer settlers face direct competition with Angolans for jobs. It is the latter who lose out, and begin to agitate for independence and an end to discrimination against Angolan people.

1956

The Popular Movement for the Liberation of Angola (MPLA) is founded, getting most of its support from the Kimbundu living around Luanda. It seeks an end to Portuguese rule. In the years that follow, other resistance movements are formed, including the Union for the Total Independence of Angola (UNITA) and the National Front for the Liberation of Angola (FNLA). UNITA draws most of its support from the Ovimbundu; the FNLA from the Kikongo.

1961

The war of independence begins. MPLA militants storm Luanda's prisons. At the same time Portuguese targets are attacked in north west Angola. The Portuguese army responds by bombing villages and using napalm. Over 60,000 refugees flee to Zaire.

1965

The war has forced 400,000 Angolan refugees into Zaire. Most settle in the border area.

1968

The war spreads south and refugees flee to Zambia.

1970s

The MPLA, FNLA and UNITA fail to resolve disagreements. More Angolans are killed because of fighting between the three liberation movements than are killed fighting the Portuguese. The super-powers worsen the conflict by arming different groups. The West backs UNITA, the Chinese back the FNLA and the Soviet Union backs the FNLA.

1974

Dr Salazar's dictatorship is overthrown in Portugal. Within days the new government announces it will leave its colonies. The three independence movements sign a cease-fire.

1975

The MPLA, FNLA and UNITA meet in Portugal and sign the Alvor Agreement. This outlines the structure of an interim government and plans for free elections. But by March violent clashes erupt between UNITA, the FNLA and the MPLA. The MPLA then establishes a government in Luanda. The FNLA and UNITA establish an alternative government in Huambo.

In late 1975 South African troops invade Angola. The South African government sees Angola as a potentially wealthy rival in southern Africa. Also, under MPLA rule Angola is a socialist and multi-racial country. Furthermore, the MPLA allows the African National Congress and the South West Africa People's Organisation to have bases in Angola, and both these organisations were fighting a guerrilla war against South Africa.

The South African army comes within 200 kilometres of Luanda. Cuban troops arrive to support the MPLA, and together they manage to drive back the South Africans.

1976-1980

The US Congress stops much military aid to UNITA. As a result UNITA is less active. There is a lull in the fighting and some economic recovery. The Angolan government is able to make big improvements in healthcare and education.

1980

Ronald Reagan, newly elected as President, promises more US military aid to UNITA. South Africa also increases aid to UNITA and resumes bombing parts of southern Angola. Many economic targets such as railways and factories are destroyed.

1982-84

Refugees continue to flee to Zambia and Zaire. By 1984 over 600,000 people are internally displaced in Angola.

1984

Drought and the spread of civil war lead to severe food shortages. The South African and Angolan governments sign a peace agreement. But UNITA continues to receive South African military aid.

1987
The MPLA shifts away from strict Marxist policies and moves towards a mixed economy.

1988
The US and African states put pressure on UNITA and the MPLA to negotiate a peace settlement. A cease-fire is signed in June but, due to different interpretations, hostilities are resumed by August. Both sides of the conflict are accused of human rights violations.

1989-1990
Over 400,000 Angolans are refugees in Zaire and Zambia. There is famine in rural areas.

1991
A peace agreement is signed by UNITA and the MPLA. A cease-fire is agreed, the peace agreement to be monitored by the UN.

1992
General and presidential elections are held in September 1992. In the general election the MPLA secures 57 per cent of the vote and UNITA 32 per cent. UN monitors declare the elections to be generally free and fair. But despite the international presence, Jonas Savimbi, President of UNITA, refuses to recognise the result. UNITA soon reorganises its army and begins to seize towns and villages.

1993-94
The civil war escalates and attempts to negotiate a cease-fire fail. The MPLA is reduced to maintaining control in western Angola and some towns in the central provinces. Over two million people are internally displaced and over 500,000 are refugees in neighbouring countries.

Angolan Refugees in Britain

Statistics

Year	Applications for Asylum	Refugee Status	ELR	Refusal
1989	235	35	15	10
1990	1685	5	10	30
1991	5780	5	10	665
1992	245	10	5	3845
1993	320	10	5	1510

Source Home Office.

The number of Angolans fleeing to Britain reached a peak in 1991 but has since fallen. Today most Angolan refugees who have the financial means of escape to Europe are finding it difficult to apply for asylum. Since the implementation of the 1993 Asylum and Immigration (Appeals) Act all asylum-seekers who wish to apply for asylum in Britain have to make a direct unbroken journey. This is very difficult to accomplish. In 1994 nearly half of all Angolan asylum-seekers are being refused at the port of entry, because they have passed through a safe third country.

Angolan refugees in Britain have often fled human rights violations. Both UNITA and the MPLA government have killed, imprisoned or executed people suspected of supporting opposition groups.

The Angolan community in Britain numbers about 10,000. Most are living in Greater London. They face many of the problems common to refugees, such as difficulty in finding permanent accommodation, employment and ESL classes. There is a community organisation working with Angolan refugees.

☐ Refugees from Eritrea

About 8,000 refugees from Eritrea have fled to Britain over the last 20 years. Although Eritrea is now enjoying peace, Eritrean refugees are unlikely to return in the near future.

Eritrea has a population of 3,500,000, plus 1,100,000 refugees and expatriates in other countries. 89 per cent of the population live rural areas. The capital is Asmara.

Ethnic Groups

Most people in Eritrea identify themselves as Eritrean although there are nine different ethno-linguistic groups in the country.

Languages

About 50 per cent of the population speak Tigrinya and another 30 per cent speak Tigre. Tigrinya is spoken in the Central Highlands of Eritrea, Tigre in north west and northern Eritrea. Most Tigre speakers are Muslim.

Tigrinya and Tigre, like Amharic, are descended from Ge'ez, the ancient religious and literary language of Ethiopia. Both are written in the Ethiopic script, from left to right. There are 35 letters in the alphabet, plus seven vowel sounds to add to the consonants. Two dots are placed after each word to separate it from the next.

Arabic is spoken as a first language by the Rashaida people, who live in the coastal region. There are another six languages spoken in Eritrea: Saho, Beja, Danakil, Baza, Barya, Bilen. Until independence these were not scripted. The Department of Education has now scripted them in the Roman script.

All Eritrean languages belong to the Hamito-Semitic language family. Tigrinya and Tigre are Semitic languages and most closely related to Arabic and Hebrew. The other six are Cushitic languages and more closely related to Somali.

Most Eritrean refugees in Britain speak Tigrinya, although a few speak Tigre. Many can understand Arabic, particularly Muslims or those who have travelled to Britain via the Sudan. Eritrean refugees who have been educated in Ethiopian or Italian schools will have been taught Amharic, English or Italian.

Names

Eritrean Christians use a first personal name, followed by a Christian name and their father's first name. The naming system is the same as that used by Ethiopian Christians. On official documents Eritreans may list their first personal name, followed by their father's and grandfather's name.

Some Eritrean women take their husband's father's name on marriage; others keep their own father's name.

Eritrean Muslims use a traditional Islamic naming system: a personal name followed by their father's name and then their grandfather's name.

Religion

About 50 per cent of Eritreans are Christian; the remainder are Sunni Muslim. In the central highlands most of the population are Christians in the coastal region and western lowlands most are Muslim.

The majority of Christians belong to the Ethiopian Orthodox Church. This church uses a Coptic Rite, very similar to the Egyptian Coptic Church, but has its own archbishop. Eritrean Christians celebrate Christmas, Epiphany and Easter, but on different days to those observed in Britain. This is because the Ethiopian religious calendar is divided into 13 months: 12 months of 30 days, plus another month of five days.

During the time of Haile Selassie, the Ethiopian Orthodox church was used as a means of cultural and political domination. The new government of Eritrea has tried to diminish the power of religious groups. Eritrean refugees in Britain may worship at the Ethiopian Orthodox Church in Ladbroke Grove, London W2. Others may attend Russian Orthodox or Greek Orthodox churches. Some Eritrean Christians are Roman Catholic, particularly the families of people who went to Italian schools. Eritrean Muslims may celebrate the main Muslim festivals and observe the same dietary laws as other Muslims.

Education System

Eritrean refugees in Britain may have attended one of four different types of school: Ethiopian schools in occupied Eritrea or in Ethiopia, Italian schools, schools in the liberated areas or schools in refugee camps in Sudan.

In the Ethiopian system children start school at six years. They remain in primary education for six years, moving on to junior high school for two years. After which they may attend senior high school for four years.

Amharic was the medium of instruction in primary schools during the Ethiopian occupation, while English was the language of instruction in secondary schools. At this time about 50 per cent of teachers in Eritrea were Ethiopian. There was very little investment in state education in Eritrea. Schools were starved of resources and the University of Asmara was closed down. These factors caused many middle class Eritreans to send their children to private schools, mostly run by Italians.

The Eritrean People's Liberation Front (EPLF) ran its own schools in the liberated areas. Education was mostly in the local language and for older students through the medium of English. The EPLF developed its own curriculum and teaching resources, which have now been modified for use throughout Eritrea. Very few Eritrean refugees in Britain will have attended schools in the liberated areas.

Children who live in refugee camps in Sudan may have attended Sudanese or Islamic schools.

The literacy rate in Eritrea is very low, only 12 per cent. Only those who live in urban areas have access to education. The majority of Eritrean children are forced to leave school to work the land or may live too far away from a school.

Economy

Eritrea can be divided into three regions: the Central Highlands, the Western Lowlands and the Eastern Lowlands. The Central Highlands rise to 2,500 metres. They are bisected by fertile valleys. Most people who live in this region are settled farmers. The Western Lowlands extend to the Sudanese border. The land is semi-desert. Most people who live here are nomadic, although there are regions fertile enough to support settled agriculture. Soil erosion is a major problem in this region. The Eastern Lowlands consist of a narrow coastal plain stretching along the Red Sea. It is a desert and the few people that live there are nomadic.

Under Italian rule Eritrea developed light industries. These were mostly located in Asmara, or in the ports of Massawa and Assab. The first car factory in Africa, built by Fiat, was located in Asmara.

After 1952 these industries were dismantled by the Ethiopian government. Factories were taken apart and transported to Ethiopia. The railway from Massawa to Asmara was ripped up. There was virtually no investment in Eritrea's infrastructure. At independence in 1991 there was 150 kilometres of all-weather road in the country. The lack of agricultural investment contributed to the disastrous famines of 1974 and 1982-85.

Eritrea's economy also suffered war damage. Today most Eritreans rely on agriculture as a means of livelihood. Eritrea's main exports are hides and other animal products. The country also relies on the repatriated earnings of refugees and migrant workers.

Nearly 70 per cent of Eritrea's food is in the form of food aid. Agricultural self-sufficiency is a major economic target of the new Eritrean government.

A Chronology of Events

Until the late 19th century Eritrea was a collection of small kingdoms ruled by local nobles. The country was influenced by many of the great powers in the region, including the Turks, Greeks, Arabs, Egyptians and Persians. In 1871 Yohannes IV, an Ethiopian, united Ethiopia and Eritrea into a modern nation state. At the same time colonial powers were beginning to take an interest in the Horn of Africa. The Italians attempted to colonise the country, but in 1889 they were routed in battle.

1889

Menelik becomes Emperor of Ethiopia. He signs a peace agreement with the Italians but is unable to drive them from Eritrea. It becomes an Italian colony. In the next 30 years over 60,000 Italian settlers arrive. They build roads, factories and a railway. Eritrea is also an important military base. Eritrean national identity begins to grow under Italian occupation.

1930

In Ethiopia Emperor Menelik's daughter is succeeded by Ras Tafari, a nobleman. He takes the name of Haile Selassie.

1934-36

Italy is ruled by the fascist Mussolini. Using Eritrea as a base, the Italians invade Abyssinia (Ethiopia).

1940-50

Britain declares war on Italy. Using Somali, Ethiopian and Eritrean soldiers, the British army drives the Italians out of the Horn of Africa. Eritrea is ruled by a British military administration and then as a British Protectorate until 1950. The Allied powers call on the UN to decide Eritrea's future. There are three options: incorporation within Ethiopia, federation with Ethiopia or independence.

1950

The UN decides that Eritrea should be federated with Ethiopia. Eritrea would have a regional government and other safeguards to preserve its autonomy. Undoubtedly Emperor Haile Selassie's pro-western stance influenced the UN, as the USA and Britain, key members of the Security Council, wished the important Red Sea ports of Massawa and Assab to remain in the hands of a friendly government.

1952

The UN agreement comes into operation. Almost immediately, Ethiopia begins to ignore large parts of the UN plan which were meant to safeguard autonomy. Eritrean factories are closed and moved to Ethiopia. There is no investment in the economy. Tigrinya and Arabic are no longer taught in Eritrean schools. Eritrean political parties and trade unions are banned. The Ethiopian government begins to imprison its Eritrean opponents. By 1960 there are about 3,000 Eritrean political prisoners in Ethiopian jails.

1961

The Eritrean Liberation Front is founded to fight for independence.

1962

The Ethiopian government manages to get a majority of its supporters elected to the Eritrean assembly. It then votes for complete unity with Ethiopia.

1974

Famine hits large parts of Ethiopia and Eritrea. Haile Selassie's government collapses and a new military government under Colonel Mengistu takes power. The Eritrean people hope that the new government will restore autonomy but these hopes are short-lived. The new government draws its support from the same people who backed Haile Selassie. Fighting continues with the Eritrean Liberation Front and the Eritrean People's Liberation Front.

Colonel's Mengistu's government — called the Derg — increases military spending and receives military aid from the Soviet Union, its ally. The policy of neglect in Eritrea, Tigray and other provinces continues.

1977

Civil war worsens in Eritrea. Over 30 per cent of the population flee from their homes. Some 250,000 refugees flee to the Sudan.

The Eritrean People's Liberation Front (EPLF), now the main group fighting for independence, makes many military gains. It controls much of Eritrea. In the liberated zones it sets up democratic local government and builds schools and clinics. The EPLF also enacts land reform.

1978

Faced with a new scale of warfare, the EPLF makes a strategic withdrawal from the cities which it controls. The Ethiopian government continues to launch attacks in Eritrea.

1983-85

Two disastrous famines strike Eritrea and Ethiopia. Soil erosion and the continued lack of agricultural investment have reduced farmers to a subsistence level. They have no savings, so when drought strikes in 1983 they cannot buy food. Up to 300,000 people die, and millions of Eritreans and Ethiopians walk to refugee camps.

1987
Further famine hits Eritrea.

1988
The EPLF makes military gains in western and northern Eritrea.

1989
Further food shortages in Eritrea.

1990
The EPLF captures Massawa, a Red Sea port. The Ethiopian government bombs the city, destroying it. The EPLF offers to open the port for food aid shipments, but the Ethiopian government does not allow this. Over 750,000 refugees are in the Sudan, some living in appalling conditions in refugee camps. Asmara and other towns held by the Derg are under nightly curfew. Human rights violations continue.

May 1991
The Derg collapses as the EPLF and opposition forces in Ethiopia make military gains. The EPLF forms a provisional government to rule the country until a referendum in April 1993. A transitional government is established in Ethiopia, and relations between Eritrea and Ethiopia are good. The provisional government offers the Ethiopians access to Assab, a Red Sea port.

1993
The majority of the Eritrean population vote for independence in a referendum held in April 1993. In May 1993 Eritrea becomes Africa's newest country.

Eritrean Refugees in Britain

Eritrean refugees have been fleeing to Britain since the mid-1960s. From 1989-1990, as repression and war worsened, the numbers of Eritrean refugees arriving in Britain increased. Among the refugees who arrived at this time were over 250 unaccompanied children. The Eritrean community in Britain now numbers about 8,000 people, mostly located in central London.

The majority of Eritrean refugees in Britain are from the central Highlands, mostly Asmara. As the ability to flee to Europe depends on having savings, most Eritrean refugees in Britain are from the commercial or professional middle classes. They may suffer a considerable drop in their living standards when coming to Britain. The unemployment rate among Eritreans is, however, less than among many other groups of refugees.

Many secondary schools and colleges in central London have received unaccompanied Eritrean children. In 1990 over 250 unaccompanied Eritrean children arrived in the UK. They had fled from Addis Ababa and other parts of Ethiopia and Eritrea. The majority were boys, fleeing the threat of conscription into the Ethiopian army.

A few children arrived alone. Other children arrived with agents or friends and relatives. Most parents used agents: they paid an agent about US $2,000 to buy tickets. The children were brought to Britain and either abandoned or taken to Eritrean community organisations. Most of the children ended up in West Sussex or the London Boroughs of Hillingdon, Camden, Westminster, Islington, Lambeth or Kensington and Chelsea.

The overall arrangements made for this group of children were poor. There was no reception policy for unaccompanied refugee children, and most local authorities received no extra funding to meet childcare needs. Some local authorities refused to take responsibility for the children. Others were slow to assume their obligations, and some children were cared for by the churches for many months.

There were, however, some examples of excellent childcare: children's homes staffed by Eritreans, and fostering arrangements made within the Eritrean community. But some Eritrean children ended up living in children's homes without any contact with members of their own community. Other local authorities used crude racial criteria when fostering Eritrean children and put them without much thought into African-Caribbean foster homes. Not surprisingly, many of these foster placements broke down.

This group of young Eritrean refugees need a great deal of support by teachers, the youth service, social services and by non-governmental organisations. The crisis often comes when they leave care at 18.

Some Eritrean refugees have lived in Ethiopia before fleeing to Britain. Others fled via the liberated areas or via Sudan. Some Eritrea refugees have experienced imprisonment and torture at the hands of the Ethiopian government. Families coming from outside Asmara may also have experienced aerial bombardment and warfare.

Eritreans are usually highly motivated students, coming from families who value education. They may see their life in the UK as a time in which to acquire education and skills which can be used to rebuild Eritrea. Many Eritrean refugees wish to return home as soon as is practical. The majority of Eritrean refugees in Britain support the policies of the present Eritrean government (although some do not). There are several Eritrean community organisations in London.

☐ Refugees from Ethiopia

There are about 7,000 Ethiopian refugees in Britain.
Ethiopia has a population of 48 million, of which 12 per cent live in urban areas.
The capital is Addis Ababa.

Ethnic Groups

Ethiopia is a multi-ethnic country; conflict between different ethnic groups has resulted in refugee movements. The largest ethnic group are the Oromo, who comprise about 40 per cent of the population. The Amhara make up 26 per cent of the population and live in central Ethiopia, around Addis Ababa. Other minority groups have accused the Amhara of dominating government, and this has been one of the root causes of conflict in Ethiopia.

Tigrayans make up 9 per cent of the population and live in the province of Tigray. The Sidama (9 per cent) mostly live in South West Ethiopia. Some 6 per cent of the population are ethnic Somalis who mostly live in the disputed Ogaden region. Smaller ethnic groups include the Afars and the Gurage.

Languages

Amharic is the official language, and is spoken by about one third of the population. Tigrinya is spoken by about five million people in the province of Tigray. These languages belong to the Hamito-Semitic language family and are derived from Ge'ez, the ancient literary and religious language of Ethiopia. Amharic and Tigrinya are written in the Ethiopic alphabet, and from left to right. There are 247 letters. Each consonant can be modified by additions which symbolise vowel sounds. Both languages have an extensive literature.

Other major languages include Galle (sometimes called Oromo). This is spoken by about 20 million Oromo in southern Ethiopia. Sidamo is spoken by five million people in South West Ethiopia. Somali is spoken by another two million people in South East Ethiopia. Galle, Sidamo and Somali are related languages. Galle has been scripted using an Ethiopic script, and today there are a few Oromo newspapers and journals. There have also been various attempts to transcribe Galle into a Roman script. Galle does not have an extensive literature, the only published books being those translated by missionaries. Somali uses the Roman script. Sidamo is not scripted.

There are many other languages and dialects in Ethiopia. Most Ethiopian refugees in Britain speak Amharic, Tigrinya or Galle as their first language and may also speak a second language.

Names

Most Ethiopian Christians have three names: a first personal name, followed by a religious name, finally that person's father's first personal name. The Christian name is determined by the day that the child is born or baptised.

A few Ethiopians use just one personal name. On official documents the religious name may not be used. Ethiopian Christians may list their first personal name, their father's name followed by their grandfather's name.

Women usually keep their name when they marry. Ethiopian Muslims use Islamic names, having a first personal name, followed by their father's and their grandfather's name.

Religion

Some 59 per cent of Ethiopians are Christian, 30 per cent are Sunni Muslim and 11 per cent practice traditional religions. Afars and ethnic Somalis are mostly Muslim; Oromo are usually Muslims or animists.

Ethiopian Muslim refugees will celebrate *Eid ul Fitr, Eid ul Adha* and the *Hijra.* They may observe the Ramadan fast and have the dietary restrictions of other Muslims.

The majority of Christians belong to the Ethiopian Orthodox Church. This church uses a Coptic Rite, very similar to the Egyptian Coptic Church, but has its own archbishop. Ethiopian Christians celebrate Christmas, Epiphany and Easter but on different days to those celebrated in Britain. This is because the Ethiopian calendar is divided into 13 months: 12 months of 30 days, plus another month of five days.

Church services are held in Ge'ez. Some Ethiopian refugees are devout. They might abstain from eating meat during Lent, demand that meat is slaughtered in special manner and might not eat pork. A child's birth is a time of great celebration: baby boys are usually circumcised at eight days, and children are baptised on the 40th day after birth. Ethiopian Orthodox refugees in Britain may worship at the Ethiopian Orthodox Church in Ladbroke Grove, London W2. Others may attend Russian Orthodox or Greek Orthodox churches.

A few Ethiopians are Roman Catholic or belong to Protestant or independent churches.

Education System

Since the 1974 revolution there has been large scale educational reform in Ethiopia.

Primary, secondary and tertiary education is free. Education is compulsory until the completion of the ninth year.

There is some nursery provision but most children start school at six. Primary education lasts for six years. At the end of primary school a child will take an examination called the Primary School Certificate. After primary education a child moves on to secondary school. At present students spend two years at junior high and then four years at senior high school. This is being changed as the Ethiopian government is in the process of reorganising secondary education.

Students take an examination at the end of junior high school. At the end of senior high, students sit for the Ethiopian School Leaving Certificate. This examination is considered to be the equivalent of a GCSE pass at grades A, B or C on a subject-for-subject basis (British Council, 1991).

The medium of instruction in primary schools is Amharic. In secondary schools the medium of instruction is English but local languages are extensively used in the classroom.

The literacy rate is 47 per cent for men and 43 per cent for women. Many more people are literate in urban areas. In 1971 only nine per cent of men and one per cent of women were literate. On gaining power in 1974, the Derg declared education to be a priority and instituted a major literacy campaign.

Economy

Much of Ethiopia is mountainous, reaching heights of over 4,000 metres. The eastern part of the country — bordering Somalia — is desert. This region is called the Ogaden. The central highlands, around Addis Ababa, are the most densely populated part of the country.

Most people rely on agriculture. Ethiopia is one of the poorest countries in the world, with a GNP per head of about £90 per year. Under the Governments of Haile Selassie and Colonel Mengistu there was very little investment in agriculture and in the infrastructure of many parts of Ethiopia. Tigray, Gondar and the Ogaden (and also Eritrea) were treated rather like colonies. Amharic landlords extracted money from tenant farmers while investing very little in the regions. As a consequence most farmers existed (and still do) at a subsistence level. Farmers have few savings to see out natural disasters such as drought.

Ethiopia's main exports are coffee, animal hides and vegetables such as beans and lentils.

A Chronology of Events

Ethiopia has been the seat of ancient civilisations, including the Kingdom of Axum which came into existence around 500 BC. But although an Ethiopian kingdom existed in various forms at different points in history, power lay in the hands of local nobles. It was not until 1871 that the country was effectively united.

1871

Yohannes IV, a northern noble manages to unite Ethiopia.

1889

The Italians attempt to colonise Ethiopia but lose in a battle which also kills Emperor Yohannes. The Italians withdraw to Eritrea which becomes an Italian colony. Menelik becomes the new Emperor, and signs a peace treaty with the Italians.

1930

Ras Tafari, a nobleman, become Emperor. He takes the name of Haile Selassie. During his rule there is continued neglect of regions of Ethiopia such as Tigray and Gondar. Much land is owned by wealthy landlords who reap the profits of tenant farmers but do not put money back. As a result peasant farmers exist at a subsistence level.

1934-36

Ethiopia (then called Abyssinia) attracts the attention of Italy's fascist government. Using Eritrea as a military base Italy prepares for war, and by late 1935 invades the country. Haile Selassie flees to Britain.

1941

The Italians are forced out of Ethiopia by British and African troops. Ethiopia and Eritrea are placed under British rule until 1952.

1952

Ethiopia gains independence and is federated with Eritrea. Haile Selassie is restored as Emperor. He gains most support from the Amhara and his government continues to neglect the needs of the non-Amharic majority. In Tigray, a province of six million people, there is only one road and five secondary schools in 1973.

1974

Ethiopia suffers a famine. Haile Selassie is criticised for his policies during the famine and overthrown by a group of army officers. There are hopes that the new government, led by Colonel Mengistu, will improve the lot of Ethiopians and Eritreans, but these hope are short-lived. The new government draws its support from the Amharic minority, the same people who backed Haile Selassie. The policy of neglect of Ethiopia's regions continues, whilst the new government, called the Derg, increases military spending.

Human rights violations increase and many opponents of the regime are imprisoned.

1975

The Tigrayan People's Liberation Front is formed to fight for regional autonomy for Tigray. Somalis and Oromo also form armed organisations, and fighting erupts in Tigray and in the Ogaden.

1983-85

Most of Ethiopia suffers from serious food shortages after rains fail. Eritrea and Tigray are particularly badly hit. Fighting means that food cannot reach starving people. Over six million people are forced to leave their villages and walk to refugee camps in Sudan and Ethiopia.

1987

Famine hits Ethiopia again. Parts of Eritrea and Tigray are are also threatened by swarms of locusts because fighting prevents the aerial spraying of the insects. The Ethiopian government resettles thousands of people on to collective farms in southern Ethiopia.

1990

Parts of Ethiopia are again threatened by famine, made worse by civil war. Opposition groups in Ethiopia unite to form the Ethiopian People's Revolutionary Democratic Front (EPRDF). This grouping is dominated by the Tigrayan People's Liberation Front and operates in co-operation with the Eritrea People's Liberation Front.

1991

The military successes of the EPRDF puts the Derg under increasing strain. In May 1991 the Ethiopian government collapses, and the EPRDF marches into Addis Ababa. It forms a transitional government and announces its commitment to democracy.

1992-94

Daily life is much easier for most Ethiopians, and human rights violations decrease. Nevertheless there are still major human rights concerns such as the imprisonment of opposition journalists. The EPRDF also attracts opposition from Addis Ababa's urban and Amharic speaking middle class. They fear that the government is dominated by Tigrayans and does not take their needs into account.

In February 1994 the elections were postponed.

Ethiopian Refugees in Britain

There are over 7,000 Ethiopian refugees in Britain. They have been arriving in small numbers since the mid-1970s. Until May 1993 the Home Office did not keep separate statistics for Ethiopians and Eritreans. Since this date over 600 Ethiopians have applied for political asylum in Britain.

Ethiopian refugees in Britain come from several ethnic groups. The majority are Amhara from Addis Ababa and its environs. They include opponents of the Derg and, most recently, opponents of the new government.

Britain has also received smaller numbers of Tigrayan and Oromo refugees. Oromo refugees are still fleeing to Britain due to fighting in south east Ethiopia, as well as repression of Oromo nationalists. Britain's Oromo community numbers about 1,000 and there are about 800 Tigrayan refugees. Both Tigrayan and Oromo refugees have their own community associations.

In the last three years over 600 unaccompanied refugee children have sought asylum in Britain. They are mostly the sons and daughters of people associated with the previous regime. Since the fall of the Derg there has been a slimming down of the army and civil service, and people closely associated with Colonel Mengistu have been replaced.

Most of the children are brought out of Ethiopia by an agent and taken to Ethiopian community organisations in central London. Most Ethiopian refugees live in Greater London with the largest numbers living in Camden, Westminster and Kensington and Chelsea.

The majority of Ethiopian asylum-seekers are being granted exceptional leave to remain (ELR). In 1993 some 98 per cent of Ethiopians who received a decision on their case were granted ELR.

☐ Refugees from Ghana

About 9,000 Ghanaians have fled to Britain as refugees, joining an existing Ghanaian community in Britain.

The Republic of Ghana has a population of 15 million, of which 33 per cent live in urban areas. The capital is Accra.

Ethnic Groups

There are six main ethnic groups in Ghana. The Akan (Ashantis) form 44 per cent of the population and live in the central and southern part of Ghana. Some 13 per cent are Ewe (pronounced ay way) and 8 per cent are Ga-Adangbe; both these groups live in southern Ghana. The Mole-Dagbane (16 per cent), Guan (4 per cent) and Gurma (3 per cent) mostly live in northern Ghana.

Languages

The official language is English which is widely spoken in Ghana. The main indigenous languages are Twi and Fanti, spoken by about six million people in southern Ghana. Twi and Fanti are very closely related languages and belong to the Niger-Congo language family.

Other important languages are Ewe, spoken by about two million people, Ga and Adangme, each spoken by one million people, and Gurma and Dagbane, each with about 300,000 speakers.

Names

Several different naming systems are used in Ghana. The Akan name their children after the day of the week on which the child is born. All the days of the week are derived from the names of gods, and have a male and female form.

Day of the Week	Name of God	Male Name	Female Name
Monday/Dwowda	Adwo	Kwadwo	Adua
Tuesday/Benada	Akena	Kobna	Abena
Wednesday/Wududa	Aku	Kwaku	Akua
Thursday/Yaw'da	Ayou	Yau	Yaa
Friday/Fida	Afi	Kofi	Efua
Saturday/Mememda	Amen	Kwame	Ama
Sunday/Kwasida	Assi	Kwasi	Essi

Children are given additional personal names, one of which is the name of a close relative or family friend. Sometimes the father's name is used as a family name. Women keep their names when they marry.

Other ethnic groups have a system of personal names and family names. Ghanaian Muslims use an Islamic naming system, comprising personal name, father's name and grandfather's name.

Religion

About 40 per cent of the population practice traditional religions, particularly in rural areas. Another 43 per cent are Christians and about 12 per cent are Muslims. People from northern Ghana are more likely to be Muslims or Roman Catholics. Those living in central and southern Ghana are more likely to be Anglicans, Methodists, Seventh Day Adventists or to belong to a wide range of smaller African churches. Church membership plays an important part in the life of many Ghanaians in Britain.

Education System

Education is free in Ghana and primary education is compulsory. Primary education lasts for six years and most children enrol at the age of six. Children then move on to a junior secondary school for three years, then to senior secondary school for a further three years, after which students take GCE O-Level examinations, administered by the West African Examinations Council. A pass at grades 1-6 is considered to be the equivalent of a GCSE pass at grades A, B or C.

A limited number of senior secondary schools offer two year GCE A-Level courses, considered to be the equivalent of a British A-Level (British Council, 1991).

English is the medium of instruction, although some primary schools are now teaching through the local language during the first two years. Children arriving from Ghana may need some additional help with their English.

The literacy rate is 43 per cent for men and 18 per cent for women. Even today only about 35 per cent of girls start secondary education.

Economy

Southern Ghana is covered in dense rainforest which has been partially cleared for small farms and plantations of oil palm, cocoa, coffee and bananas. Savannah covers northern Ghana. The main exports are coffee, cocoa, aluminium, fish, tropical hardwood and precious stones.

Ghana is poorer than many of its West African neighbours. There is a large urban/rural divide.

Causes of Flight

Ghana has been a trading nation for hundreds of years, first with other African kingdoms and later with European countries. The slave trade decimated the economy of coastal regions. Later Ghana became a British colony — the Gold Coast.

Despite numerous religious and ethnic divides, Ghanaian nationalism began to emerge at the beginning of the 20th century. The desire for independence was taken up by newly founded political parties such as Kwame N'Krumah's Convention People's Party. N'Krumah is remembered as one of the founding fathers of African nationalism and the Movement of Non-Aligned Nations. He became Prime Minister in 1952, and in 1957 Ghana became one of the first colonies in Africa to win its independence. His government began an ambitious programme of agrarian and social reforms. His party built up a solid political party structure and consequently an active trade union movement. This is still in evidence today, even though many political activists have been forced into exile.

But conservative elements in Ghanaian society conspired against the government, and in 1966 N'Krumah was overthrown in a coup d'etat. Nearly thirty years of political instability has followed.

Ghana returned to civilian rule in 1969 but the new government did not last long. In 1972 the government of Dr Kofi Busia was overthrown in a military coup. The new government embarked on policies which proved to have disastrous economic consequences on the poor and middle classes. By 1977 Ghana had a huge foreign debt and high inflation. Those who questioned the government's policies were often imprisoned. In 1977 the 'revolt of the middle classes' took place. There were strikes and demonstrations. Colonel Acheampong, President from 1972, was replaced by another military ruler. Later another military coup led by Flight-Lieutenant Jerry Rawlings overthrew this government.

At first excitement greeted Rawlings' coup. It promised an end to years of military misrule, corruption and repression. Ghanaians, politically sophisticated and well-organised, elected a civilian government within months. But the optimism was to be short-lived. Two years later Rawlings again assumed power. The 1979 commitments to 'freedom, justice and accountability' were soon swept aside. Rawlings started to suppress opposition. Amnesty International and other human rights organisations report detentions, imprisonment, executions and the activity of death squads. Not even the churches have been immune from oppression.

Most of those escaping human rights abuse fled to neighbouring countries. But in Togo, Ivory Coast and Nigeria some refugees have been deported. Britain has the largest Ghanaian refugee community in Europe. There are also sizeable numbers of Ghanaian refugees living in Germany.

Ghanaian Refugees in Britain

Statistics

Year	Asylum Applications	Refugee Status	ELR	Refusal
1983	689	199	126	199
1984	337	73	59	157
1985	141	37	24	135
1986	196	22	21	38
1987	125	19	50	82
1988	172	23	79	44
1989	330	30	115	25
1990	1,330	5	30	50
1991	2,405	10	20	100
1992	1,600	5	20	1,210
1993	1,785	5	10	925

These figures exclude dependants after 1985. Source Home Office.

About 9,000 Ghanaian refugees have arrived in Britain since 1982, joining an existing Ghanaian community of about 50,000 people. In everyday situations it is often difficult to distinguish between Ghanaians who are refugees and those who have migrated for other reasons.

Ghanaian refugees started arriving after 1981 (Lieutenant J. J. Rawlings' military coup). Most of the early arrivals were political opponents and trade unionists. Today's Ghanaian asylum-seekers come from a wider spectrum of society, including rural people whose only 'crime' was to be involved with their church.

The majority of Ghanaian asylum-seekers are now being refused refugee status or ELR.

Most Ghanaian refugees live in Greater London alongside other compatriots. The largest communities are in the London Boroughs of Lambeth, Southwark, Tower Hamlets and Hackney. There are several community organisations offering advice, legal representation, employment training and cultural activities.

☐ Refugees from Iran

Since 1980 over 20,000 Iranian refugees have arrived in Britain.

The Islamic Republic of Iran has a population of 53 million, of whom 54 per cent live in urban areas. The capital is Tehran.

Ethnic Groups

Over the last 3,000 years different invaders and migrants have settled in Iran. Although 60 per cent of the population identify themselves as Persians, the culture and people of Iran reflect these many waves of immigrants.

Another 40 per cent of the population belong to minority groups, the largest of which are the Azeris, comprising 27 per cent of the population. Other minority groups include the Kurds (15 per cent of the population), Turkmen (3 per cent), Baluchis (2.5 per cent), Arabs (2.5 per cent), Armenians (2 per cent of population), Assyrians and Jews. Refugees from all these minority communities have fled Iran, in particular Kurds, Armenians and Jews.

Languages

Persian is the official language, spoken by the majority of people in Iran and also in western Afghanistan. In Iran the language is generally referred to as Farsi; in Afghanistan it is called Dari.

Persian is one of the world's oldest languages. Since the 7th century it has been written in the Arabic script with a number of additional letters to accommodate extra sounds. Persian is an Indo-European language.

Azeri is spoken by about five million people in the Province of Azerbaijan. Azeri is linguistically related to Turkish. Other languages include Gilaki and Mazanderani: both are related to Persian and are spoken in northern Iran along the shores of the Caspian Sea. Kurdish is spoken by many of Iran's five million Kurds, although the use of the language has been heavily discouraged. Between 1946 and 1979 it was forbidden to speak or write Kurdish. As a result many younger Kurds are not literate in the language.

Baluchi is spoken by about 500,000 people in South East Iran. Other languages include Arabic (500,000 speakers) Turkmen (500,000 speakers) Armenian (250,000 speakers) and Assyrian (100,000 speakers). Britain has received Iranian refugees from the Armenian and Assyrian communities, who speak these languages and generally also speak Persian.

Names

Iranian men and women have a first personal name. This can be followed by their father's name and a family or descriptive name. Women usually retain their family names on marriage but the children adopt their father's family name. In Britain a few Iranian women are now changing their family names when they marry.

Religion

Some 80 per cent of Iranians are Shi'a Muslims. The Kurdish minority are mostly Sunni Muslims. Other religious groups include Armenian Christians, Assyrian Christians, Baha'is, Zoroastrians, Jews and a small number of Catholics and Protestants.

In the late 1970s soaring inflation and discontent with the Shah's autocratic regime led to the development of an active opposition. The exiled Ayatollah Ruhollah Khomenei, supported by Islamic clergy, inspired millions of ordinary Iranians who were clearly disappointed with the failures of Western capitalism. For them Islamic fundamentalism offered a radical alternative.

In 1979 the Shah was forced to flee and his government was replaced by a fifteen-member Islamic Revolutionary Council. Supreme power was vested in a religious leader — initially the Ayatollah Khomenei. After a brief power struggle, the Islamic clergy emerged as the only force capable of taking control of Iran. A new constitution and legislative changes were introduced, both based on *sharia* — Islamic law and religious teaching.

As part of the new ideology women were rapidly removed from public life. An Islamic dress code was adopted. The age of marriage was reduced from eighteen to nine years. Divorce laws were changed, preventing women from obtaining a divorce save under the most extreme circumstances. Married women convicted of adultery are punished by being stoned to death. Sexual segregration in education has drastically reduced the opportunities available to women. Certain professions are also barred to women.

Many secular Iranians actively supported the overthrow of the Shah but soon became disillusioned with the new regime. As the Government adopted more repressive measures secular Iranians began to flee. The majority of Iranian refugees living in Britain are not religiously observant.

A small number of Mujahideen Khalq have fled to Britain. The Mujahideen Khalq are a Shi'a political group whose ideology is a mixture of socialism and Islam. Most of the Mujahideen Khalq are exiled in Iraq.

Iran's Islamic constitution recognises the rights of other religions, and Sunni Muslims, Christians, Jews and Zoroastrians are all represented in the *Majlis* — the Parliament. But Iranian Jews and Armenians have nevertheless been forced to flee.

In 1979 Iran's Jewish community comprised about 70,000. After the revolution Iran immediately aligned itself against Israel and made Zionist activity a crime punishable by death. Some prominent Jews were executed. At the same time the Ayatollah Khomenei publicly reassured Jews of their safety in Iran. But in the face of blatant anti-Zionist ideology many Jews felt unsafe in Iran. Between 1980 and 1992 over 55,000 Jews fled Iran, to Israel or to European countries.

Many Armenian Christians have also fled Iran. Extremist elements in the Islamic clergy have harassed teachers in Tehran's Armenian schools, and some Armenian businesses have found it difficult to function.

Special mention must be made of the Baha'i. This is a modern religion, founded in the 19th century in southern Iran. Its roots are in Shi'a Islam, although it is a separate religion. Followers believe that God's will has been revealed throughout the ages by a series of prophets. The prophets include the Lord Buddha, Zarathrustra, Jesus Christ and Mohammed. The Baha'i faith has about five million adherents world-wide, including about 200,000 followers in Iran.

The Baha'i do not have the recognition afforded to other religious minorities and have suffered extensive persecution since 1979. Many holy places have been destroyed and the Baha'i have been ordered to recant their faith in public. In some parts of Iran local government officials have treated the Baha'i with great harshness. Over 200 Baha'i have been murdered. Many hundreds of others have been detained or imprisoned. Whilst in prison they have been tortured in an attempt to force them to recant their faith. They have also suffered systematic economic discrimination. The Baha'i have been denied welfare benefits and pensions. In some parts of Iran the Baha'i have lost land or been denied business licences.

Iranians of all religions celebrate the Yalda and Nourouz festivals. The Yalda festival marks the longest night of the year, and has its roots in the Zoroastrian religion and in the ancient traditions of Persia. Nourouz is the Iranian New Year and is celebrated in the Spring.

Education System

Education is compulsory for eight years. Children may attend nursery classes but for most children primary school starts at six years. Primary education lasts for five years; at the end of which students sit an examination. Success in this examination entitles students to enter secondary education.

Secondary education can last for seven years. Schooling is divided into two cycles: a three year guidance cycle and a two or four year intermediate cycle. At the end of the guidance cycle students take a national examination. Those who pass are entitled to enter the intermediate cycle.

Intermediate education offers the opportunity for specialisation. Students chose one of four types of course: academic, industrial, service industry related or rural and agricultural.

Students choosing academic courses study a general curriculum for three years. The final year offers specialisation into arts, natural science, physics and mathematics or social sciences. On completion of the intermediate cycle students take a national examination called the *Concours*. A pass at *Concours* is deemed to be the equivalent of a GCSE pass, grades A, B or C on a subject-by-subject basis. Students choosing vocational courses may study in programmes lasting for two or four years (British Council, 1991).

The medium of instruction in all schools is Farsi.

Since the Islamic Revolution there have been extensive educational changes. All schools were immediately segregated, including nursery schools. In the early 1980s the curriculum was rewritten to reflect Islamic ideology. Many teachers and educational administrators left at this time. Religious teaching plays a major role in the curriculum and in school life. The Armenian and Jewish communities have their own schools, as do other recognised religious minorities. These schools are obliged to follow the national curriculum and use Farsi as the medium of instruction. Private schools and co-educational schools are banned.

The literacy rate is 71 per cent for men, compared with 50 per cent for women. Levels of literacy are higher in urban areas and lowest in rural Baluchistan and Iranian Kurdistan.

Economy

About 30 per cent of the population are employed in agriculture, the production of wheat and fresh and dried fruits being important. Carpet manufacture also employs many people. Iran has substantial oil reserves, which account for most of its export earnings. Central Iran and the areas around the Caspian Sea are the most fertile regions. Baluchistan is dry and infertile and one of the most impoverished regions of Iran.

A Chronology of Events

Iran has been inhabited by peoples speaking Indo-European languages since the 18th century BC. From the 10th century BC a recognisable Persian culture had developed, and by 500 BC the Persians controlled a large Empire, stretching as far as the Mediterranean and India. The Persian Empire then fell into the hands of Alexander the Great. After Alexander's death parts of the Empire were conquered by the Seleucid Turks and the Romans.

The area which is now Iran was brought under the control of the Arab Caliphate of Baghdad in the seventh century AD. Islamic thought and practice were introduced during this period. After the collapse of the Caliphate of Baghdad, Persia attained autonomy under the rule of Seleucid and Persian dynasties. This was a time of great scientific and cultural achievement.

In 1258 Persia was invaded by the Mongols. For three centuries political life was dominated by conflicts between the Mongols and the Ottoman Turks. Eventually a Persian monarch united the country, expelling the Turks. Persia was then ruled by a succession of dynasties.

1906

Persia becomes a constitutional monarchy ruled by a Shah.

1909-1921

A treaty divides Persia into two areas — one under the economic influence of Britain and the other of Russia. Britain exploits the oil fields. During the First World War Persia is occupied by the British and Russians. Foreign occupation and widespread government corruption lead to popular unrest. In 1921 the Government is overthrown by Reza Khan, commander of the National Guard.

1923-25

Reza Khan becomes Prime Minister. In 1925 he ousts the Shah and takes the throne. He attempts to turn Persia into a modern and neutral state. Among other things he abolishes the obligatory wearing of the veil, and modernises the health and education systems. He cancels British oil concessions.

1935

Persia is renamed Iran.

1941

Reza Shah refuses to allow a consignment of Allied arms to pass through Iran. After issuing an ultimatum, the British and Soviet armies invade Iran. Reza Shah abdicates in favour of his son, Mohammed Reza Pahlavi. Educated in Europe, the new Shah is perceived to be more amenable to British interests.

1949-53

The 1949 constitution restricts the powers of the Shah. Prime Minister Mossadegh attempts to reduce economic dependence on Britain and tries to nationalise the oil fields. In 1953 Mossadegh is overthrown in a CIA backed coup, and much political power returns to the Shah. Mossadegh is imprisoned and thousands of socialist and nationalist politicians are killed or detained.

1961-73

Iran experiences a period of increasing westernisation, greater penetration by transnational companies, rapid economic growth, but increasing urban poverty. These changes are known as the 'White Revolution'.

1963

The Islamic clergy oppose the Shah's modernisation policies. Peaceful demonstrations inspired by the Ayatollah Khomeini are crushed by the armed forces and many demonstrators are killed. Khomeini is forced into exile.

1974

A huge rise in oil prices causes an increase in Iran's oil revenue. The Shah launches an ambitious spending programme which fuels inflation and exarcerbates tensions within Iranian society. The spending boom is followed by harsh austerity measures to control inflation. The poor suffer most from government spending cuts. Antagonism towards the Shah's regime increases.

1975

All political parties with the exception of the Resurgence Party are banned. The Shah declares that all those who oppose the new order 'can take their passports and leave the country'.

1977

Amnesty International criticises the Iranian government's record on human rights. Protests mount in Iran, with numerous strikes and demonstrations. The best organised opposition to the Shah's regime comes from the exiled Ayatollah Khomeini.

1978

Another year of protests, many of which are violently suppressed. Martial law is declared at the end of the year.

1979

On January 6th Shahpur Bakhtiar forms a new government in a a last ditch attempt to avert a revolution. But the Shah flees the country soon after. The Ayatollah Khomeini arrives in Tehran and on 11th February Iran is declared an Islamic Republic. Governing powers are initially vested to a fifteen-member Islamic Revolutionary Council.

The new regime launches an attack on Iranian Kurdistan. Other breaches of human rights soon become apparent.

1980

There is an intense power struggle within the government, which continues for two years. An election results in Abol-Hasan Bani-Sadr becoming President, and more elections are held for the *Majlis* (parliament). The Islamic Revolutionary Council is then dissolved.

Women are expelled from government offices. The universities are closed. There are numerous border conflicts with Iraq, tension is heightened when Khomeini calls for the Shi'a of Iraq to rebel against the 'atheistic Ba'athist regime'. In September 1980 Iraqi troops cross the Shatt-al-Arab Canal to claim territory. The Iran/Iraq war begins; it is to last for eight years.

1981

President Bani-Sadr is deposed. A bomb attack on the offices of the ruling Islamic Republic Party kills 70 politicians. A further bomb in October kills the President and Prime Minister. Hojatolislam Ali Khamenei becomes the new President. The Revolutionary Guards continue a campaign of terror, executions and arrests as the regime crushes all internal opposition.

1982

Iranian students in foreign universities are banned from receiving money from Iran.

1983-87

Human rights abuses continue, Kurdish and Baha'i minorities are subject to widespread persecution.

1988

After signs of internal dissent, there is a new peak of arrests and executions of political opponents. At least 2,500 people are executed. Faced with an ailing economy and no prospect of winning the war with Iraq, President Khamenei agrees to a cease-fire and to accept UN Resolution 598, calling for an end to the war.

1989-91

Ayatollah Khomeini dies and Ayatollah Khameini becomes Iran's new spiritual leader. Another power struggle ends with the 'reformist' Hashemi Rafsanjani being elected as President. There are further constitutional changes, and the post of Prime Minister is abolished.

The 'reformists' indicate that they would like to improve relations with the West. During the Gulf War Iran maintains a neutral position. There are a few signs of improvements in human rights, such as an amnesty for draft evaders and war deserters. But arrests and executions of political activists continue.

Former Prime Minister Bakhtiar is assassinated in Paris. Rafsanjani states that any returning refugees 'must adapt themselves to the country's revolutionary code of conduct'.

1992

Rafsanjani is re-elected as President. There are disturbances in some of Iran's main cities due to dissatisfaction with government policy, followed by mass arrests and executions.

Iranian Refugees in Britain

Statistics

Year	Asylum Applications	Refugee Status	ELR	Refusal
1980	1,421	876	44	150
1981	1,547	1,171	66	331
1982	2,280	1,355	144	383
1983	1,862	547	599	51
1984	1,310	320	506	90
1985	861	262	562	144
1986	897	136	300	216
1987	649	69	291	126
1988	393	45	456	62
1989	350	95	485	15
1990	455	45	100	10
1991	530	55	60	10
1992	405	110	605	60
1993	365	100	130	50

These figures exclude dependants after 1985. Source Home Office.

Iranian refugees come from different ethnic groups and have very many different political sympathies. Many Iranian refugees in Britain have previously studied here.

Some of those who sought asylum in the early 1980s were supporters of the Shah. They may have already been in Britain, usually as students, and could not return. Other Iranians with monarchist sympathies fled immediately after the revolution. But at the same time many politically active Iranians, particularly on the left, welcomed the revolution and took the opportunity to return home. Most soon found themselves opposing the new regime, when its abuse of human rights and fundamentalist policies became apparent. They fled Iran. Those who had studied abroad often returned to exile in the countries and towns where they had studied. Other refugees who had not been politically active at the time of the Shah's regime increasingly found themselves in conflict with the post-revolutionary government.

Most Iranian refugees live in North and West London and in Leeds, although most university towns have small Iranian communities.

Iranian refugees encounter many of the same problems faced by other groups of refugees: unemployment, lack of recognition of qualifications and, for some, language problems. But Iranians who previously studied in Britain have generally faired better than other groups of refugees.

A visa requirement for Iranians was imposed in 1979, making it difficult for people to escape the country. A growing proportion of recent Iranian refugees are being awarded ELR, making family reunion difficult.

Refugees who have been imprisoned in Iran are quite likely to have been tortured. The Medical Foundation for the Care of Victims of Torture has seen more Iranians than any other national group.

Iranian students are still coming to Britain, including those who support the regime. In 1986 a bomb killed an Iranian student who was a known opponent of the Iranian government. This shocked the Iranian community. The bombing, and the obvious political differences between different groups of Iranian refugees, engender distrust — some Iranians might appear to be suspicious of other groups of Iranians and/or students.

There are Iranian community organisations in London and Leeds, and a supplementary school for children in London.

□ Refugees from Iraq

Throughout the 1980s refugees have fled Iraq to Britain. The refugees are from three ethnic groups: Arabs, Kurds and Assyrian Christians. Today about 9,000 Iraqi refugees live in Britain.

Iraq has a population of 18 million, of which 73 per cent live in urban areas. Nearly 4,000,000 Kurds now live in autonomous Iraqi Kurdistan. The capital is Baghdad and the administrative headquarters of Iraqi Kurdistan is Arbil.

Ethnic Groups

About 70 per cent of the population are Arabs. Another 23 per cent are Kurdish, mostly living in Kurdistan. About two per cent of the population are Turkmen, and another two per cent Assyrian Christians. Iraq also has a small Armenian community.

The majority of Iraqi refugees in Britain are Kurdish. The origins of the Kurdish people are uncertain; some anthropologists believe that the Kurds are an amalgamation of Indo-European tribes who have lived in the Zagros mountains for over 4,000 years. Kurdish society has developed its own distinct culture and Kurds have a strong sense of identity. In rural areas Iraqi Kurds have strong clan loyalties which still determine which political parties they support.

Within Iraqi Kurdistan other minority groups such as Jews and Assyrians have been absorbed into the predominantly Kurdish culture. The Assyrians are the other victims of the Iraqi government's persecution, and many of their villages and churches have been destroyed. They live in towns and villages in Iraqi Kurdistan but, unlike the Kurds, their first language is Assyrian. They are generally more prosperous than their Kurdish neighbours and many have relatives in the US or in Europe. During the Gulf War Assyrians were identified as being pro-western whatever their real views were.

Many Turkmen also live in Iraqi Kurdistan; their population is estimated to be between 350,000 and 900,000. They speak Turkmen, a language closely related to Turkish and used also in Turkmeniya and Afghanistan. The Turkmen allege that they have suffered persecution at the hands of the Iraqi government. Relations between Turkmen and Kurds have often been tense, and no ethnic Turkmen have seats in the Kurdish parliament.

Languages

Arabic is the official language of Iraq and is also spoken by many Kurds and Assyrians as a second language. Arabic is a Semitic language, mostly closely related to Hebrew and Aramaic. Classical Arabic — the language of the Koran — is taught in Madrassah and in schools. A modern simplified standard form of classical Arabic is used as a written language throughout the Arab world. Spoken Arabic varies from country to country, and the Iraqis have their own dialects.

Iraqi Kurds speak Kurdish as their first language. It is an Indo-European language, most closely related to Persian. There are two main Kurdish dialects: Kurmanji and Sorani. Kurmanji is spoken in Turkey and in Iraq northwards from Mosul to the Caucasus. Kurmanji has been scripted in Roman and Cyrillic script. Sorani is spoken in western Iraqi Kurdistan and is written in a modified Arabic script. It is now the official Kurdish language used in Iraqi Kurdistan. It is also the dominant literary form because of the relative cultural freedoms granted to Iraqi Kurds.

Assyrians speak Assyrian. The language is sometimes incorrectly called Aramaic or Syriac. Assyrian is a Semitic language and developed from Aramaic, the language used in the Middle East from about the 4th century BC. At this time it was written in Hebrew script. Aramaic was the language of Jesus Christ. After the 7th century AD Aramaic was gradually replaced by Arabic and Turkish in most of the Middle East. The Aramaic language has survived as Assyrian and Syriac. The latter is the liturgical language of the Chaldean, Nestorian, and Maronite churches. Syriac is written in several different scripts.

Assyrian is the first language of the Assyrian people. They live in northern Iraq but also in Syria, Turkey, Lebanon and Iran. Assyrian is written in the Nestorian script. The script has developed from cursive Hebrew and is written from right to left.

Kurdish Jews also speak Assyrian. Turkmen and Armenian are spoken by the respective minority groups.

Names

Iraqi Arabs use an Islamic naming system. They have a first personal name, followed by their father's personal name, then that of their grandfather. Women keep their own names on marriage. Many Iraqi Kurds use this naming system. Some Kurds may have a personal name and use their grandfather's name as a family name. Other Kurds may have personal name, their father's name and then a family name reflecting a place or clan membership. In western countries many Kurds adopt their grandfather's name as a family name.

Assyrian Christians may use a European naming system. Others have a first personal name, followed by their father's name and then their grandfather's name. The names used by Assyrian Christians are often the names of saints.

Religion

Shi'a Muslims make up 55 to 60 per cent of the total Iraqi population. The majority of Shi'a Muslims live in southern Iraq and in the poorer suburbs of Baghdad. Sunni Muslims make up 20 per cent of the Iraqi population and live mostly in northern Iraq. Most Iraqi Kurds are also Sunni Muslims, although religion is not a major component of Kurdish identity.

The most important Shi'a shrine is at Kerbala in Iraq. Despite being in the majority, the Shi'a population has historically been underprivileged and politically weak. Few Shi'a hold senior government positions.

Since the late 1970s the Iraqi government has operated a carrot and stick policy towards the Shi'a. The Government has provided some economic assistance to southern Iraq and dispensed rewards to communities willing to co-operate. At the same time many religious Shi'a were suspected of having links with fellow Shi'a in Iran, and were ruthlessly oppressed.

The 1991 uprising in southern Iraq was started by dissident army personnel — not all Shi'a — fleeing from Kuwait . For a brief period repressed political forces — both Shi'a and secular — were active. Within a few weeks the uprising was ruthlessly crushed, suppressing both political and religious activity. Many clergy were arrested and Shi'a shrines desecrated.

The Marsh Arabs of southern Iraq are Shi'a Muslims. They have seen their settlements bombed and marshlands drained. Chemical weapons were probably used against the Marsh Arabs in 1993.

Assyrian Christians belong to two sects: Chaldeans and Nestorians. The Chaldeans recognise the Roman Catholic Pope as their patriarch but use the Eastern Rite when worshipping. The Nestorians are followers of Saint Nestor, excommunicated for heresy by the Roman Catholic church in the 5th century. The Nestorians have their own patriarch who lives in Chicago, USA. Both groups consider themselves ethnic Assyrians, and sometimes share the use of a church.

Education System

Up until May 1992 all primary and secondary education was under the control of the Ministry of Education. The medium of instruction in all schools was Arabic.

Some pre-school education is available. Primary education starts at six and lasts for six years. Progress from class to class is dependent on passing examinations. At the end of primary schooling a Primary Baccalaureat examination can be taken.

Secondary education is divided into two three year cycles. During the first or intermediate cycle all students follow a common curriculum. At the end of three years students sit for the Third Form Baccalaureat. Those with the highest pass marks can progress to the second cycle. Those with lower marks only have the option of attending vocational secondary schools. In the second or Preparatory Cycle, students can choose between arts and science subjects. At the end of three years a Sixth Form Baccalaureat is taken, which is a basic qualification for university entrance.

There are four types of vocational secondary school in Iraq: agricultural, industrial, veterinary and commercial. Courses last for three years (British Council, 1991).

The literacy rate is 90 per cent for men and 88 per cent for women. Literacy is lower is rural Kurdistan and in southern Iraq.

In October 1991 the Iraqi Government withdrew all troops, funds and services from Iraqi Kurdistan (with the exception of the Kirkuk governorate). The Kurds then started to set up their own administration, although they lacked funds and international recognition. Schools are functioning, but lack basic equipment. The Kurdish administration has kept the basic structure of the system but all teaching is now through the medium of Kurdish.

Economy

Iraq can be divided into three geographical regions. To the north are the mountains of Iraqi Kurdistan. The majority of the population are rural, and many are pastoralists. The plain of Mesopotamia runs through central Iraq, between the River Tigris and River Euphrates. This area is Iraq's food producing region; wheat and dates are the most important crops. Iraq is the world's largest date producer but has to import most of its basic foodstuffs. Southern Iraq is arid.

Iraq is a middle-income country whose major source of income comes from the production of crude oil. Iraqi oil sales are now restricted by UN resolutions, as is other trade with Iraq. Economic life has been severely affected by the embargo. Unemployment has risen and spare parts are in very short supply. Although food and medicine are exempt from sanctions, Iraq now lacks foreign exchange to purchase these goods and the UN embargo has hurt the poorest most of all.

Causes of Flight

Iraq

The territory which is now Iraq has been the cradle of many ancient civilisations. The Sumerians, Akkadians, Babylonians and Assyrians all had their homes in Iraq. The Greeks called the region 'Mesopotamia'. But the area paid dearly for its fertility and location, and was conquered by many foreign powers. From the 16th century it was ruled by the Ottoman Empire.

During the First World War the Arab population of the region rose up against their Turkish rulers. The British, keen to protect their oil interests, occupied the country which was to become Iraq. After the First World War Iraq was placed under a League of Nations mandate administered by Britain. Amir Faisal ibn Hussain, a member of the Hashemite family of Arabia, was nominated as monarch. Iraq gained full independence in 1931.

The 1940s and 1950s saw a rise in Arab nationalism throughout the Middle East, in particular the growth of Ba'athism, the political ideology developed in Syria in the 1940s. It emphasised Arab unity and promoted the idea of a single Arab nation. The Ba'athists advocated a secular socialist state which would redistribute wealth, but played down Marxist class conflict. Ba'athist parties gained a great deal of popular support in Iraq in the 1950s and were perceived as being a threat to the monarchy. As a result all opposition parties were banned in 1953.

In 1958 the monarchy was overthrown in a military coup which brought General Abdullah Karim Qasim to power. Initially he drew support from Ba'athists, communists and some Kurds. But over the next four years he lost his popularity and was overthrown in 1963 by a coalition of Ba'athist and Iraqi nationalists.

The Ba'athists were quickly driven from power. Iraq was then ruled by a series of unstable governments. In 1968 the Ba'athist party staged a coup d'etat. Major General Ahmad Hassan al-Bakr became President, Prime Minister and Chairman of the Revolutionary Command Council (RCC). In 1979 Saddam Hussain, then Vice-Chairman of the RCC replaced al-Bakr as the President and Chairman.

Political power has been concentrated in the hands of the Ba'ath party. By establishing overlapping and competing security services and undermining the influence of alternative centres of power, Saddam Hussain has crushed any alternative political organisation. Since the 1970s Amnesty International has regularly documented extra-judicial executions, detentions, torture and large-scale disappearances. Up to 150,000 Kurdish people have disappeared. In the 1970s up to 100,000 people were deported to Iran, including a community of Shi'a Faili Kurds. At the beginning of the 1980s there was a second wave of deportations: up to 200,000 people, mostly Shi'a Muslims, were transferred to Iran when the Iraqi government claimed that they were Iranian.

In 1980 the Iraqi government entered an expensive and bloody war with Iran following increased tensions between the two countries. In September 1980 Iraqi troops crossed into Iran to reclaim the Shatt-al-Arab Canal which had been ceded to Iran in 1975. The war lasted eight years and cost thousands of lives. At this time the Iraqi government received economic aid from Saudi Arabia and Kuwait, and was favoured by western powers who seemed oblivious to human rights violations. After the Iran-Iraq war ended, the Iraqi government launched a military campaign against the Kurds.

In August 1990 Iraq marched into oil-rich Kuwait. To protect western interests the UN launched a military campaign against the Iraqi regime. Kuwait was liberated, but the campaign stopped short of toppling Saddam Hussain. Many Kurds and Iraqi Arabs saw it as the time to act. During March/April 1991 there were uprisings in Kurdistan and in southern Iraq. But the uprisings were met with brutal repression by the army and security services, causing two million people to flee the country. In southern Iraq an estimated 150,000 people were arrested as a result of the uprising. Today human rights violations continue unabated. The Marsh Arabs have been a particular target.

Since the Gulf War there have been moves among Iraqi opposition parties to develop a common platform. An alliance known as the Iraqi National Congress was formed in 1992 and is based in London (Graham-Brown 1994).

Kurds

The Kurds mostly live in the mountainous areas of eastern Turkey, northern Iraq, north west Iran and the southern Caucasus. In the years before the First World War Kurdistan was divided between the Ottoman and Persian Empires. The largely nomadic Kurdish population was afforded autonomy in return for policing this border.

When the Ottoman Empire was broken up the Kurds had many hopes for independence. The Treaty of Sevres, signed in 1920, promised autonomy for both Armenians and Kurds. But it was vetoed by the Turkish government, and in 1923 the Treaty of Lausanne divided Kurdistan between Turkey, Iran, Iraq, Syria and the Soviet Union. The reaction of the Kurds was to rebel.

The early revolts were not nationalistic. But in 1958 a group of Kurds, led by Mullah Mustafa Barzani, returned from exile and founded the Kurdish Democratic Party (KDP). It called for Kurdish autonomy in a bi-national state. This demand was rejected by the Iraqi government and Barzani returned to Kurdistan and launched a guerrilla war.

Following nearly ten years of hostilities, the Iraqi government agreed to Kurdish autonomy in 1970. But mutual suspicion and Baghdad's reluctance to cede the oil-rich city of Kirkuk caused the agreement to break down. A much diluted autonomy agreement was offered to the Kurds in 1974. It was rejected and a fierce war followed in which the Kurds were supported by Iran. In 1975 Iran signed an agreement of co-operation with Iraq and withdrew its support for the Kurds, in exchange for territorial concessions in the Persian Gulf. After this Kurdish resistance collapsed.

In 1975 the Patriotic Union of Kurdistan (PUK), led by Jalal Talabani split from the KDP. Several smaller leftist parties also emerged, together with an Islamic Party and an Assyrian party. The KDP began to revive its fortunes in the 1980s and is now led by Masoud Barzani, son of Mullah Musafa Barzani.

During the Iran-Iraq war (1980-88) Kurdish guerrillas — known as *peshmergas* — were again backed by Iran. From the mid-1980s the Iraqi government began an operation to clear parts of Iraqi Kurdistan of their predominantly Kurdish population. An estimated 500,000 Kurds were deported from their homes on the Turkish and Iranian frontiers. Their villages were destroyed, making return impossible.

The deliberate policy of clearing Kurdish villages culminated in the 1988 *Anfal* campaign. Up to 5,000 Kurdish villages were razed and many former inhabitants were deported to towns in southern Iraq. Others were put in camps or simply disappeared. An estimated 100,000 people remain unaccounted for from 1988 alone.

From 1987 the Iraqi regime began to use chemical weapons against the Kurds. In March 1988 some 6,000 people were killed in a chemical weapons attack on the town of Halabja.

The Iran-Iraq war came to an end on 20th August 1988. During the next two weeks the Iraqi army drove Kurdish guerrillas out of their strongholds. They used saturation bombing and chemical weapons in this assault. Despite a UN Resolution condemning Iraq's use of chemical weapons, no member of the UN Security Council took any action against Iraq.

Up to 150,000 innocent people were killed during the *Anfal* campaign. By the end of 1988 340,000 Iraqi Kurdish refugees were living in Iran and another 90,000 in Turkey. Refugees also fled to European countries.

After the 1991 Gulf War there was a short-lived uprising in Kurdistan. It was followed by massive Iraqi reprisals. More than 1,500,000 Kurdish refugees fled to Turkey and Iran. In April 1991 the Gulf War allies imposed a 'safe haven' covering north east Kurdistan. Subsequently they created a no-fly zone above the 36th parallel. This led to the return of many of the refugees, although Iraqi forces remained in the Kurdish areas outside the safe haven.

Kurdish leaders held talks with the Iraqi government in mid-1991 but these broke down, mainly over the issue of access to oil-rich Kirkuk. There were also skirmishes between Iraqi troops and *peshmergas*. In October 1991 the Iraqi government withdrew all troops, funds and services from most of Kurdistan (apart from the governorate of Kirkuk). It imposed an embargo on goods crossing the de facto border.

The Kurds have now set up their own administration and a Kurdish parliament was elected in May 1992, with the KDP and the PUK dividing most of the seats between them. The Kurdish administration is able to raise taxes but it lacks funds and international recognition.

There are many strains on the new Kurdish administration. There have been clashes between different political parties in parts of Kurdistan. The continuation of the UN no-fly zone and the passage of basic supplies is dependent on the Turkish government. The latter is violently opposed to any separate Kurdish state. The Turkish army has made numerous incursions into Iraqi Kurdistan, and Iraqi Kurds have become involved in efforts to crush Turkish Kurdish guerrillas. The Iranian army has also made incursions into Iraqi Kurdistan. (Graham-Brown, 1994, McDowall, 1991).

Iraqi and Iraqi Kurdish Refugees in Britain

Statistics

Year	Applications for Asylum	Refugee Status	ELR	Refusal
1982	271	61	21	76
1983	298	65	43	55
1984	348	55	65	30
1985	251	57	103	16
1986	210	30	112	56
1987	210	15	81	46
1988	163	12	98	22
1989	215	55	215	5
1990	985	65	130	10
1991	915	45	115	15
1992	700	190	1210	40
1993	495	185	300	30

There are about 12,000 refugees from Iraq currently living in Britain. The largest group are Iraqi Kurds whose community numbers about 6,000 people. The majority of Iraqi Kurds arrived in Britain after 1988.

Most Iraqi Kurds live in Greater London. The Kurdish Cultural Centre is one of several community organisations working with Iraqi Kurdish refugees. It provides an advice and casework service for newly-arrived refugees. The Kurdish Cultural Centre also organises many cultural events, the most important of which are the Nawroz festivities. Nawroz is the Kurdish New Year, celebrated in March 21st. It is a time for picnics in Kurdistan but the British weather does not permit such celebrations. Iraqi Kurdish children also have the opportunity to attend a supplementary school in London.

Although Iraqi Kurds and Turkish Kurds both have a distinct Kurdish identity, there are important social and political differences between these two groups. Different community organisations represent the needs of the two communities.

Most Iraqi Kurds arrived in Britain speaking little or no English. Access to ESL classes remains a major need of this group of refugees.

The Iraqi Arab community numbers about 3,000. Most Iraqi Arab refugees have been active in opposition politics and some come from prosperous backgrounds. Several community organisations serve their needs.

Britain also hosts a small Assyrian community numbering about 3,000 people. Most Assyrian refugees live in west London, in Ealing, Kensington and Chelsea and Hammersmith. The Nestorian Patriarch stayed in Kensington on his way to the USA. He established an Assyrian Christian church in the locality; other refugees settled near the church and their compatriots. There is an active Assyrian community organisation which runs a supplementary school among many other activities.

There are very small numbers of other Iraqi minority groups living in Britain including Jews, Armenians and Turkmen.

□ Refugees from Lebanon

About 3,000 Lebanese refugees have fled to Britain, most of them between 1989 and 1991.

Lebanon has a population of 3,500,000, of which 82 per cent live in urban areas. The capital is Beirut.

Ethnic and Religious Groups

Lebanon's main communities are

Maronite Christians	900,000
Orthodox Christians	250,000
Greek Catholics	150,000
Shi'a Muslims	1,100,000
Sunni Muslims	750,000
Druze	200,000
Armenians	175,000
Other Christians	50,000
Palestinians	350,000
Kurds and Syrians	100,000

The Druze practice a faith that developed out of Shi'a Islam in the 11th century, a form of Islam which holds that Jethro is a major prophet.

Most Kurds and Palestinians are not Lebanese citizens.

Languages

Arabic is the official language. The Lebanese speak their own dialect, although newspapers and books are written in a simplified version of classical Arabic which is used throughout the Arab world.

Armenian, Kurdish and Assyrian are spoken by the respective minority groups.

Names

Lebanese Christians have adopted a European naming system. Many Lebanese Muslims use this system as well, having a first personal name, sometimes followed by their father's name, and then a family name.

Education System

There are four kinds of school in Lebanon: state schools, private tuition-free schools, fee-paying schools and the schools administered by UNRWA for Palestinian refugees. Arabic is the main language of instruction but some private schools use French and English as the medium of instruction.

Primary education starts at six and runs for five years. Students then spend three or four years in intermediate schools, where three types of courses are offered. Some students attend a four year academic course. Others spend three years in academic courses, followed by one year preparing to enter vocational schools or teacher training institutes. Other students study vocational course for three years. At the end of intermediate education students receive a certificate called a *Brevet*.

After intermediate schooling students can attend upper secondary schools, where three types of programme are available. Students can study academic courses leading to the Baccalaureat. There is a programme for prospective primary and intermediate school teachers, finishing with a teaching diploma. There are also vocational courses in subjects such as commerce, nursing and electronics, finishing with a *Baccalaureat Technique 11* (British Council, 1991)

Private tuition-free schools, private schools and UNRWA schools are organised in much the same way as state schools. The literacy rate is 86 per cent for men and 69 per cent for women. Literacy rates in rural areas are lower.

Economy

The Lebanese economy has been devastated by the civil war. Before 1975 Lebanon was the banking and commercial capital of the Arab Middle East. Textiles and agricultural products were also important exports.

A Chronology of Events

Lebanon was ruled by the Ottoman Turks for more than 400 years, as part of the Ottoman Empire's Syrian Province. For most of this time Lebanon's different communities lived in peace, although in 1860 and 1861 there were clashes between Maronite Christians and Druze which left 2,000 people dead.

1920-23

The French take control of Syria and Lebanon after the defeat of the Turks in the First World War. New borders for Lebanon and Syria are draw up, giving Lebanon a small Christian majority.

1943

Lebanon gains independence. An agreement is reached to try and satisfy all Lebanon's minority communities: the 'National Pact'. Parliamentary seats are divided between Christians and Muslims in a ratio of six Christian seats to five Muslim. The president is a Maronite Christian and the prime minister a Sunni Muslim. Other top administrative posts are divided between the different communities.

1958

Tensions grow between people who see Lebanon as an Arab nation and those who believe Lebanon should be closely linked with European countries. These tensions cause a brief civil war in 1958.

1970s

Poverty and the destabilising effect of Palestinian refugees cause tensions to rise. Parts of Lebanon are very wealthy but Beirut and Tripoli are surrounded by slums and much of the countryside is impoverished. The poor are mostly Muslim and lack political representation. Their numbers are swelled by Palestinian refugees and Kurdish and Syrian migrant workers. The urban poor include a number of educated young men who can find no work. In such conditions many of these young men turn to armed struggle to try and change Lebanon's political system.

Some 350,000 Palestinian refugees are living in camps in southern Lebanon and on the outskirts of Beirut. During the 1960s Palestinian guerrillas living in the camps start raiding northern Israel. The Lebanese Government, particularly Maronite Christian politicians, become increasingly hostile to the Palestinians, believing they are trying to create 'a state within a state'. But there is another point of view held by some intellectuals and the poor, mostly Muslim Lebanese. They admire the Palestinians courage and hope that they will be able to help change Lebanon.

1975

Phalangist Christian militia attack a bus of Palestinians in Beirut. (The Phalangists are a right-wing political organisation.) The civil war begins. The Phalangists and other Christian groups fight against the National Movement which is made up of several political organisations, with mainly Muslim support.

Muslims are forced to leave their homes in Christian neighbourhoods and vice versa.

1976

Syria intervenes to support the Christian Lebanese forces.

1978

Israel invades southern Lebanon, displacing 200,000 people, but is forced to withdraw after UN and US pressure.

1982

Israel launches another invasion called 'Operation Peace for Galilee'. It aims to defeat the Palestinian fighters once and for all. During the next two months some 19,000 people are killed in fighting and Israeli air raids.

Israeli forces reach West Beirut within a few days. They lay seige to the city. A multi-national peace-keeping force of US, British, French and Italian troops arrives. They attempt to supervise the withdrawal of Palestinian guerrillas and guard the refugees living in camps. Israel withdraws its troops and promises not to enter West Beirut.

The peace-keeping force leaves as soon as the Palestinian guerrillas flee. Israeli troops enter Muslim West Beirut. With Israeli co-operation Christian Lebanese forces enter Sabra and Chatilla refugee camps. Some 2,000 Palestinian refugees are murdered on 16th, 17th and 18th September 1982.

1983

Israel is forced to withdraw to a 'security zone' in southern Lebanon after losing many troops. But it arms and trains another force called the South Lebanese Army. This comprises Christian troops who fight Palestinians and other militia, working with the Israeli government to police a *cordon sanitaire* in southern Lebanon.

1984-89

The civil war worsens. Christian and Muslim militia splinter. Christians fight Christians in East Beirut. Amal, a Shi'a Muslim group, fights Palestinians and Hizbollah, an Islamic fundamentalist group. The Israelis continue to bomb southern Lebanon. Food and water become scarce in much of Beirut and thousands of civilians are killed.

1989

The increased violence prompts Syria to take a more active role. Its troops enter Lebanon. In October 1989 a peace agreement is signed, and the Syrians force the Lebananese to form a government of national reconciliation. Thereafter there are attempts to disarm the militia.

1990-92

The Syrian-backed government continues to disarm the militia. In August 1992 elections are held for a new government in which the power of the Christian majority will be slightly reduced. Some Christian extremists hold strikes on the day of the elections. The Syrian army continues to hold large parts of Lebanon, and the Israelis continue to back the South Lebanese Army and maintain control in the security zone.

1993

Some 200,000 Lebanese flee their homes in southern Lebanon after suffering bombardments by the Israeli airforce, the latter retaliating after Hizbollah guerrillas shell northern Israel.

Lebanese Refugees in Britain

Statistics

Year Asylum	Applications	Refugee Status	ELR	Refusals
1988	148	1	37	6
1989	180	5	200	10
1990	1,110	5	180	5
1991	755	5	110	20
1992	380	25	610	65
1993	285	15	270	90

Lebanese refugees are a very diverse population. In Britain fall they fall into four groups:

— Lebanese Christians and Muslims who fled during the civil war of 1975-1991;
— supporters of General Michel Aoun and those who have been associated with the South Lebanese Army who have fled since 1991;
— Palestinians who fled during the civil war or have more recently fallen victim to inter-communal conflict;
— Armenians and other minority groups who fled during the civil war.

Lebanese refugees have joined an existing Lebanese migrant community, mostly living in the London Boroughs of Westminster, Kensington and Chelsea and Hammersmith and Fulham. The migrant community is more prosperous than the refugees; most Lebanese migrants are professionals or involved in commerce or the Arab media. Some Lebanese refugees and most stateless Palestinians arrive speaking little or no English. The latter group need most support so they can rebuild their lives.

For many years the British Government awarded most Lebanese asylum-seekers exceptional leave to remain. In December 1992 the Home Office announced that, due to the end of the civil war and significant improvements in the situation, the circumstances in Lebanon no longer justified awarding ELR.

☐ Refugees from Sierra Leone

Since 1991 small numbers of refugees from Sierra Leone have fled to Britain.

Sierra Leone has a population of 4,000,000 of which 31 per cent live in urban areas. The capital is Freetown.

Ethnic Groups

The Temne and Mende are the largest ethnic groups, together forming about 30 per cent of the population. The Lokko, Sherbor, Limba, Sussu, Fulah, Kono and Krio are other major groups. The Krio are the descendants of African slaves returned from the West Indies by the British in the 19th century, after a court ruling in London. There is also a Lebanese minority living in Freetown.

Languages

English is the official language. Nearly one million people speak Mende, mostly in southern Sierra Leone. Temne is spoken by about 750,000 people in central and North West Sierra Leone; Vai is spoken on the coast and along the southern border with Liberia. Limba, Kissi, Gola and Krio are other common languages. All languages in Sierra Leone belong to the Niger-Congo language family, with the exception of Krio which is derived from English.

Names

Most Sierra Leoneans have a first name, followed by a family name. The Krio descendants of freed slaves usually have English first and family names.

Religion

Most Sierra Leoneans follow traditional beliefs. About 30 per cent are Muslims, mostly from the north. There is a Christian minority living in Freetown.

Education System

School starts at seven years and primary education lasts six years. Secondary education lasts another five years. Schooling is meant to be compulsory until 16 but there is a high drop out rate among the poor. Male literacy rate is 38 per cent: female literacy rate is 21 per cent.

Economy

Sierra Leone is one of the world's poorest countries, despite its many natural resources such as gold, diamonds, iron ore and tropical timber. Government corruption and economic mismanagement have meant that only the elite has benefited from the country's wealth.

The country's infrastructure is undeveloped. Basic services do not meet the population's need, and Sierra Leone has the world's highest infant mortality and the lowest life expectancy.

Reasons for Flight

Sierra Leone has been consumed by civil war since 1991. The civil war is closely linked to war and instability in neighbouring Liberia. The two countries have similar histories. Sierra Leone was a British colony until 1961. It was, and still is, a potentially rich country but its wealth is held by Krio, Lebanese and foreign interests. Most diamonds and gold are smuggled out of the country.

In the late 1960s and early 1970s there were attempts to reform the economy but they were opposed by those who owned the country's wealth. Sierra Leone has been a one-party state since 1978. From 1985-1992 the country's President was Major-General Joseph Saidu Momoh. In April 1992 he was overthrown in a military coup led by Captain Valentine Strasser. The new government has promised elections.

In March 1991 forces of Charles Taylor's National Patriotic Front of Liberia (NPFL) invaded Sierra Leone. The invaders were supported by Sierra Leonean opposition and soldiers from Libya and Burkina Fasso. Sierra Leonean government forces managed to take back most of the land held by the rebels.

In the wake of the invasion there have been gross violations of human rights by both the rebels and the Sierra Leone government. Thousands of civilians have been detained, tortured or killed because they were suspected of supporting the rebel forces. The NPFL army has also killed civilians. Another major cause for concern is the conscription of children into the Sierra Leonean army and into the NPFL forces.

Some 260,000 Sierra Leoneans are internally displaced and another 400,000 have fled as refugees, mostly to Guinea.

Although the Sierra Leone government has managed to recapture land, it remains a very unstable country. As long as the country's wealth is held by a tiny, corrupt minority there will always be discontent. There is also potential for inter-ethnic conflict.

Sierra Leonean Refugees in Britain.

There are probably less than 1,000 Sierra Leonean refugees in Britain. Most live in Greater London. They fall into two groups: opposition politicians, and middle class families who have left since 1991.

☐ Refugees from Somalia

Since the mid-1980s over 15,000 Somali refugees have arrived in Britain, joining existing communities in London, Cardiff, Liverpool and other industrial areas.

The region comprises Somalia and the Republic of Somaliland, the latter being an unrecognised state.

The population is about seven million, of whom 37 per cent live in urban areas. At least 500,000 people died in the famine of 1992/93, including half of all children under five years. The capital is Mogadishu.

Ethnic Groups

The Somalis form one of the most homogeneous populations in Africa. But in other ways they are very divided. They consider themselves to be one ethnic group and have a strong sense of linguistic and cultural unity but clan affiliation has proved to be an increasingly divisive factor, culminating in the present crisis.

There are six major clan families:

— the Dir, living in northern Somalia

— the Daarood, a pastoral clan family living in the north, east and southern parts of the country

— the Issaq, a pastoral clan family living in the north — to which the majority of Somali refugees in Britain belong

— the Hawiye, a pastoral clan family whose members predominate in parts of the south and around Mogadishu

— the Digil, a clan whose members mostly live in the south

— the Rahawayn, a clan whose members mostly live in the south.

Each clan family is divided into many clans. For example, the Daarood clan family contains clans such as the Ogaadeen, Majeerteen and Mareehan. Clans may range in size from an few hundred members to several thousand. Somalis identify more with their clans than with the larger clan families.

Clans are divided into branches, down to the level of extended families. The office of clan leader is usually hereditary but clan elders, called Sultan, are normally figure-heads. Political decisions are made by clan elders.

The clan system is patrilineal: a person's clan, branch and family loyalties are determined by his or her father. In Somalia most families take their genealogy very seriously, as it locates them within Somali society. In Britain clan affiliations are less important among the older established migrant Somali communities. But among newly-arrived refugees the clan system is still a very important factor in community life.

Clan membership impinges on a person's political affiliations. The Somali National Movement has tended to represent members of the Issaq clan family, whilst the United Somali Congress drew its support from the Hawiye clan family.

Clan politics have also influenced the activities of some Somali refugee community organisations in Britain.

Languages

Somali is the first language spoken by the great majority of the population of Somalia, as well as another 1.5 million people in Ethiopia, 300,000 in Kenya and about 125,000 in Djibouti.

Somali became the national and official language of Somalia in 1973, after being transcribed into a written form in the early 1970s. Prior to this Arabic and English were used in written communication, and English was the language of administration. Somali belongs to the Hamito-Semitic language family. Linguists place Somali in the Cushitic sub-group, closely related to Eritrean languages such as Afar and Saho.

After much debate in the 1970s, it was decided to use a Roman script for the Somali language. Although a Roman script is used, the ordering of the alphabet is similar to Arabic. There are 21 consonants and 15 vowels and diphthongs; the letters 'p', 'v' and 'z' are not used. Pronunciation of letters is also different, for example 'x' is pronounced as an 'h'. It is likely that Somali children who are literate in their own language may initially find the different ordering and pronunciation confusing when learning English.

Standard Somali, as spoken in the North, is universally understood and used. There are also a number of dialects spoken, such as Digil and Rahanweyn in southern Somalia.

Somali has a rich oral and poetic tradition. Story-telling plays an important part in Somali cultural identity. The implementation of the written form of the language had a profound effect on its development. A new vocabulary had to be created to cover aspects of life such as science, technology and social sciences and many new words have been borrowed from English. Standard Somali also contains many words of Arabic origin.

Arabic is also widely understood in Somalia, due to the long-standing influence of traders, who also brought Islam. Many town-dwelling Somali boys attend Madrassah and learn classical Arabic and the Koran. English and Italian were introduced as colonial languages in the 19th century and Swahili is also spoken in southern coastal towns.

Names

Somalis use an Islamic naming system, taking three names: a first name, followed by their father's and grandfather's name. A woman usually keeps her name on marriage. The names are Islamic. Nicknames are also frequently used.

Religion

The majority of Somalis are Sunni Muslims. As Muslims Somalis are expected to live according to Koranic law. They celebrate all the main Muslim festivals and have the same dietary restrictions as other Muslims.

Education System

In precolonial Somalia few people received a formal education. Most Somalis were nomadic; story-telling provided the main means of teaching children the cultural and moral values of Somali society, although some boys who lived in coastal towns attended Madrassah.

After British and Italian Somaliland were colonised there was an expansion of urban education. The main aim was to provide an educated middle class to service the administrative and trading interests of the respective colonial powers. In British Somaliland the educational system was based on a British model and the medium of instruction was English. In Italian Somaliland the medium of instruction was Italian. At independence and the unification of the two former colonies, two different educational systems were operating. By 1965 the Somali government had unified them. English and Arabic were the languages of instruction in the north; Italian and English the languages of instruction in the south.

Education policy changed rapidly after a military coup in 1969 and the coming to power of a government which proclaimed a socialist ideology. In 1972 the government adopted the newly scripted Somali language as the official language. This was followed by the launch of a literacy campaign in 1973. Schools and colleges were closed for one year, and school students, college students and teachers were sent out to teach the new alphabet. By 1980 Somalia had a literacy rate of 60 per cent — no mean achievement in a country where about 60 per cent of the population are nomadic.

Schools were also nationalised in 1972. In 1975 Somali replaced English as the language of instruction.

Many children in urban areas attended Madrassah for about 12 months before starting state education at six. In theory, education is compulsory up to the age of 14 years. State education is at three levels: elementary, intermediate and secondary schools, each lasting for four years.. Children are tested every term and through an annual examination, failure in which requires the student to repeat the year. As in many poor countries classes include students of many different ages. Girls and boys are taught together, although many more boys than girls attended school. Most Somali schools only operate in the morning.

During the first eight years Somali, Arabic, religious studies, mathematics, history, geography, sciences, social science, art, physical education and home economics are taught, also English in the last four years of secondary school. At the end of secondary education the Secondary School Leaving Certificate is taken.

Education is considered a high priority by Somali families. But Somalia is a very poor country and there have always been limited resources. Even before the current crisis school buildings were in poor condition and books in short supply. Class sizes were very large, with up to 60 children. Teaching methods in Somalia were very formal, with an emphasis on learning facts. Somali children will not have experience of laboratory practicals, nor of group and collaborative learning methods. In Somalia parents had very little involvement with schools, so refugee parents in Britain may be reticent about visiting schools or becoming involved in their activities.

Siad Barre's assault on northern towns, followed by the collapse of the Somali government, has had a very grave effect on education. In the north — now the Republic of Somaliland — most urban schools were destroyed in 1988. After 1988 many children from northern Somalia were unable to attend school. Teachers of Somali refugee children can expect this group to have a severely interrupted education or never to have attended school.

The Republic of Somaliland is an unrecognised state, without a national budget. A handful of schools are operational, mostly in Hargeisa, and the teachers are working without wages. More Madrassah are operational.

In the south the educational system stopped operating in early 1991, as governmental authority declined. A few families have made informal arrangements for their children to be taught, and Madrassah are also providing a religious education for some children (Kasabova, 1991).

Economy

Most of Somalia is semi-desert, with the exception of a the Juba Plain in southern Somalia, where export and subsistence crops are grown. Despite recent urbanisation Somalia is essentially a pastoral society, with about 60 per cent of the people grazing camels, sheep, goats and cattle. About 80 per cent of Somalia's exports come from livestock; other exports include fish and fresh fruit such as bananas. The major market for Somalia's exports is Saudi Arabia and other other Gulf States. Much livestock is provided for the pilgrims attending the *Haj*. Somalia's trading links with the Arabian Peninsula stretch back thousands of years.

Towns are the centre for livestock trading. Town-dwelling Somalis keep strong links with their relatives in the countryside. Urban Somalis often have joint shares in livestock with their rural kin, and children are frequently sent to spend holidays with relatives who live in the interior.

In the 20th century foreign remittances have become increasingly economically important. Somalis were recruited into the British armed forces during the Second World War and later into the British merchant navy. Today many Somalis are also working in the Gulf States.

A Chronology of Events

2000-1500BC

Archaeologists first identify Somali people in the Horn of Africa. Somalia is known as 'the Land of Punt' by the Egyptians, meaning the land of frankincense, and close trading relationships are developed between Red Sea villages and towns and Egypt.

900-1300AD

Somalia nomads are living in present-day Somalia, and parts of present day Ethiopia, Djibouti and Kenya. Islam replaces animism as the religion of Somali people. Somalia gradually emerges as a centre of trade.

19th century

Somalia begins to attract the attention of colonial powers, as it is of strategic importance at the mouth of the Red Sea. The Berlin Conference in 1884 divides up the African continent between various European imperial powers. The northern part of Somalia becomes a British colony — British Somaliland — while the Italians take control of the south.

1897

The Anglo-Abyssinian Treaty allocates the Ogaden region of British Somaliland to the Ethiopians.

1899-1920

Sheikh Mohammed Abdilleh Hassan, called by the British the 'Mad Mullah', leads rebellions against the Ethiopians, British and Italians. Although unsuccessful in his attempts, he is credited with the origins of modern Somali nationalism.

1939-45

Britain and Italy are on opposing sides in the Second World War. British Somaliland is used as a base to fight the Italians in Eritrea, Abyssinia and Italian Somaliland. Many Somalis join the British armed forces during this campaign. Italian Somaliland is captured from the Italians.

1950-60

Somalia is again divided. The Italians return to the south with UN backing, and the British continue to administer British Somaliland. At this time nationalists, led by the Somali Youth Club, begin to demand independence and national unity.

1960

British and Italian Somaliland gain independence and unite to form one country. But there are many problems for the new government: the country is very poor and the north and south have experienced different colonial and administrative systems. There are deep clan and political divisions in the country. But despite these challenges the Somali Republic is a democracy, and human rights are respected.

Many Somalis are living outside the new nation, in Ethiopia, Djibouti and Kenya.

1969

The democratically elected Somali government loses public support. President Abdirashid Ali Shermaarke is assassinated and a group of army officers seize power in a military coup. Major General Mohammed Siad Barre becomes president of the newly named Somali Democratic Republic and the country is ruled by an unelected body called the Supreme Revolutionary Council. Nevertheless the government affirms that the country will be returned to democracy and promises to introduce policies to improve the lives of ordinary people. In the next five years there is a large-scale literacy campaign, coupled with ambitious rural development projects.

1970

The Somali Democratic Republic announces its commitment to socialism and looks to the Soviet Union for support. Financial and military aid is given, and the country soon has one of the largest armies in Africa.

At this time the Somali Democratic Republic experiences severe food shortages. The government organises an efficient relief operation that prevents people dying of starvation.

1977

War breaks out between the Somali Democratic Republic and Ethiopia over the disputed territory of the Ogaden, which President Barre wanted to bring into 'Greater Somalia'. The Somali army joins the Ogaden-based guerrillas of the Western Somali Liberation Front. The Soviet-Somali alliance ends, as the new Ethiopian regime develops its own ties with the Soviet Union. The USA steps into the shoes of the Soviet Union and gives military aid to the Somali government. Neither super-power contributes much to the economic development of the country.

1978

Ethiopia wins back control of the Ogaden but the guerrilla war in this disputed territory continues. The conflict with Ethiopia is not settled until 1988.

Present Barre begins to experience the first opposition to his rule. Oil price rises hit Somalia very badly and the country falls deeply in debt. The International Monetary Fund steps in, forcing the Somali government to cut public spending and adopt a structural adjustment policy. Food subsidies are cut, causing hardship among the urban population.

Prompted by rising popular discontent members of the Majeerteen clan back a coup d'etat. This fails and President Barre launches reprisal attacks on the Majeerteen. Army units destroy the Majeerteen's water sources and over 2,000 clan members die or are killed. Other government opponents are killed or imprisoned.

1982

Three opposition parties are formed, including the Somali National Movement (SNM). All three parties soon commit themselves to armed struggle in their desire to overthrow President Barre. Civil war has begun. President Barre unleashes terror against clans associated with opposition parties. Northern Somalia is worst affected, with members of the Issaq clan facing repressive measures ranging from imprisonment to execution of those suspected of supporting the SNM.

1988

In retaliation for attacks on the Issaq clan, the SNM launches a military offensive in northern towns. The Government responds with extreme force destroying the northern towns of Burao and Hargeisa by shelling and aerial bombardment. Over 72,000 people are killed in Hargeisa and 400,000 flee as refugees. Some of the refugees subsequently seek asylum in Britain.

1989

Persecution shifts to the Hawiye clan in central Somalia. They form the power-base of the United Somali Congress (USC), another opposition group. Civilians are imprisoned and killed. The USC is better able to challenge Siad Barre's misrule and oppression.

1991

Following popular discontent, the USC marches into Mogadishu. Siad Barre is forced to flee. But the USC splits into two groups almost immediately, one led by General Aidid and the other by interim President Ali Mahdi Mohamed. Each is backed by a sub-group of the Hawiye clan. Both factions are heavily armed by Soviet and US weaponry left in the country. In other parts of the country political parties and factions fail to unite and inter-clan conflict worsens. Nearly one million people are forced into exile or internally displaced.

By the end of 1991 it is obvious that Somalia is facing severe food shortages as a result of drought and the war's disruption of the agrarian economy. UN relief agencies are criticised for their slow response.

In May 1991 the SNM declares independence in the north. There is a fragile peace in the new Republic of Somaliland. But it is an unrecognised state, and does not qualify for international aid, which it desperately needs for the reconstruction of the country.

1992

The International Committee of the Red Cross warns that 4,000,000 Somalis are at risk of starvation. Diplomatic solutions to the conflicts fail. Fighting prevents food aid from being distributed. Aid agencies are forced to hire militia to protect food convoys and their employees. Some 500,000 Somalis die of starvation in 1992, including half of all children under five. By the end of the year one million people are displaced and a further one million are refugees in Ethiopia, Kenya, Yemen and European countries. Non-governmental organisations become increasingly frustrated with the UN's slow reaction to the worsening crisis.

On 8 December 1992 US troops land in Mogadishu, in Operation Restore Hope. The international response is mixed. Some aid agencies feel that without the full co-operation of the Somalis, the move would end in disaster. Others have become convinced that the need to stop the dying justified military intervention. Food security is assured but attempts to disarm the militias are of limited success.

1993

A UN peacekeeping force takes over from the US operation. No transitional government or united leadership has emerged, and the country remains divided.

Somali Refugees in Britain

Statistics

Year	Asylum Applications	Refugee Status	ELR	Refusal
1986	152	17	7	27
1987	202	19	43	62
1988	305	192	63	8
1989	1,850	815	260	10
1990	2,250	275	75	25
1991	1,995	50	225	40
1992	1,575	25	2,210	320
1993	1,465	45	3,075	210

The figures exclude dependants. Source Home Office

There are about 35,000 Somalis in Britain. This country has hosted a Somali community since the early years of the 20th century when sailors from British Somaliland settled in the ports of London, Cardiff and Liverpool, and in industrial cities such as Sheffield, Middlesborough, Manchester and Birmingham. Since the assault on the northern towns in 1988, Britain's Somali community has grown. The new arrivals are refugees and, like the immigrant community before them, most of them are from the former British Protectorate.

The largest Somali community is in Greater London. Somalis live in all London boroughs, and almost every London secondary school has received Somali refugees, as have many primary schools. The Somali community is concentrated in the London Boroughs of Tower Hamlets, Hackney and Newham, and in Ealing and Brent.

Many of Britain's Somali refugees are now living in very deprived conditions. Almost all London-based Somali refugee families spend considerable periods of time in bed and breakfast hotels. Somalis are over-represented in hard-to-let local authority accommodation. Extended family often join relatives who have housing; it is estimated that 88 per cent of Somali families in East London live in overcrowded conditions. (London Borough of Tower Hamlets, 1992). Most adult Somali refugees are likely to have completed secondary education and to speak some English. But despite high levels of literacy, unemployment among Somali refugees remains very high: over 85 per cent among refugees of 35-50 years.

Bad housing, poverty and unemployment are all sources of stress in the Somali community. Racial harassment is another stressor: on one east London housing estate there were 123 racial attacks on Somalis in a 12-month period. These attacks ranged from spitting and verbal abuse to more serious incidents such as assault and arson. For recently arrived refugees this is a new and terrifying experience.

Somali refugees also have unique health problems, caused by recent events in Somalia, by life in refugee camps in East Africa and by poverty and stress in Britain. The assault on Hargeisa in 1988 left 72,000 people dead and a further 290,000 civilians injured. Some Somali refugees still bear their war injuries. Others may bear psychological scars.

Over 400,000 refugees fled from the northern towns to camps in Somalia and in neighbouring countries. Conditions in the refugee camps were harsh, access to food and clean water problematic. Most refugees from these camps suffered from malnutrition and gastro-intestinal infections.

Many Somali refugee organisations feel that the NHS has not responded to the needs of their community. Surveys have found that the refugees have difficulty in gaining access to healthcare, due to lack of knowledge about their basic rights and the type of services available.

There are Somali community organisations in all parts of Britain with substantial Somali populations. Some of these community organisations are running supplementary schools for the children of their members.

Despite being a well-qualified group, Somali refugees are probably among the most deprived refugee communities in Britain. In responding the the needs of Somali children, LEAs and schools must develop educational policies to support low income families.

☐ Refugees from Sri Lanka

Over 22,000 Sri Lankan Tamil refugees have arrived in Britain since 1983.

The Democratic Socialist Republic of Sri Lanka has a population of 17 million, of whom 21 per cent live in urban areas. The capital is Colombo.

Ethnic Groups

About 74 per cent of the population are Sinhalese. It is believed that the Sinhalese migrated from India in waves after the 5th century BC. Another 18 per cent of the population are Tamils and includes Tamils who migrated to Sri Lanka 2,500 years ago, around the same time as the Sinhalese. They mostly live in northern and eastern Sri Lanka. About one million 'plantation Tamils' live in the tea-producing areas of central Sri Lanka. They are the descendants of indentured labour brought by the British in the 19th century to work on the tea plantations. Most Tamil refugees in Britain are from northern and eastern Sri Lanka.

Muslims make up about seven per cent of the population and are sometimes called Moors, because it was thought —wrongly — that they were the descendants of Moroccan Arabs. There are also small numbers of people of Dutch and

Portuguese descent, called Burghers, generally with Dutch or Portuguese family names.

In prehistoric times Sri Lanka was joined by land to India. A group called the Veddahs lived in Sri Lanka at this time; today small numbers of Veddahs still live in southern Sri Lanka.

Languages

The Sinhalese population speaks Sinhala as its first language. Sinhala, unlike Tamil, is an Indo-European language descended from Sanskrit. This would seem to indicate that the Sinhalese originally migrated from North India. But the Sinhala alphabet, with its rounded letters, more closely resembles the Dravidian languages of South India.

The Tamil and Muslim populations speak Tamil. Tamil belongs to the Dravidian language family. Other closely related languages are Kannada and Malayalam, both spoken in south India. About 60 million people speak Tamil throughout the world: 50 million in south India, four million in Sri Lanka, and others in Malaysia, Singapore, Fiji, Trinidad, Guyana, and parts of East Africa. Tamil has a standard written form but the dialects spoken in Sri Lanka and south India differ.

The Tamil alphabet has 247 letters. There are 12 vowel sounds and 18 consonants. Each vowel sound then modifies a consonant, giving an extra 216 letters; there is also a special letter which represents the 'f' sound.

Language issues are an integral part of the conflict in Sri Lanka. Under British rule English was the language of government and the medium of instruction in schools and higher education. Up until 1948 an educated Tamil would speak Tamil as a first language and English as a second. From independence until 1956 English was still the language of government. But in 1956 Sinhala became the sole official language and the language of government. Overnight, hundreds of Tamil civil servants lost their jobs because they lacked proficiency in Sinhala. Twelve Tamil MPs and their supporters staged a peaceful protest outside Parliament about the change in language policy. A Sinhalese crowd stoned the demonstrators and then killed 150 Tamils in subsequent riots.

In 1989 Tamil became an official language. But the language of government is still Sinhala.

Names

Tamil names are complicated because Tamil refugees may use two different naming systems.

To illustrate — two Tamil men's names are:

R. Sivanandan

M. V. Vijayapalan

'Sivanandan' and 'Vijayapalan' are the persons' names. They are neither first names nor family names. They would be called Sivanandan or Vijayapalan, and a polite form of address would be Mr Sivanandan and Mr Vijayapalan.

The initials 'R' and 'V' refer to the person's father's name. A few Tamils also have family names, particularly if they have well known and respected forebears whose name they might wish to remember. Vijayapalan's family name is Malavarayan, and is written down as the first initial. When a woman marries she takes her husband's name as an initial before her name.

Many Tamils also have nicknames or pet names, sometimes shortened versions of their name. Vijayapalan and Sivanandan may be called 'Vijay' or 'Siva'.

In both Britain and Sri Lanka some Tamils use the European naming system. As Home Office, school and medical records are not designed to cope with different naming systems, many Tamils living in Britain feel obliged to use the European system. Additionally if they have a well known forebear they might want to keep that name as their family name. For example Gopal Sivalingham and Parvathi Sivalingham are brother and sister. Their parents have adopted Sivalingham as their family name.

Sri Lankan Christians use a European naming system and usually have an English first name. Sri Lankan Muslims use the Islamic naming system. The Sinhalese population use a first name and a family name, as is the practice in North India and Europe.

Religion

Most Sri Lankan Tamils are Hindu. Tamil houses may have a shrine to a particular god or goddess, and Tamils are generally more religiously observant than most people in Britain. Many Tamils also visit Hindu temples; each temple is dedicated to one particular god or goddess.

The main Tamil festivals are:

> Pongal — the harvest festival, celebrated on 14 January.
>
> Navarathiri — celebrated for nine days in October in honour of the goddesses Parawathy, Lakshmi and Saraswathy.
>
> Divali — the Hindu festival of lights, celebrated in November. In Tamil this festival is known as Deepavali.

Tamils will also celebrate the temple festivals of their own temple.

Sri Lankan Tamils are not strict vegetarians and usually eat meat and fish, although very few will eat beef. Many Tamils do not eat meat on Fridays or religious holidays.

Like all Hindu societies Tamils belong to different castes. Allegiance to caste is still an important factor in social relations in Sri Lanka's villages, though less so in towns and in Britain. Caste allegiance does not impinge on refugee community groups but is still an important factor when arranging a marriage.

A few Sri Lankan Tamils are Christians. Britain has also received Tamil-speaking Muslim refugees, but these two groups are in the minority.

Education System

Education is held in high esteem by Tamils, in both Sri Lanka and Britain. Tamil refugee children are usually very highly motivated.

Almost all Sri Lankan children attend primary schools. Education is compulsory from five to 14 years and is free from kindergarten to university level in state institutions. There are also fee-paying schools. The Sri Lankan education system is probably the best in south Asia and, consequently, the literacy level is very high: 81 per cent for women and 91 per cent for men.

Despite these educational achievements access to higher education is a major grievance of the Tamil community. In the 1960s proportionally more Tamils entered universities than did Sinhalese students. Sinhala nationalists responded by putting pressure on the government to restrict the numbers of Tamil students in higher education. In 1970 they were told that they would need higher marks in their A-Level examinations than Sinhalese students in order to enter university. This caused enormous discontent among Tamil students, many of whom became politically active.

Education has also been disrupted by the civil war and by the siege of the Jaffna Peninsula. The children of displaced people are not usually enrolled in school. In many parts of northern and eastern Sri Lanka the army has intimidated and arrested students during school hours. Papers for O-Level and A-Level examinations have arrived late, or not at all. Many Tamil school students are now travelling to Colombo to take examinations.

The Jaffna Peninsula has been under total blockade for three years. The Sri Lankan Air Force has bombed schools and other civilian targets, and children have been killed. The Sri Lankan government has prevented many essential goods from reaching the Jaffna Peninsula, including basic foodstuffs, medicines and paper. Despite the destruction of some schools and the absence of exercise books, desks and other equipment, schools are still open. Sri Lankan government examinations are not running in the Jaffna Peninsula.

Until the early 1960s English was the medium of instruction in schools and colleges in Sri Lanka. Now Sinhala and Tamil are the media of instruction in schools and Sinhalese and Tamil students are usually educated in separate institutions. English is taught as a second language from the fourth year at primary school but is not compulsory either for Ordinary Level or for university entrance. Tamil refugee children will require language support, although most will be familiar with the Roman alphabet. Their parents are likely to speak English and, if encouraged, will be able to help their children learn the language.

In 1985 Sri Lankan education was reorganised. Schooling is at four levels: six years of primary education, two years in a junior secondary school, three years in a senior secondary school and two years on pre-university courses.

School students enrol at primary schools when they are five or six years old. Primary school lasts six years (years I-VI). Students the spend another two years at junior secondary school (years VII-VIII), school being compulsory up to 14 years.

Senior secondary school lasts another three years (years IX-XI). At the end of year XI students sit for Sri Lankan GCE O-Levels. Students take the examination in eight subjects and must pass six including mathematics and Sinhala or Tamil. A credit or distinction in a Sri Lankan O-Level subject is considered to be the equivalent of a GCSE pass at grades A, B or C.

Pre-university courses last for two years (years XII-XIII). At the end of year XIII students sit for Sri Lankan GCE A-Levels. Students sit the examination in four subjects and must pass at least three to be considered by universities. The Sri Lankan A-Level is considered to be equivalent to a British A-Level. Students can also sit for the National Certificate in English examination while on pre-university courses; this is at a higher level than the Sri Lankan O-Level English.

Economy

About 45 per cent of the population are employed in agriculture, fishing or forestry. The agricultural workforce is employed on plantations or small farms. Rice is one of the main crops grown on these farms.

Tea is Sri Lanka's main export and is produced on the state-owned tea plantations in central Sri Lanka. Other plantation crops include rubber, coconut and fruit.

Sri Lanka produces many precious and semi-precious stones and these are another important export, as is clothing. The tourist industry has been devastated by the civil war.

There is presently very limited economic activity in the Jaffna Peninsula, save for the cultivation of subsistence crops. The naval blockade prevents fishing. Farmers cannot obtain diesel and fertilisers, and merchants have no produce to sell.

A Chronology of Events

During the 11th and 12th century AD there was a Tamil kingdom in northern Sri Lanka. Between the 14th and 16th century three kingdoms existed: a Tamil kingdom in northern Sri Lanka, the Sinhalese Kingdom of Kotte and the Sinhalese Kingdom of Kandy.

1505
The Portuguese arrive in Sri Lanka. Over the next 120 years they trade in spices, and capture the Kotte and Tamil kingdoms.

1656
The Dutch colonise Portuguese Ceylon and introduce plantation crops to the island; coffee, sugar cane, spices and tobacco are important produce. Like the Portuguese before them, the Dutch are unable to capture the Kandyan kingdom in central Ceylon.

1796
The Tamil and Kotte Kingdoms are handed over to the British East India Company after an agreement between the British and Dutch government. Plantation agriculture and the spice trade are expanded.

1802
Ceylon becomes a British colony. In 1815 the Kandyan Kingdom is brought under British rule.

1833
The former Tamil and Sinhalese kingdoms, previously ruled separately, are brought under one administration.

1840
The British pass a new law called the 'Waste Lands Ordinance'. This allows the British to claim any land where ownership cannot be proved. As most farmers lack title deeds, the British colonial administration is able to claim much land. This is then sold very cheaply to plantation owners. Coffee, coconuts and rubber are grown on the plantations. Over 200,000 Indian Tamils are brought as indentured labour to work on the new plantations.

1870
The coffee crop is killed by a fungal disease. Tea bushes are planted and tea replaces coffee as Ceylon's main export.

By the end of the 19th century Ceylonese Tamils begin to obtain jobs in the British colonial administration.

1911
There are now more Plantation Tamils than Ceylonese Tamils. Working mainly on the tea plantations of central Ceylon, they are poorer than Ceylonese Tamils.

1944
The Soulbury Commission arrives from London to prepare Ceylon for independence. Tamil politicians request legal safeguards to protect minorities. Mr D. S. Senanrayake, President of the Ceylon National Congress, promises that the rights of Tamils and other minority groups will be protected.

1948

Ceylon gains independence from Britain. One of the first actions of the new government was to pass the Citizenship Act. This made all Plantation Tamils stateless, as citizenship had to be proved by descent or by registration. In 1949 another new law removed the right of stateless Tamils to vote.

1956

Sinhala becomes Ceylon's official language, replacing English as the language of government. Many Tamils protest, believing that they will be excluded from government employment. Twelve Tamil MPs and their supporters stage a peaceful protest outside Parliament. A Sinhalese crowd stones the protesters whilst the police take no action. Rioting spreads to many parts of Colombo and over 150 Tamils die.

1958

Protests about the language issue continue in an atmosphere of great tension. In May 1958 Sinhalese crowds attack Tamils and over 1,000 people are killed. Some 12,000 Tamils are rescued from Colombo by British and French ships.

1964

An agreement is signed between India and Ceylon, to allow 525,000 Plantation Tamils to be given Indian citizenship and be repatriated over the next 15 years. Some 300,000 Plantation Tamils will be given Ceylonese citizenship and allowed to stay. The agreement is supplemented in 1974 by a further treaty which gives the remaining Plantation Tamils Indian and Ceylonese citizenship but the process is very slow.

1972

Ceylon becomes Sri Lanka and Buddhism is declared the religion of the state. There are no longer any legal safeguards to protect the rights of minorities.

1976

Tamil leaders meet and call for a separate state for Tamils. This move is supported by the majority of Tamil people. Tamil Eelam, the proposed state, would comprise northern and eastern Sri Lanka.

In the same year young Tamils form a group which later becomes the Liberation Tigers of Tamil Eelam (LTTE). This organisation soon resorts to armed struggle.

1977

Over 500 Tamils are killed in communal violence while the police and army do nothing.

1978

Tamil becomes a national language, according to the Sri Lankan government, but in practice this means little.

1981

There is further communal violence.

1983

Communal violence flares up again. In July 1983 a week of rioting leaves 2,500 Tamils dead, 150,000 people in refugee camps, and 23,000 homes and businesses destroyed. Many Tamils leave Colombo for good, fleeing to northern and eastern Sri Lanka where they are not in a minority. Others flee to India, North America and Europe.

1985

The Indian government arranges peace talks between the Sri Lankan government, the Tamil United Liberation Front (a political party with no guerrilla wing), and the five main Tamil guerrilla groups. The talks soon break down as the Sri Lankan government is unable to make proposals that satisfy the Tamils.

1986

The LTTE murder 146 Sinhalese Buddhist pilgrims. This triggers intense violence between the Sinhalese and Tamil communities. The Sri Lankan government is condemned by Amnesty International for the torture of Tamil prisoners and for extrajudicial executions.

Fighting breaks out between some Tamil guerrilla groups. By the end of 1986 at least 85,000 Tamils have fled to southern India, where many live in poverty.

1987

The LTTE leadership is forced out of India and returns to Sri Lanka, establishing a parallel government in Jaffna. The Sri Lankan government retaliates with an armed offensive and an economic blockade of the Jaffna Peninsula. The armed offensive stops just short of Jaffna.

India arranges further peace-keeping talks. Among the provisions is the return of refugees and the dispatch of an Indian Peace Keeping Force (IPKF) to northern Sri Lanka. But by October 1987 fighting breaks out between the LTTE and the IPKF. The latter is also accused of human rights violations, in particular extra-judicial executions.

In southern Sri Lanka the Janata Vimukti Peramuna, a Sinhalese political party, begins guerrilla activity. This organisation espouses a mixture of Marxist and Sinhala nationalist policies. Violence perpetrated in the struggle between the Janata Vimukti Peramuna and the Sri Lankan army leaves at least 1,000 people dead. Foreign diplomats estimate that 40,000 Sri Lankans disappeared in 1987.

1989

After a violent start to the year the LTTE and the Sri Lankan government agree to begin peace talks. The Indian Peace Keeping Force agrees to leave Sri Lanka.

1990

In June 1990 the LTTE attacks 17 police stations and executes 110 police officers. The Sri Lankan army retaliates, and the war enters a new stage. Within two weeks over 1,000 people are killed and 200,000 left homeless. The Sri Lankan government operates an economic blockade of the Jaffna Peninsula; food, medicines and many other essential goods are banned from sale in northern Sri Lanka. There is no electricity in the Jaffna Peninsula, and universal malnutrition.

1991

The blockade and bombing of the Jaffna Peninsula continues. Over 1,000,000 people are now internally displaced in Sri Lanka. Some 220,000 refugees have fled to southern India, and 400,000 Tamils have sought asylum in Europe and North America.

At the end of 1991 the governments of India and Sri Lanka announce they are collaborating on a plan to encourage the early return of refugees living in India. Aid agencies oppose this, as they believe Sri Lanka to be unsafe.

1992-93

The blockade of the Jaffna Peninsula continues. India returns 25,000 refugees to Sri Lanka. UNHCR has no access to these returnees and cannot ascertain whether they returned voluntarily or were coerced. Those who return find their houses destroyed or looted and they receive very little resettlement assistance to enable them to rebuild their homes.

Switzerland and Norway announce plans to return Tamil refugees to Colombo.

Tamil Refugees in Britain

Statistics

Year Asylum	Applications	Refugee Status	ELR	Refusals
1982	16	0	2	27
1983	380	0	13	31
1984	548	2	31	100
1985	1,893	10	669	11
1986	1,275	5	1,488	5
1987	992	7	732	64
1988	402	6	226	52
1989	1,790	10	840	30
1990	3,330	15	455	5
1991	3,765	20	730	20
1992	2,085	40	4,265	215
1993	1,965	10	2,420	60

Figures exclude dependants after 1985. Source Home Office.

The European response to Tamil refugees has been to view them as economic migrants who needed some kind of temporary protection. Since 1983 very few Tamil refugees have been given refugee status in Britain and other European countries (with the exception of France). In Britain Tamil refugees are most often given ELR; in other European countries they are afforded similar kinds of temporary protection.

But until 1992 very few Tamil refugees were returned. There was one well-publicised deportation case in 1988: five Tamils who had been refused refugee status in Britain were returned to Sri Lanka and on arriving three were arrested by the Indian Peace Keeping Force and another arrested by the Sri Lankan police. Three of the five were beaten in custody. They later submitted an appeal, asserting they had been unfairly denied refugee status. The immigration adjudicator ordered that the five applicants be returned to Britain for a reconsideration of their asylum case.

In late 1992 the Swiss government announced plans to return some groups of Tamils who had been refused asylum in that country. Sri Lanka was to be divided up into four regions: Greater Colombo, southern Sri Lanka, central Sri Lanka and northern and eastern Sri Lanka. The Swiss government stated that some Tamils could be returned to Colombo. (Human rights organisations presently believe Colombo to be unsafe for Tamil returnees). Other European governments seem likely to follow the Swiss policy and return Tamils.

Tamil refugees can be divided into two social groups: young single men who have been politically active in Sri Lanka, and those of an older age group, usually with a family. Many young Tamil men have been held in police or army custody, and may have been tortured. They may have missed large parts of their school or university education. Many young Tamil men are finding it difficult to find employment in Britain.

Refugees who came to Britain with qualifications and work experience have generally integrated well into British society. Some have achieved success in commerce or as professionals.

Most of Britain's Tamil refugees live in Greater London, in particular in South London (in the London Boroughs of Croydon, Merton and Sutton), and in East London (in the London Boroughs of Newham and Redbridge). There a several active community organisations and supplementary schools for Tamil children.

☐ Refugees from Sudan

About 4,000 Sudanese refugees live in Britain, a few fleeing in the early 1980s but the majority after a military coup in 1989.

Sudan has a population of 23 million. Before the civil war intensified in 1987 about 80 per cent of Sudanese lived in rural areas. Fighting has driven many southern Sudanese to take refuge in shanty towns surrounding Khartoum and other towns. The capital is Khartoum.

Ethnic Groups

Sudan is an ethnically diverse country. Some 40 per cent of the population identify themselves as Arabs, although the claim of Arab descent is much more a matter of cultural allegiance rather than ethnic origin. Since the Arab conquest in the 7th century there has been much intermixing of Arabs, Nubians and other African peoples.

Sudanese Arabs live in northern Sudan. Non-Arab groups living in northern Sudan make up another 20 per cent of the population. They include the Nile Nubians, who consider themselves the descendants of the ancient Kingdom of Nubia, and live in the Nile Valley north of Khartoum. Under the influence of Ethiopia, the Nubians embraced Christianity in the 6th century, later converting to Islam. They speak a dialect of Nubian. There are also many other smaller ethnic groups such as the Beja, Nuba, Ingessana, Fur and Massalete. The non-Arab peoples of northern Sudan speak many different languages. The extent of the mixing of ethnic groups is such that languages from three major linguistic families (Hamito-Semitic, Chari-Nile and Niger-Congo) are spoken in northern Sudan, plus a number of independent languages.

Much has recently been written about the Nuba. They are diverse group of peoples living in the Nuba mountains of southern Kordofan. They number about one million people and are culturally different from their Arab neighbours. Many speak a dialect of Nubian, although they look like southern Sudanese. Their relationship with the Nile Nubians is a matter of anthropological debate. Some retain their traditional beliefs, others have converted to Islam or Christianity.

Cattle-herding Arabs, known as Baggara Arabs, also live in the Nuba mountains. There has been competition between the two groups for land and wells. Since the civil war began, the Sudanese People's Liberation Army (SPLA) has been trying to recruit support among the Nuba mountain groups. The SPLA murdered Nuba leaders who refused to co-operate with them.

The Sudanese government's response to Nuba insurgency has been to arm Baggara Arabs, who then raid Nuba villages. Thousands of Nuba have been killed in what amounts to 'ethnic cleansing'. The Sudanese government has also arrested and killed large numbers of educated Nuba. Since October 1990 the

Nuba mountains have been sealed off and in 1992 a *jihad*, or Holy War, was declared against the Nuba. The Army and armed militia moved into Nuba villages, destroying them and moving people to relocation camps. Other Nuba peoples were murdered: up to 6,000 were killed near the village of Heiban in 1992.

About 500,000 Eritrean refugees live in towns and camps in western Sudan and in Khartoum.

Southern Sudanese form about 30 per cent of the population. As in the north there has been much intermixing of different ethnic groups. The southern Sudanese can be divided into two groups: those living in the central grasslands and south east Sudan, and the peoples living in the forests along the border with the Central African Republic, Zaire and Uganda.

The Dinka, Nuer and Shilluk belong to the first group. All speak Nilotic languages. The peoples of the south west Sudan are linguistically more diverse, and include ethnic groups such as the Azande and Bari.

Almost all ethnic groups are represented among the Sudanese refugees who have fled to Britain.

Languages

Arabic is the official language of Sudan and is spoken by about 50 per cent of the population, mostly in northern Sudan. It is the medium of instruction in schools. Almost all Sudanese refugees in Britain speak Arabic, whether they are from the north or south.

Arabic is a Semitic language, written from right to left. It has an alphabet of 28 letters, mostly consonants. Vowel signs are added by dots marked above or below the letters, although such pointing is only usually shown in religious texts and in children's books.

Classical Arabic — the language of the Koran — is taught in the Madrassah and in schools. A modern, simplified standard form of classical Arabic is used as the written language throughout the Arab world.

Spoken Arabic varies from country to country and the Sudanese speak their own dialects. When Sudanese Arabs meet Arabs from another country they usually converse in classical Arabic.

Other main languages are dialects of Nubian, spoken in northern Sudan and Kordofan. Beja, a Hamito-Semitic language is spoken in eastern Sudan. Dinka, Nuer, Shilluk, Zande and Bari are the languages most frequently spoken in southern Sudan. English is widely spoken in government and academic circles.

Names

Several different naming systems are used. In northern Sudan Islamic names are used among the Muslim population. A person has a first name, followed by the father's first name, and the grandfather's name. Women keep their names after they marry. Sometime the grandfather's name is not used.

Among the Copts, and in western and southern Sudan the same system of a first name, father's name and grandfather's name may be used but the names themselves are Sudanese or Christian rather than Islamic. Some Sudanese Christians also have a baptismal name, which they use every day but which may not be written on official papers. Other southern Sudanese may use different naming systems, for example a person may have a first personal name, followed by a name indicating the circumstances in which they were born. They may also have a family name or use their father's name as a last name.

Other Copts and Southern Sudanese have adopted a western naming system: a Christian name followed by a family name.

Some southern Sudanese use a naming system similar to that used in Uganda. A child will have a first name, then a name which relates to the circumstance in which he or she is born, followed by the father's name. Women will tend to keep their names when they marry.

Religion

About 70 per cent of the population are Sunni Muslims, 18 per cent animists, eight per cent Roman Catholic, 0.5 per cent Protestant and 0.5 per cent Coptic Christian.

Islam has a strong Sufi element in the Sudan. The majority of Sudanese Muslims claim allegiance to the Khatmiya or the Tiganiya Sufi order. These sects preach a Sudanese version of Islam, characterised by austerity, mysticism, a direct relation with God, and tolerance of other religions.

In recent years other Islamic sects and groupings have flourished, including Islamic fundamentalist organisations. The economic crises of the 1970s and 1980s have undoubtedly led to a rise in religious fundamentalism. In 1983 *shari'a* — Islamic laws — were introduced by President Nimeiri. These were extended in 1991 and 1992, although *shari'a* does not apply to southern Sudan. Human rights activists have expressed concern about *shari'a*: penalties such as stoning an amputation are cruel and degrading. Non-Muslims no longer share the same rights of citizenship as others.

Most Sudanese Christians live in southern Sudan, except the Coptic Christians. This community numbers about 200,000 people, mostly living in Khartoum, Omdurman, Dongola, Atbara, Wad Medani, Port Sudan and El Obeid. They speak Arabic, although Coptic is still used as a liturgical language. Since 1989 the Sudanese government has enacted policies which are intended to drive them out of the country. Hundreds of Copts have been dismissed from their jobs simply because they are Christian. About 1,000 Sudanese Copts have fled to Britain.

Education System

Primary education is free in Sudan and lasts for six years. Most children enrol when they are about six years old. Primary education is followed by an intermediate course lasting for three years at the end of which students have to pass an examination to gain access to secondary schooling.

Secondary school courses last between two and four years. There are three types of secondary schools: academic, technical and national industrial schools.

In academic secondary schools students follow a three year course. In the first two years they study a common curriculum, specialising in arts or science subjects in the third. Arabic, mathematics, religion and English are compulsory. At the end of three years students sit for the Sudan Secondary School Certificate which requires passes in six subjects. The Secondary School Certificate is considered comparable to a GCSE pass at grades A to C, on a subject-for-subject basis.

The medium of instruction in northern Sudan is Arabic. English is a compulsory subject from the intermediate stage. In southern Sudan primary and intermediate schools teach through the medium of Arabic or through the local language where it is scripted. Secondary schools teach through the medium of Arabic or English (British Council, 1991).

The education system has been in turmoil since the late 1970s. Many teachers have left Sudan, as refugees or migrant workers. Cuts in public spending forced upon Sudan by the International Monetary Fund have restricted educational expenditure. Sudanese schools are consequently badly equipped and classes are very large. Teaching is formal and offers little experience of laboratory practicals or subjects such as drama.

The literacy rate is 36 per cent for men and six per cent for women. In urban areas the literacy rate is much higher but only 12 per cent of all Sudanese girls are enrolled at secondary schools.

Economy

Sudan can be divided into four geographical regions: the northern deserts, the Nile Valley, the savannah of central and south east Sudan, and the rainforests bordering Zaire. Most people live along the Nile.

Sudan is a predominantly agricultural economy — some 62 per cent of all Sudanese work on the land. The main export crops are cattle, cotton, sesame and gum arabic.

A Chronology of Events

Sudan was called Kush by the Egyptians and Nubia by the Greeks, and has come under the influence of many different cultures.

Until the 16th century there were Christian kingdoms clustered along the Nile. At the start of the modern period these kingdoms collapsed and gave way to a series of Muslim states. In 1889 an Anglo-Egyptian army defeated the Sudanese army of Mohamed Ahmad al Mahadi (a self-claimed Muslim redeemer) at the Battle of Omdurman. The two countries then established joint rule over Sudan.

1920s

The British move to separate the Arab and Muslim north from the African south. The two parts of Sudan are ruled separately and colonial policies are enacted that accentuate the differences.

1930s and 1940s

The northern Sudanese begin a campaign of independence. Many southern Sudanese, fearing they would be dominated by the north, are less intent on immediate independence.

1956

Sudan becomes independent. Even before independence there is fighting between the Sudanese army and rebel soldiers in the south. Their rebellion forms the basis of a larger separatist movement which fights Sudan's first civil war, lasting until 1972. During this time the Sudanese government spends large sums of money on weapons and army pay. There is little investment in Sudan's infrastructure. Thousands of people are killed and many more flee as refugees to Ethiopia, Zaire, the Central African Republic and Uganda.

1969

A coup d'etat brings Colonel Nimeiri to power.

1973-79

The world market price of cotton begins to fall in the 1970s. This crop is a major Sudanese export. Following the rise in oil prices Sudan faces a huge balance of payments deficit and economic crisis. The International Monetary Fund (IMF) is eventually called in by the Sudanese government. It recommends a series of austerity measures, including the abolition of food subsidies and other cuts in public spending.

By the end of the 1970s food prices begin to rise. Many Sudanese join protests against the IMF programme. Other Sudanese turn to Islamic fundamentalism. President Nimeiri is eventually forced into coalition with the fundamentalist Muslim Brothers.

1981

Food supplies run short in southern Sudan.

1983
President Nimeiri imposes *shari'a* law on Sudan. He also divides the south into three administrative regions. Both decisions cause much discontent and civil war breaks out again between the government and the Sudan People's Liberation Army (SPLA), led by Colonel Garang. They fight for the abolition of *shari'a* and for political autonomy.

1984
Drought from the early 1980s turns to widespread famine in Sudan.

1985
The IMF forces the Government to raise food prices. There are widespread demonstrations and Nimeiri is overthrown. The transitional government promise to hold elections and to review *shari'a.*

1986
A coalition government is formed after elections, led by Sadiq al Mahadi. But the civil war continues in southern Sudan. Several southern cities are kept under siege by the SPLA.

1987-89
The civil war intensifies. In 1988 over 250,000 people starve to death in southern towns because both the government and the SPLA prevent food aid reaching the starving. Refugees flee to Ethiopia and Uganda. Over 1,000,000 people flee to Khartoum to escape fighting and famine. Most of the internally displaced live in slums around the edge of the city.

Islamic laws are not abolished. There are also attacks on Dinka people by Arab militias armed by the Government.

1988
Shari'a is frozen, pending a constitutional conference.

1989
Another military coup d'etat installs Brigadier Omar al Bashir as President. He has much support from fundamentalist elements in Sudanese society. The coup puts paid to any peace agreement between the government and SPLA. Human rights violations worsen, include mass detentions, extrajudicial executions, the banning of political parties and trade unions, media censorship and the abolition of an independent, secular judiciary.

1990
There is widespread famine in southern Sudan.

1991
Shari'a is again imposed on northern Sudan. More than 5,000 people are murdered in and around the town of Bor in a feud between two factions of the SPLA.

1992

The Sudanese government expels more than 400,000 displaced people from their homes in Khartoum's squatter camps. They are transferred to the desert, without adequate food, water or shelter.

A military offensive forces the SPLA from many of their positions.

1993

The Sudanese government declares their war in the south to be a *jihad*— a holy war. The famine in southern Sudan worsens. Over 400,000 people flee to Ethiopia, Kenya, Uganda, Zaire and the Central African Republic, and up to four million are internally displaced.

Sudanese Refugees in Britain

Statistics

Year	Asylum Applications	Refugee Status	ELR	Refusals
1989	110	45	0	5
1990	340	10	5	5
1991	1,150	10	5	10
1992	560	150	115	125
1993	300	740	660	75

Source Home Office.

Before 1989 most Sudanese refugees who fled to Britain were from southern Sudan and their numbers were very small. Most Sudanese refugees in Britain have arrived since the 1989 coup d'etat.

Sudanese refugees are a diverse group. They include southern Sudanese, Copts, people associated with Nimeiri's regime, politicians from different political parties, trade unionists and other opposition activists. What draws them together is their opposition to the current government and its fundamentalist policies.

The largest Sudanese communities are in London, Brighton and Manchester. About 2,000 Sudanese refugees live in London.

Over 1,000 Sudanese refugees live in Brighton — the largest refugee group in the area. The Brighton community are 70 per Coptic Christian, and 30 per cent Muslim, mostly from northern Sudan. Most come from middle class backgrounds and have strong hopes of returning to Sudan when it is safe to do so.

Sudanese refugees face many of the problems that other refugee groups encounter in the UK. A recent survey indicted that 65 per cent of adult Sudanese refugees lacked fluent English. Sudanese women in particular faced this language barrier and it prevented them gaining access to other services. Housing was another problem cited in the survey, with many Sudanese being continually rehoused in various forms of temporary accommodation.

Many Sudanese have complained that they have suffered racial harassment in their homes. (A Sudanese man was murdered in Brighton in November 1993 in a racially motivated attack.)

Sudanese community organisations have been formed in Brighton, London and Manchester.

☐ Refugees from Turkey

Over 12,000 Turkish refugees have arrived in Britain since 1988. Some 95 per cent of the refugees are Turkish Kurds.

Turkey has a population of 54 million, of whom 48 per cent live in urban areas. The capital is Ankara.

Ethnic Groups

About 80 per cent of the population are ethnic Turks, the descendants of people who migrated from central Asia. Another 19 per cent are Kurds. The majority of Kurds live in eastern Turkey.

Almost all Turkish refugees in Britain are Turkish Kurds. In Turkey they are the largest minority group. It is estimated that there are some 9,600,000 million Kurds comprising 19 per cent of the total population. The majority of Kurds live in the mountainous parts of south-east Turkey.

The origins of the Kurdish population are uncertain; they have lived in the region for at least 4,000 years. Most anthropologists believe that the Kurds are made up of an amalgamation of Indo-European tribes who lived in the Zagros mountains. Even in modern Turkey Kurdish people have a cultural identity distinct from their Turkish neighbours. In rural areas Kurds have strong clan loyalties.

There are also smaller communities of Armenians, Arabs, Georgians and Greeks living in Turkey.

Languages

Turkish is the official language of Turkey. It belongs to the Altaic language family so is not Indo-European; its structure is very different from most European languages. Today Turkish is written using the Roman alphabet, modified by accents.

Most Kurdish people speak some Kurdish; it is central to their ethnic identity. Kurdish is an Indo-European language, most closely related to Persian, and has two main dialects: Kurmanji and Sorani. Kurmanji is spoken in Turkey and also in Iraq, from Mosul northwards to the Caucasus. Zaza is another dialect, spoken in the western parts of Turkish Kurdistan. Kurmanji is written in Roman script. But few Turkish Kurds are literate in their first language. From 1935 until 1991 speaking Kurdish was illegal. It is now legal for colloquial use but its use is forbidden in political speeches or any form of the media.

Names

Most Turkish Kurds now use a Turkish naming system: a first name followed by a family name.

Religion

The majority of Turkish Kurds are Sunni Muslims but there are also Shi'a Muslim groups including the Alevis. In the area around Tunceli both Kurds and ethnic Turks belong to the Alevi sect. The Alevis observe few of the fundamental tenets of Islam such as fasting during Ramadan and cleansing rituals before prayer and are considered heretics by many Islamic fundamentalists. About one million Turkish Kurds belong to the Alevi sect. But for all Kurds their distinct identity is ethnic and national rather than religious.

Education System

Education is compulsory between the ages of six and 14. Primary education usually lasts five years, although there are some schools which run an eight year programme. The primary curriculum covers Turkish, maths, science, social studies, religious education, art, music and physical education. Children must pass class examinations in every subject to progress to the following year.

After completing five years of primary education, a student can move to a middle school. Here schooling lasts for three years, assuming a child passes all the class examinations. Students will start to learn a foreign language in a middle school. A middle school or Basic Education Diploma is awarded at the end of this stage of education.

There are several types of secondary schools, and programmes can last for three or four years, at the end of which a leaving certificate — *Lise Diplomasi* — is awarded. General high schools offer a three year general curriculum. So do science high schools, but with more emphasis on sciences and mathematics and vocational and commercial high schools, preparing students for work in agriculture, industry or commerce. Technical high schools offer four year programmes preparing students for employment or university. Anatolian high schools are selective and teach some courses in a foreign language. Competition for places is intense and students normally progress to university (British Council, 1991).

All state education is carried out through the medium of Turkish. The drop out rate in Kurdistan is high. Because young people often leave school to work on family farms and because many villages do not have an accessible school, illiteracy in Kurdistan is much higher than the national average. There is only one university in Kurdistan, and it is often difficult for Kurds to obtain higher education outside the region.

Overall some 86 per cent of Turkish men and 62 per cent of Turkish women are literate. But in Kurdistan the literacy rate is only 48 per cent. Only 18 per cent of Turkish Kurds start secondary education, and only 9 per cent complete it.

Economy

Turkey is a middle income country whose main exports are textiles, fruit, iron and steel and petroleum products. Some 45 per cent of the workforce are employed in agriculture. Most Turkish Kurds work on the land although Kurdistan is a mountainous region, and snow covers the southern districts for about half the year, cutting some villages off for months. In summer temperatures can reach 35C.

The majority of Turkish Kurds are landless peasants or small farmers. Kurdish provinces are the poorest in Turkey and per capita income is half the national average, while unemployment is twice the national average. There is a less developed infrastructure and the standard of healthcare is lower than in the rest of Turkey. This is reflected in infant mortality and life expectancy statistics: in Kurdistan infant mortality is 150 deaths per 1,000 live births; in Turkey it is 70 deaths.

Causes of Flight

The Kurds mostly live in the mountainous areas of eastern Turkey, northern Iraq, north west Iran and the southern Caucasus. In the years before the First World War Kurdistan was divided between the Ottoman and Persian Empires. The largely nomadic Kurdish population was afforded autonomy in return for policing this border.

Kurdish national identity began to develop in the 19th century, resulting in several revolts against Ottoman rule. It was at this time that the Turks began the deportation of Kurds. Whole villages were transferred to areas deemed less susceptible to insurgency. This policy is still being practised.

During the early years of the 20th century the Kurds suffered at the hands of Turkish nationalists. In 1908 there was a coup d'etat in Turkey and the Sultan was replaced by a more democratic government. The coup was led by the 'Young Turks', who were very nationalistic. Minorities such as the Armenians and Kurds became victim to repressive legislation. The new government denied that Kurds were a different ethnic group. Instead they were deemed to be 'mountain Turks'.

When the Ottoman Empire was broken up the Kurds hoped for independence. The Treaty of Sevres signed in 1920 promised autonomy for both Armenians and Kurds. But it was vetoed by the Turkish government and, in 1923, the Treaty of Lausanne divided Kurdistan between Turkey, Iran, Iraq, Syria and the Soviet

Union. The reaction of the Kurds was to rebel. Two rebellions, in 1923 and 1927, were put down very harshly. At least 100,000 Kurds were killed and anti-Kurdish legislation was drafted. Use of the Kurdish language was banned, as were Kurdish schools, associations and publications. In 1932 there were large scale deportations of Kurds to Turkish areas.

During the 1960s and 1970s Kurdish political parties were formed. Almost all of them call for political independence for Kurdish people. The best known is the *Partiya Karkeren Kurdistan* (PKK) which is committed to armed struggle against the Turkish state.

From 1978 onwards there have been increased human rights violations in Kurdistan. In 1978 there was a massacre of Kurds at Maras, organised by the neo-fascist Grey Wolves. Martial law was proclaimed in Kurdish provinces in 1979, followed by a state of emergency in 1987. Large numbers of soldiers are stationed in Kurdistan. Since 1980 some 250,000 Kurdish men have been detained and tortured in prisons. About 4,000 civilians have been killed every year since 1980. The Turkish army often enters villages which it suspects of being sympathetic to the PKK. The army attempts to intimidate. Men are randomly detained and tortured, others are executed.

Refugees in Britain

Statistics

Year	Asylum Applications	Refugee Status	ELR	Refusals
1987	121	3	5	8
1988	337	5	13	30
1989	2,415	205	765	75
1990	1,590	265	675	60
1991	2,110	90	200	80
1992	1,865	460	1,535	645
1993	1,480	340	855	710

Turkish Kurds are one of the largest groups of refugees to arrive in recent years. Since 1980 nearly 11,500 Turkish Kurds have come to Britain. The majority have arrived since 1989: in mid-1989 there were local elections in south east Turkey, in which right wing and Islamic parties made many gains. Among the election winners was a man suspected of organising a massacre of Kurds. For many Kurdish people in the Maras region this was the last straw, and some sought asylum in western countries.

An increased number of Turkish Kurds started arriving in May 1989 and by June Britain imposed a visa requirement on Turkish nationals to prevent more refugees arriving. Many Kurds were detained on arrival, some in prisons.

Almost all Turkish Kurds have remained in Greater London. There is a large community living in the London Boroughs of Hackney and Haringey.

Some 92 per cent of Turkish Kurds arrived in Britain speaking little or no English. Although colleges have organised some excellent ESL programmes for Kurdish refugees, demand far outstrips the numbers of places. This, coupled with the fact that most Kurds worked as farmers in Turkey, makes finding jobs difficult. Even highly-skilled or well-educated Kurds have difficulty finding work. Those who are working mostly have found menial jobs in the clothing trade or hotel and catering industry.

The Kurdistan Worker's Association estimates that 60 per cent of Kurdish refugees are single men and 10 per cent single women. Others have left family behind and, as most Turkish Kurds who are allowed to stay are granted exceptional leave to remain, they may have to wait for four years before being granted family reunion. This causes a great deal of distress to many people. Turkish Kurds have mounted several family reunion campaigns.

Many Kurdish refugees have also been detained and tortured in Turkey. The Medical Foundation for the Care of Victims of Torture has many Turkish Kurds as clients.

Most Kurdish refugees have strongly held political beliefs. There are several community organisations working with Turkish Kurds, representing different political views. The largest group is the Kurdistan Worker's Association, located in Haringey. It offers general advice, language courses and employment training.

☐ Refugees from Uganda

In 1972 29,000 Ugandan Asians were expelled from Uganda and came to Britain. Since then another 7,000 Ugandan refugees of African origin have fled to Britain.

Uganda has a population of 19 million, of which 10 per cent live in urban areas. The capital is Kampala.

Ethnic Groups

There are over 30 different ethnic groups in Uganda. These diverse groups can be divided into peoples of three different language families: Bantu languages, Nilotic and Central Sudanic.

The ethnic groups who speak Bantu languages mostly live in southern and western Uganda. They include the Baganda, Banyankole, Batutsi, Bahutu, Banyoro and Batoro. With the exception of the Batutsi, most practice settled agriculture.

Two of these groups, the Batutsi and the Bahutu, have arrived in Uganda in the last 100 years. Many became citizens of Uganda when Belgium and Britain redrew colonial boundaries. Others were encouraged by the British to move from densely populated Rwanda to Uganda, to increase Uganda's labour force.

The ethnic groups speaking Nilotic languages mostly live in northern Uganda. They include the Acholi, Langi and Karamojong. The ethnic groups who speak Central Sudanic languages live in north west Uganda.

There are also minorities of Indian and European origin.

Uganda's recent history has been characterised by conflict, which has ethnic as well as religious and economic dimensions. Prior to colonisation the ethnic groups from southern Uganda, who spoke Bantu languages were mostly settled farmers, and lived in well-organised kingdoms with a developed commercial life. The Nilotic speaking groups from northern Uganda consisted of a mixture of pastoralists and settled farmers and lived in societies which were more loosely structured.

British colonisers regarded southern Uganda as more developed and made it the centre of their administration. They placed greater educational and infrastructural resources there and preferred southern Ugandans for important administrative posts. Northern Ugandans were favoured for jobs in the police force and the army. The British allowed ethnic rivalry to develop, as part of a deliberate divide and rule policy. These divisions remain today.

Languages

The official language is English and is widely spoken and understood. The most important African language is Luganda, a Bantu language spoken by over three million people around Kampala. Other important Bantu languages include Swahili, Nkole, Chiga, Gisu, Toro and Nyoro. Swahili is rarely the first language but it is often used as a means of communication between different ethnic groups.

Nilotic languages include Acholi, Lango, Alur and Karamojong. Central Sudanic languages include Lugbara and Madi. Many of the African languages are scripted using Roman letters.

Names

Ugandan Muslims follow an Islamic naming system: a first personal name, followed by the father's name and then the grandfather's.

Ugandan Christians and animists use an African naming system. People are given a first personal name, often European in origin, then a second name which relates to the circumstances of their birth. Finally they use their father's name or a family name. In Uganda women usually keep their own family name after marriage. In European countries, and sometimes in urban Uganda, women take their husband's family name after marriage.

Religion

Over 60 per cent of the population are Christian, another 25 per cent follow traditional beliefs, and about 15 per cent are Muslim.

There is a religious element to conflict in Uganda. British and French missionaries arrived in Uganda at the same time. In the late 19th century there were many conversions to the Anglican and Roman Catholic faith. Today many political parties draw their support from members of particular religious groups.

Education System

Private nursery schools are available in some parts of Uganda. Most children, however, start school at six (some may start later). Primary education lasts for seven years. The medium of instruction is English and students study mathematics, science, English, the major local language, religious education, arts and crafts, music, physical education and social studies. At the end of seven years students sit the Primary Leaving Examination.

Secondary education is divided into two cycles: lower and upper. Lower secondary education runs for four years, at the end of which students may sit for the Uganda Certificate of Education, equivalent to GCSE.

After two years of upper secondary education students can sit for the Uganda Advanced Certificate of Education. Technical schools are alternatives to secondary schooling, offering a three year full-time course in vocational subjects to students who have passed their Primary Leaving Examination. (British Council, 1991).

The literacy rate is 65 per cent for men and 40 per cent for women.

Economy

Uganda is a fertile country. Many people are subsistence farmers, cultivating small plots of rice and maize. Cash crops such as coffee, cotton, tea and tobacco are grown on small farms as well as plantations. Most people who live in rural southern Uganda are settled farmers. In northern Uganda many more people are pastoral nomads or semi-nomads, living alongside pockets of settled agriculturalists. Northern Uganda is less prosperous, and this north/south divide is a source of tension.

Fishing is an important occupation for those who live near Lake Victoria or other rivers and lakes. Uganda also has copper reserves.

A Chronology of Events

Prior to European colonisation Uganda was made up of many small kingdoms, some of which had a well-developed commercial life. During the mid 19th century Uganda attracted the attention of European explorers who found a fertile and beautiful country. In order to counter the spread of Islam and to secure to

Uganda for their own use, European governments dispatched missionaries to convert the local population. There was much rivalry between the French Roman Catholic and Anglican missions.

1884-1894

The Berlin Conference grants the territory of Uganda to the British, who draw up the borders. People from many ethnic groups are now ruled as one colony.

1950s

Ugandan nationalist parties begin to agitate for independence. Milton Obote leads the United People's Congress which draws its support from Protestants and people from northern Uganda. Other parties represent Roman Catholics and southerners.

1962

Uganda wins independence. Milton Obote is the country's first Prime Minister.

1966

The first human rights abuses are reported. Disagreements about government policy and accusations of corruption lead Milton Obote to dismiss the Kabala (the king), install himself as President and make Uganda a one-party state. Colonel Idi Amin leads an armed services attack on the Kabala's palace.

Late 1960s

Idi Amin gains more popular support and political power. This period is marked by many political and economic problems.

1971

Idi Amin takes advantage of Milton Obote's absence from Uganda and seizes power in a coup d'etat. He publicly lifts the state of emergency and frees some political prisoners. But at the same time he imprisons and kills many of his opponents. Within three months of taking office he suspends all democratic rights, makes himself president for life, and gives the army unlimited powers to arrest all opponents.

1972

Over 60,000 Ugandan Asians are expelled from Uganda, as part of Idi Amin's plan to 'Africanise' the country. The Ugandan Asians constitute an important foundation for the economy, and further economic chaos follows their expulsion. The British government agrees to accept 29,000 Ugandan Asian refugees and others resettle in India and Kenya.

Human rights abuses continue to increase. During Idi Amin's rule up to 500,000 people are murdered, mainly Acholi and Langi people. Other victims include the Anglican Archbishop of Uganda. Thousands of people become refugees.

1978

Idi Amin overstretches himself. In an attempt to distract attention from the terrors and collapsing economy he orders the invasion of neighbouring Tanzania. The Ugandan National Liberation Army, a composite group of exiled civilians, joins the Tanzanian army and invades Uganda. They depose Amin and install a coalition government.

1978-80

The coalition partners are unable to agree among themselves and there are two years of short-lived governments.

1980

The United People's Congress, led by Milton Obote, comes to power after rigged elections. Obote becomes president for the second time and uses his power to suppress all opposition. Nearly 300,000 people are killed by the army. In the Luwero triangle, north of Kampala, as many as 200,000 people are murdered. Thousands of people are illegally detained. Bahutu and Batutsi minorities are forced out of Uganda. Some 450,000 people flee as refugees to Sudan and Zaire.

1983-85

The National Resistance Army (NRA), a guerrilla army founded by Yoweri Museveni, works to overthrow Milton Obote. It slowly gains control of large parts of the country.

1985

Milton Obote is overthrown in a military coup led by two high-ranking Acholi officers, one of whom, Tito Okello, becomes Uganda's new president. Some political prisoners are released but army killing continues.

1986

The NRA takes Kampala, and Okello is overthrown. Yoweri Museveni, a Muslim from southern Uganda, becomes the new president.

Restoring respect for human rights is an important part of the new government's programme. Almost all army looting and killing ceases in southern and western Uganda. Nearly 400,000 refugees return home from neighbouring countries. But there are still many human rights concerns. There is still habitual indiscipline in the army and reports of the NRA killing people in northern Uganda suspected of supporting opposition groups. The Acholi are worst affected. Other groups at risk are ex-soldiers in Milton Obote's army, members of the Ugandan People's Congress and human rights activists.

1989

Increased numbers of Ugandan refugees begin to flee to Britain and other European countries. Others are internally displaced or flee to Zaire. They are mostly Acholi who have fled northern Uganda. Counter-insurgency operations against remnants of Milton Obote's army have targeted the Acholi.

Ugandan Refugees in Britain

Over 29,000 Ugandan Asian 'refugees' arrived in Britain in 1972 — not refugees in the legal sense, as they had been given British travel documents. They came with few belongings and, after initial periods in reception centres, were settled in many parts of Britain. Today they are a very successful community and. children of Ugandan Asian refugees achieve high results in school.

Statistics for Recent Arrivals

Year	Applications for Asylum	Refugee Status	ELR	Refusal
1982	66	25	36	0
1983	199	15	69	12
1984	165	46	28	10
1985	203	25	74	19
1986	189	4	37	22
1987	318	11	53	54
1988	414	20	314	19
1989	1235	40	560	10
1990	2125	10	295	25
1991	1450	10	85	75
1992	295	10	1160	305
1993	595	5	1125	435

Ugandan refugees in Britain have fled for many different reasons. They may have been associated with opposition parties; the frequent changes of government means that Ugandan refugees have many different political opinions. The largest group of refugees are Acholi who fled during 1989-1991.

Until recently most Ugandan refugees were granted exceptional leave to remain (ELR). The Home Office is now refusing an increasing number of asylum-seekers, and there are reports of ELR not being extended. The UNHCR has organised a voluntary repatriation programme for Ugandans and this has led the British Home Office to consider Uganda as a safe country. Although Uganda is certainly safer, the Refugee Council believes that certain people may be at risk if returned. These include Acholi, and those associated with the Obote and Okello governments.

Most Ugandan refugees have settled in Greater London, where they face many of the same problems as other refugees. Adults are likely to speak fluent English and parents can be asked to help their children learn English.

There are several Ugandan community associations in Greater London, representing people of different political opinions.

☐ Refugees from Viet Nam

Over 1,400,000 refugees fled from Viet Nam between 1975 and 1990. Britain has accepted 24,000 Vietnamese refugees.

Viet Nam has a population of 65 million, of whom 21 per cent live in urban areas. The capital is Hanoi.

Ethnic Groups

Some 98 per cent of the population are ethnic Vietnamese, the rest ethnic Chinese, Cambodian or belonging to indigenous minority groups. Until 1978 Viet Nam had an ethnic Chinese community — artisans or merchants in towns — amounting to two per cent of the total population. In 1978, after a border dispute between Viet Nam and China, anti-Chinese racism increased. The ethnic Chinese faced restrictions on movement and some had their businesses confiscated. Many Chinese fled Viet Nam.

Languages

Vietnamese is spoken by almost everyone in Viet Nam. It does not appear to be closely related to any other major language of south east Asia but it has borrowed about half of its vocabulary from Chinese.

Vietnamese has a standard written form, and many regional dialects. It is a tonal language — different levels of pitch are used to convey different meanings. The language is written in Roman script, modified by accents which alter the tone or inflection on each syllable.

Cantonese Chinese was spoken by most ethnic Chinese in Viet Nam, although a few spoke other Chinese dialects. Cantonese is written in characters known as ideographs, which have no relation to the sound of the word but represent the word. All written Chinese languages use the same ideographs. This means that a text written by a Cantonese speaker can be read by a Mandarin Chinese speaker, even though the two people cannot communicate verbally.

Chinese ideographs are very complex: the number of strokes it takes to draw some can exceed 30. A Chinese child will learn about 2,000 ideographs by the age of ten. A newspaper or novel may contain 5,000-6,000 ideographs. Cantonese is, too, a tonal language.

Khmer is spoken by about 400,000 people living near the Cambodian border. The indigenous minority groups speak many different languages, the most important of which are Muong, Nung, Miao and Yao. French is also spoken by some older people and by civil servants.

Most ethnic Chinese refugees in Britain speak Cantonese as their first language and also good Vietnamese. Most will be literate in Cantonese and many in

Vietnamese too. A small minority speak not Cantonese but another Chinese dialect such as Fukienese, Wu or Hakka Chinese.

Ethnic Vietnamese refugees speak Vietnamese and many people are literate. Some ethnic Vietnamese who married into Chinese families will speak Cantonese or other Chinese dialects.

Names

The naming system used by Vietnamese and ethnic Chinese is different from the European naming system.

Vietnamese and Chinese names have three parts: a family name, a middle name and a personal name. The family name is always written first, followed by the middle name and then the personal name.

Family Name	Middle Name	Personal Name	
Tran	Van	Tai	(M)
Hoang	Khin	Chan	(M)
Nguyen	Thi	Hoa	(F)
Ly	Nhi	Mui	(F)

Children use the same family name as their father. Women do not change their names on marriage but are often addressed formally by their husband's family name. There are about 25 common Vietnamese family names and about 100 common Chinese family names. Some family names such as Tran and Vuong can be either Vietnamese or Chinese.

The middle name is a second personal name and may add meaning to the first personal name, for example Minh Chau: Beautiful Pearl. Among the Vietnamese the middle name might be a male or female title. Van as a middle name indicates a male; Thi female. Among the Chinese community the middle name can also be used as a generational name: in some families all brothers, sisters and paternal cousins are given the same middle name.

The personal name comes last. Not all personal names are specifically male or female.

In Britain some refugees have reversed the order of their names to fit in with European filing systems. It is best to ask people for their family names, middle names and personal names. In school records a mother's family name should also be recorded, as it differs from the father's.

Both Vietnamese and ethnic Chinese refugees may have nicknames. To address a Vietnamese informally usually the personal name is used; for ethnic Chinese the middle name and personal name are used.

To address a Vietnamese formally the title and personal name should be used:

Mr Tai

A married women should be addressed by her title and her husband's personal name:

Mrs Tai

To address an ethnic Chinese refugee formally, the title and family name are used:

Mr Tran

A married women should be addressed by her title and her husband's family name:

Mrs Tran.

Religion

Religious belief is an integral part of Vietnamese culture. Although most Vietnamese do not have specific religious affiliations their lives will have been influenced by Buddhist, Taoist, Confucian and traditional belief systems.

Buddhists believe in reincarnation and the possibility of achieving Nirvana — release from the endless cycle of rebirth. Some Buddhists may be vegetarian, although very few Vietnamese refugees have such dietary requirements. Instead some Vietnamese abstain from eating meat for two days every month, on the full and new moon.

Taoism (pronounced dowism) and Confucianism are sets of philosophical ideas. Taoists believe that humankind has a fixed place in the natural order of the universe. In daily life a Taoist attempts to achieve a state of harmony with the natural world. Confucians have a strict code of conduct and aim towards a state of perfection in the present world. They discourage speculation about life after death.

Many Vietnamese homes have a small shrine devoted to the memory of family ancestors. Some Vietnamese maintain very ancient customs and may believe in a spirit world of dead ancestors. Respect for ancestors and one's parents is also central to Confucian philosophy. Buddhism, Taoism and Confucianism are not mutually exclusive. Asked about religion a Vietnamese may well say he is Buddhist and Confucian.

About 20 per cent of Vietnamese refugees in Britain are practising Roman Catholics.

Education System

Before the reunification of Viet Nam in 1975 there were four almost separate educational systems: Vietnamese, Franco-Vietnamese, French and Chinese, although the latter operated only in South Viet Nam. There were also some private American schools. On reunification in 1975 the education system was reorganised along the lines of the North Vietnamese educational system and Chinese schools were gradually closed. Education is now compulsory for children aged six to fifteen.

Teaching methods in Viet Nam have always been formal and disciplined. The school curriculum is also academic. To some Vietnamese parents British schools may seem chaotic. Parents may also expect their children to pursue academic rather than vocational courses at school. It is essential to explain to parents that vocational courses, play, drama, sports and arts and crafts are part of school life in Britain, so that they and their children know what to expect.

Today the majority of Vietnamese children of school age will have been born in Britain and have no experience of the Vietnamese educational system. But some 1,850 Vietnamese left Hong Kong between 1988 and 1992 and came to Britain as part of the Third Vietnamese Programme, most of them young couples, families with young children or people with relatives in Britain.

Prior to coming to Britain this group of refugees lived in one of Hong Kong's open camps. Residents of the open camps have freedom of movement with Hong Kong, and are free to find work in the local community whilst they wait to be resettled in another country.

Within the camps education is run by non-governmental organisations, co-ordinated by UNHCR. Nurseries cater for younger children and schools for 5-16 year olds. Teachers are recruited from among the resident Vietnamese population. Children accepted for resettlement in an English speaking country usually received some English lessons. But education in Hong Kong's open camps is very basic and formal.

Economy

Over 70 per cent of Viet Nam's labour force is employed in agriculture, fishing or forestry. Rice is the main crop and an important export. Others include rubber, coffee, tea, cotton, soybeans, clothing and footwear, coal and minerals. There are substantial oil, coal and mineral reserves in northern Viet Nam.

Viet Nam's Gross National Product is estimated to be about $150 per head, making it one of the poorest countries in the world. The country's foreign debt is enormous, the main creditors being the governments of Japan, Iraq and Algeria. World Bank and IMF loans were for many years blocked by the USA, and until recently there was little foreign investment.

Concerns were expressed about the effects of the end of aid from the Soviet Union which for a long time propped up the Vietnamese economy. But apart from shortages of some agricultural spare parts, these fears have not been realised. There is a great deal of improvement in the industrial economy which is expanding at a rapid rate.

The countryside is another matter. The central provinces of Nghe Tinh and Binh Tri Thien are particularly isolated and impoverished. The land bears the scars of the intense aerial bombardments of 1968-73. Deforestation, soil erosion and flooding have worsened in recent years. Roads are poor, spare parts and fuel are always in short supply and power cuts hamper small scale industry. Halting environmental degradation and improving the economic infrastructure will be central to improving the quality of life in rural areas. These needs will only be met with substantial amounts of bilateral and multilateral aid.

The majority of Vietnamese refugees in Britain have come from the small towns and fishing villages of North Viet Nam. The continued poverty of this area makes it unlikely that Vietnamese refugees will ever return in large numbers. Vietnamese in Britain are, however, visiting their homeland in increasing numbers.

Causes of Flight

Viet Nam's early history was dominated by rivalries with Cambodian, Chinese and Thai dynasties. In 1802 Viet Nam was united under the Nguyen dynasty but unity and independence did not last long, as the French attacked Viet Nam in 1858.

By 1887 France controlled all of present day Viet Nam, Laos and Cambodia. In 1940 the Japanese invaded French Indochina. Ho Chi Minh, a communist, formed the Viet Minh, a broad-based independence movement. He led a guerrilla war against the Japanese from a cave in northern Viet Nam.

By the time the Japanese surrendered in 1945 the Viet Minh controlled most of northern Viet Nam. The victorious Allies agreed that Britain would administer the south of Viet Nam, and China the north. But the Viet Minh marched into Hanoi before the Chinese arrived, and the democratic republic of Viet Nam was proclaimed in September 1945. Not even the Soviet Union recognised the new country. The British and French ruthlessly suppressed the Viet Minh, reconquering southern Viet Nam. By March 1946 the French had installed a colonial government in southern Viet Nam, headed by Bao Dai.

The communist Viet Minh Government, lacking international recognition, were forced into fighting a guerrilla war, initially backed by China. It lasted from 1946-1954 and some 172,000 French soldiers were killed. The French were backed by the US who feared a communist take-over in South East Asia.

In 1954, after suffering a massive military defeat against the Viet Minh, the French were drawn to the negotiating table. The Geneva Accords temporarily divided Viet Nam in two, along the 17th parallel. The Viet Minh were to govern the North, while the head of government in South Viet Nam was Ngo Dinh Diem, a nationalist leader. Elections were scheduled for 1956 but were prevented by the South Vietnamese government. The Diem regime tortured and killed thousands of its opponents, including Buddhist monks. Opponents of the government formed the National Liberation Front, a communist-supported guerrilla army.

The US government provided aid to the South Vietnamese, including military aid. By 1961 US troops were taking part in action in Viet Nam. By 1965 there were 200,000 US troops in South Viet Nam, and the US began its carpet bombing of the region. Between 1968 and 1973 nearly two million people were killed. Cambodia and Laos were also heavily bombed.

In the early 1970s resistance to conscription and the gathering anti-war movement forced US President Nixon into disengaging from Viet Nam. The US signed the Paris Agreement in January 1973 and withdrew its troops. But the North and South Vietnamese armies continued fighting. In April 1975 the North Vietnamese reached Saigon, the South Vietnamese government collapsed and the country was united again.

Since 1975 the country has been economically isolated. Not one dollar of reparation has been paid to this war-damaged country. Until 1993 the US government vetoed all proposals for International Monetary Fund and World Bank loans, despite the fact that the Vietnamese government achieved the political and economic preconditions that were ostensibly preventing multilateral loans and grants.

The first refugees to leave Viet Nam were southerners who fled soon after the fall of Saigon — about 130,000. They were mostly officials in the former South Vietnamese Government or people who had close contact with the US during the war. Most were ethnic Vietnamese and most settled in the US.

The second exodus began in 1977. About 880,000 left, many of them by boat. Between 1977 and 1990 over 155,000 Vietnamese asylum-seekers died at sea, from dehydration, drowning or murder by pirates.

The refugees fled from both north and south Viet Nam. Some were opponents of the new regime who had been imprisoned in re-education camps. Others were north Vietnamese who did not want to be moved to farm the new economic zones.

About two per cent of Viet Nam's population were ethnic Chinese, many of whom were former artisans and merchants in small towns. In 1978, after a border dispute between Viet Nam and China, anti- Chinese racism increased. The ethnic Chinese faced restrictions on movement and some had their businesses confiscated. After 1978 they fled from Viet Nam.

Some 260,000 ethnic Chinese fled to China and settled there. Other refugees travelled to Malaysia, Singapore, Indonesia, the Philippines and Hong Kong. By 1979 the exodus of people from Viet Nam was so great that the UN was forced to convene an international conference in Geneva. It was at this conference that the British government agreed to accept 10,000 refugees from the camps in Hong Kong. More were accepted at a later date.

Up until 1988 all Vietnamese were automatically given refugee status on leaving the country. This policy gave a green light to all those who wanted to flee.

British and Hong Kong authorities have come under much criticism for conditions in the Hong Kong camps and detention centres, most of which have been built in former factories. Families are stacked in containers on top of each other, creating overcrowded conditions that are very stressful. Those who live in camps have been interviewed by the Government of Hong Kong and UNHCR, and accepted as refugees under the terms of the 1951 UN Convention and 1967 Protocol Relating to the Status of Refugees. This group is awaiting resettlement in a third country. They have freedom to work in Hong Kong and leave the camps when they wish. Those in detention centres are either asylum-seekers or people whose asylum application has been refused. This group has no freedom of movement.

Refugees who fled to other South East Asian countries were resettled in the US, France, Canada, Australia, Germany, Britain and other European countries. The US has the largest Vietnamese refugee community, and all its refugees come from South Viet Nam. Even today the US will not accept Vietnamese refugees from the north.

Vietnamese Refugees in Britain

Statistics

Arrivals in UK from Hong Kong 1979-1992	14,666
Arrivals from other SE Asian countries	4,420
Arrivals from the Viet Nam Orderly Departure Programme	4,475
Total UK Vietnamese population	24,000

About 65 per cent of Britain's Vietnamese community is from northern Viet Nam. This is because most refugees in this country have been resettled via camps in Hong Kong. The boat journey to Hong Kong is fairly straightforward, although not without hazards. Until January 1979 Britain received very few Vietnamese refugees. Those who did arrive had mostly been rescued at sea by British registered ships. At the UN Geneva conference the British Government agreed to accept 10,000 refugees from Hong Kong as part of the First Vietnamese Settlement Programme. This lasted until 1984.

Three NGOs — The Save the Children Fund, the Ockenden Venture, and the British Council for Aid to Refugees — administered reception centres. Refugees stayed in the reception centres for three to six months, after which they were sent to local authority accommodation throughout Britain. Here they received some initial support but then became very isolated.

In 1984 the British government agreed to take another quota of Vietnamese refugees as part of the Second Vietnamese Programme. This group mainly consisted of people who had relatives in Britain and were thus entitled to family reunion. They came from Hong Kong or were allowed to depart from Viet Nam, as part of the 'Orderly Departure Programme'. The refugees spent time in reception centres, then sent to areas where there were existing Vietnamese communities. Funding was provide to set up community groups.

In 1988 a third Vietnamese Resettlement Programme was agreed by the Home Office. This lasted until October 1992. Three different groups of people were allowed to resettle in Britain: those who were entitled to family reunion, those who met certain selection criteria and a small quota of vulnerable refugees and unaccompanied children. The selection criteria were criticised for being too rigid: those who had no family connections or were not deemed vulnerable had to be accepted as a refugee, and be under 35, be literate in Vietnamese or Cantonese and to have worked in Hong Kong. The tough selection criteria and slow administrative procedures meant that by the end of the Third Vietnamese resettlement Programme in October 1992 the quota of 2,000 Vietnamese had not been reached.

Refugee Action, a national NGOs run largely by Vietnamese, administered the reception centres for the Third Vietnamese Resettlement Programme.

The reception arrangements made for Vietnamese programme refugees have come under much criticism, particularly as regards the dispersal of refugees on the First Programme. In 1985 the Government's Home Affairs Select Committee on Race and Immigration examined the resettlement programmes. It concluded that the policy of dispersal throughout Britain was unsuccessful. Indeed its lack of success has been born out by secondary migration of Vietnamese refugees. By 1989 it was noted that 50 per cent of all Vietnamese refugees had moved from their resettlement areas. The majority moved to major conurbations, particularly London, Birmingham and Manchester. Today about 14,000 Vietnamese live in London, mostly in the London Boroughs of Southwark, Lewisham and Greenwich. About 4,000 refugees live in Birmingham and another 2,500 in Manchester. The main reason for secondary migration was the desire to live near other Vietnamese, and also to move to areas where the chances of employment were perceived to be better.

The provision of ESL in reception centres has also been criticised, as many refugees left the centres speaking little English and were unable to find classes in the areas to which they were sent. This has been a major barrier to employment. Today the Vietnamese are still one of the most disadvantaged refugee groups. Throughout the early 1980s the majority of those available for work were unemployed. Today between 40-50 per cent of single and married male Vietnamese are unemployed, well above the national average. Language barriers have also meant that many Vietnamese have not had equal access to services. This is a particular problem for elderly refugees.

☐ Refugees from former Yugoslavia

Since June 1991 and the beginning of the conflict in former Yugoslavia over 8,000 asylum-seekers have arrived in Britain, most from Bosnia, Croatia and Kosovo. Other citizens of former Yugoslavia are living in Britain on a temporary basis, or as part of a British government programme.

Populations

Slovenia 1.8 million
Serbia 9.3 million
Croatia 4.6 million
Bosnia 4.1 million
Macedonia 1.9 million
Montenegro 600,000

Ethnic Groups

Yugoslavia means 'the country of the southern Slavs' and most people are Slavs. Serbs, Croats and Bosnians are ethnically and linguistically very closely related, although there are differences in their backgrounds.

The Serbs form the largest ethnic group in former Yugoslavia. They constitute 65 per cent of the population within their own republic. There are also large numbers of Serbs outside the borders of Serbia. At present about 11 per cent of Croatia's population are Serbs. Some 30 per cent of the population of Bosnia-Hercegovina are Serbs.

The Montenegrins speak Serbo-Croat and consider themselves ethnically and politically close to the Serbs. The Croats mostly live in Croatia and in western Hercegovina. About 18 per cent of the population of Bosnia-Hercegovina are Croats.

The Slovenes make up 90 per cent of the population in their republic and there are few communal tensions in Slovenia.

Slav Muslims mostly live in Bosnia-Hercegovina where they constitute about 40 per cent of the population. They were converted to Islam during Turkish rule. Although Bosnian Muslims have a relaxed attitude to their religion, it is an integral part of their identity. Some 14 per cent of the population of Montenegro are Muslim. Slav Muslims also live in the part of Serbia called the Sandzak that borders Bosnia-Hercegovina, making up about 55 per cent of the population.

There has been much debate about the ethnic origins of Macedonian people. The Macedonians speak a language that has Serb and Bulgarian roots. But the rights of Macedonians to be identified as a distinct ethnic group are being denied. Nationalist Serbs regard Macedonians as Serbs. Greek nationalists believe Macedonians are Greeks who happen to speak a Slavic language. The Bulgarian government asserts that Macedonians are a Bulgarian people. Both Greece and Bulgaria have a minority Macedonian population within their borders. Macedonia remains a very tense region which could easily erupt into war, dragging other Balkan nations into the dispute.

Most ethnic Albanians live within the Serbian Province of Kosovo — known in Albanian as Kosova — constituting about 90 per cent of its population. In Macedonia about 20-40 per cent of the population are Albanians.

Kosovo is regarded as the heartland of Serbian culture by many nationalists. Tension has been high in Kosovo since 1989, when there were many strikes and demonstrations, followed by an abortive coup in 1990. Kosovo is currently under Serbian military control, with continued curfews in the capital Pristina. Serbo-Croat has been imposed as the medium of instruction in schools and colleges and a Serbian curriculum introduced. Thousands of Albanian teachers, lecturers, healthcare professionals and civil servants have been dismissed from their jobs. Albanian children have been denied access to healthcare, and Albanian newspapers and cultural institutions have been closed down. Owning a cassette of Albanian music is punishable by a prison sentence of 60 days. There are many reports of arbitrary arrests and beatings in custody.

The Hungarians of Voyvodina, where they make up 19 per cent of the population, have also had their rights denied and Hungarian secondary schools have been closed. Former Yugoslavia also has Europe's largest Roma (gypsy) community, numbering some 850,000 people. In all the six republics of former Yugoslavia, Roma continue to suffer from racism. Many Roma have been caught up in the Bosnian conflict and have fled as refugees. Other minority communities living in former Yugoslavia include Turks, Slovaks, Bulgarians, Vlachs and Jews.

A final casualty of the breakup of Yugoslavia are the five per cent of people who identify themselves as Yugoslavs. Since 20 per cent of all marriages took place across the ethnic divide, many of these Yugoslavs are the children of mixed marriages. Unable to identify with the nationalist wave, they feel they have lost their country.

Languages

Serbo-Croat, Slovenian and Macedonian were the official languages of former Yugoslavia, with Serbo-Croat the language of government. Serbo-Croat is generally considered as one language but the Serbs call their language Serbian and use a modified Cyrillic alphabet, while the Croats call their language Croatian and use the Roman alphabet. It is easy to identify a person's ethnic origin by their accent and use of words. Serbs and Croats may use different words for particular things, for example Serbs use the word *'igra'* for dance, while Croats use *'ples'*. But in both cases alternatives are understood by everyone.

Slovenian is spoken in Slovenia and uses the Roman script. Macedonian is spoken in Macedonia, written in the Cyrillic alphabet and is closely related to Bulgarian. Serbo-Croat, Slovenian and Macedonian are Slavic languages.

Albanian is spoken by over one million people in Kosovo and Macedonia. The Albanians call their language *shqip*. Albanian is an Indo-European language, although it is not closely related to any other European languages. There are two distinct dialects: *Toask*, spoken in southern Albania, and *Gheg*, spoken in northern Albania, Kosovo and Macedonia. Albanian is written in the Roman script.

Hungarian is spoken by about 500,000 people in Voyvodina. The Hungarians call their language Magyar. It is not an Indo-European language but Finno-Ugric, related to Finnish, Estonian and a number of language spoken in Siberia. Hungarian grammar contains many features not found in Indo-European languages and is written phonetically in a modified Roman alphabet. Yugoslav Roma generally speak Romanes as their first language. Closely related to Indian languages, it has been scripted in the Roman script. Few Roma will be literate in Romanes, although about 10 primary schools are now using the language as a teaching medium.

Names

All ethnic groups in Yugoslavia use a European naming system: a personal name followed by a family name. Women adopt their husband's family name on marriage. As in many countries, a name can indicate origin: certain names are distinctly Muslim, Hungarian or Albanian. Muslims are likely to be given personal names which are Islamic in origin: Alija, Ramiz and Amira are typical.

Religion

Yugoslavia was the land were western and eastern churches met. Some 29 per cent of the population of former Yugoslavia are Roman Catholics, mostly Croats and Slovenes. There are a small number of Roman Catholic Albanians living in Kosovo.

Another 36 per cent of the population are Eastern Orthodox Christians, including most Serbs and many Montenegrins and Macedonians. Under the communist regime the Orthodox church was receptive to government policies. Today the clergy are closely identified with nationalist sentiments, and allegiance to the Orthodox church is part of 'Serbian' identity. The Macedonian and Serbian

Orthodox church have their own Archbishops and hierarchies. There are Serbian Orthodox churches in London and Leeds.

About 14 per cent of the population are Muslim, mostly from Bosnia-Hercegovina, the Sandzak, Montenegro, Macedonia and Kosovo. Some Roma converted to Islam in the 15th century under Ottoman rule. The Muslim population are overwhelmingly Sunni Muslim. Religious observance differs between communities — less than 15 per cent of Bosnian Muslims describe themselves as religious, compared with 45 per cent of Kosovo Albanians. But for all Muslims, observant or not, religion forms part of their identity.

Education System

From 1945-1991 the education system in Yugoslavia was decentralised. Basic policy was laid down by the federal government but each republic had considerable freedom in its implementation.

There are limited places in creches and kindergartens. Primary education is compulsory and lasts for eight years. Most children start school at the age of seven, although a few schools admit children aged six. Children begin to learn foreign languages — French, German, English or Russian — at the age of twelve. Secondary education lasts for four years, up to the age of 19. Children may leave school at 15. Until 1987 young people followed a core curriculum for two years and had the opportunity to specialise during their last two years of education. Today specialisation operates throughout secondary education, affording many opportunities to study vocational subjects. At the end of four years students sit for the Secondary School Leaving Diploma. This qualification may satisfy entrance requirements for higher education in Britain (British Council, 1991).

The medium of instruction in schools in Croatia, Serbia and Bosnia is Serbo-Croat. There were many Albanian schools in Kosovo but 1991 a Serbian curriculum was introduced and Serbo-Croat imposed as the medium of instruction.

In Voyvodina there are about 200 Hungarian language schools but since 1975 some have been closed. There are several Romanes medium schools in Serbia and some Croatian schools organise Romanes classes.

The literacy rate is 92 per cent for men and 76 per cent for women. Illiteracy is more of a problem in rural areas and among some minority groups such as Albanians and Roma.

Economy

Bosnia, Kosovo, southern Serbia, Montenegro and Macedonia are mountainous, while much of Croatia, Slovenia and northern Serbia are flat. The north has always been more prosperous than the south.

Before the war tourism was a major source of income. Former Yugoslavia also had large deposits of bauxite and other minerals. Other exports include ships, clothing and footwear. Economic activity has been very severely disrupted by fighting and by the trade embargo.

A Chronology of Events

A vicious civil war now consumes part of the country that was Yugoslavia. At the time of writing over 1,700,000 people are refugees and another 2,280,000 are displaced within Bosnia-Hercegovina. The potential for further bloodshed remains high as Kosovo, Macedonia and the Sandzak are tense regions which could easily erupt into war, possibly dragging other Balkan nations into the dispute. All this is difficult to reconcile with the image of old Yugoslavia — sunny holiday resorts and an open communist government.

There is no simple explanation for the conflict. The civil war has its roots in history, in longstanding disputes between the different ethnic groups in the region, and in the bloody events of 1941-45. The seeds of today's conflict were sown as communist regimes collapsed throughout eastern Europe and the void left by communism was filled by nationalism. Aspiring leaders in different Yugoslav republics whipped up nationalist sentiment as a means to keep power.

In Yugoslavia economic factors also played a part: the prosperous republics of northern Yugoslavia sought to divorce themselves from the poorer south. There is also tension between the richer urban areas and the poorer and more conservative countryside. Nationalist leaders have found it easier to gain support from the rural population, whereas ethnic origins are less of an issue in the towns.

Some commentators also believe that the old communist system's desperate struggle for survival contributed to the war: the large Yugoslav army was brought into action to maintain a united country and ensure survival of the system and itself. Yugoslavia's armaments industry, concentrated in Bosnia and Serbia, has ensured that regular and irregular Serbian soldiers have easy access to weapons. It is also possible to view the civil war as a number of different conflicts, varying between region and between militia.

1918-1945

For many centuries Yugoslavia was divided between two great empires which cut across Europe. To the north Slovenia and Croatia were part of the Western Roman Empire and subsequently the Austro-Hungarian Empire. In the south Serbia was incorporated into the Eastern Roman Empire and later the Ottoman Empire. Yugoslavia was not a united state until the end of the First World War. The new state was proclaimed in December 1918 under the name of the Kingdom of Serbs, Croats and Slovenes. It was a marriage of convenience rather than a love affair, and from the start there was serious tension between the different ethnic groups.

Croats and Slovenes were fearful of Serbian domination and there were continual disputes between the three groups. It was these conflicts which caused the Serbian head of state, King Alexander Karadjordjevic to dissolve the democratic constitution in 1929. Five years later he was murdered on the orders of Croatian fascists, during a visit to Marseilles.

The conflict between Serbs and Croats reached a climax during the Second World War. The Nazis invaded Yugoslavia in 1941 and created a puppet state in Croatia, with the support of the Ustashe, Croatian fascists. This state included parts of Bosnia-Hercegovina and Serbia. Hundreds of thousands of Serbs, Croatian democrats, Jews and Roma were murdered by the Ustashe.

The Ustashe were opposed by the Serbian nationalist Chetniks and by Josep Broz Tito's communist partisans. The Chetniks and communist partisans also fought each other with great brutality. Over 1,700,000 people — one tenth of Yugoslavia's population — were killed between 1941 and 1945, most by fellow Yugoslavs. This period of history is subject to claim and counter claim by nationalist historians but whatever the truth, memories of the Second World War play a part in maintaining today's hostilities.

1945-1990

Tito emerged victorious in 1945 and ruled the country until his death in 1980. He chose to sweep ethnic conflict under the carpet and attempted to unite the population under the slogan 'Unity and Fraternity'.

Tito created a socialist government which stood outside the Soviet bloc. Yugoslavia was a relatively liberal society with some privatised enterprise, more prosperous than other eastern European nations. But Tito did not succeed in ironing out the great regional differences in the country. Slovenia was and still remains a prosperous central European country, while the south is largely a peasant society.

Obsessed with the threat of Soviet invasion, Tito built up the largest army in Europe — virtually all men over the age of 20 will have completed military service. The Yugoslav armaments industry is also large. Both these factors have contributed to the intensity of today's war.

Under Tito Yugoslavia was divided up into six republics and two autonomous provinces (Kosovo and Voyvodina). There was legislation to protect minority rights. It is ironic that the towns of Bosnia-Hercegovina were regarded as very cosmopolitan and tolerant at this time.

Tito played off different ethnic groups to create a stable balance of power. The Serbs dominated the army and the Communist Party apparatus. Tito tried to counter this by giving constituent republics extensive autonomy, particularly in the 1974 constitutional reforms. But on his death autonomy slowly disintegrated into chaos.

1990-1993

A common socialist ideal and an extensive party apparatus held Yugoslavia together until 1990 but with the collapse of eastern European communism the last thin threads snapped. In the summer and autumn of 1990 Kosovo Albanians took to the streets demanding greater autonomy. The demonstrations were brutally suppressed. Yugoslavia's disintegration gathered momentum in 1990 when Slovenia held multi-party elections. Other republics then held elections, and everywhere nationalist parties were victorious. Even in Serbia and Montenegro where former communists won elections, they did so by appealing to nationalist sentiments. Slobodan Milosevic, the Serbian President, made his career by the campaign against Kosova Albanians and his calls for a Greater Serbia.

After the elections the new governments of Slovenia and Croatia wished to turn Yugoslavia into a looser confederation of states and secure greater autonomy for themselves. The republics of Serbia and Montenegro wanted to retain a central government and a central army. The governments of Macedonia and Bosnia-Hercegovina initially supported a federal Yugoslavia, but nationalist fervour forced a change of policy.

On 25 June 1991 Croatia and Slovenia declared their independence. The Yugoslav People's Army was brought into action firstly in Slovenia. After a ten day war Slovenia won its independence and the conflict moved on to Croatia. Here a Serb minority rebelled against the moves towards Croatian independence. The Serbs were frightened of Croatian nationalism and the revival of many of the Ustashe symbols. Slobodan Milosevic and other nationalists stirred up these fears.

In the bloodshed thousands were killed, and towns such as Osijek, Dubrovnik and Vukovar suffered extensive damage. The Croatian war created thousands of refugees, both Croatian and Serbian. Parts of Croatia are still occupied by Serb forces.

The UN brokered a cease-fire and stationed 14,000 peace-keeping soldiers in Croatia. Under the UN Peace Plan Croatia is set to regain its occupied areas, despite statements of no surrender by Serbian leaders. The UN Mandate in Croatia has to be renewed at intervals.

After the cease-fire in Croatia the conflict moved further south and became more bloody. In Bosnia-Hercegovina Muslims make up 40 per cent of the population, Serbs 30 per cent and Croats about 18 per cent. By 1992 Bosnia-Hercegovina had a hung parliament representing different ethnic groups, and a Bosnian Muslim President. The Bosnian Parliament attempted to maintain a multi-ethnic state initially within Yugoslavia. But in February 1992 nationalist pressures caused the government of Bosnia-Hercegovina to declare independence. Bosnian Serbs then proclaimed their own state and soon after Serbian forces attacked Sarajevo and other Bosnian cities.

By the end of 1992 regular soldiers, formerly of the Yugoslav People's Army, and irregular Serbian militia gained control of 70 per cent of Bosnia-Hercegovina. Bosnian Croats have seized control of most of western Hercegovina and central Bosnia, and also proclaimed their own state. The Slav Muslims have no mother republic or powerful supporters. The international arms embargo has rendered them inferior in military terms. Although they are the largest ethnic group they have been driven out of large parts of Bosnia-Hercegovina during campaigns of 'ethnic cleansing'.

Both Serbs and Croats have been accused of using methods reminiscent of the Nazis to drive people from their homes. In some areas race regulations were enacted, whereby Muslims were put under curfew or forbidden to visit certain areas. Other towns have tried to organise population transfers through advertisements and posters: a Croat in the Serb-controlled town of Banja-Luka might, for instance, exchange a house with a Serb from the Croatian town of Split.

But 'ethnic cleansing' is rarely so peaceful. Often Muslims and Croats have been force to leave their homes after signing a document renouncing all claims to their property. If people refuse to sign away their homes they are subject to campaigns of terror. Amnesty International has reported rapes, torture, beatings and extra-judicial executions as part of the process of 'ethnic cleansing'. The Serbian forces are accused of committing the largest numbers of human rights violations but Serbs, too, are victims of 'ethnic cleansing'.

Cease-fires have come and gone, and all peace talks have failed. The UN and EC have appointed mediators: the UN mediator is currently Thorvald Stoltenberg, and the EC is represented by Lord Owen. The London Peace Talks of August 1992 resulted in a temporary cease-fire and required the Bosnian Serbs to hand over 20 per cent of land and all heavy artillery. But the cease-fire did not hold. These talks were followed by a plan to divide Bosnia into ten provinces, divided largely along ethnic lines. This peace plan failed. In August 1993 the two mediators produced another peace plan, dividing Bosnia into three separate states. But warring parties have been unable to agree on borders. The UN peace plan of summer 1994, creating a Muslim-Croat federation and a separate state for the Bosnian Serbs, has been rejected by the latter.

Former-Yugoslav Refugees in Britain

Statistics

Year	Asylum Applications
1991	320
1992	5,635
1993	1,830

Source: Home Office

There have been very few decisions made on asylum applications.

Refugees have been fleeing former Yugoslavia since 1991. The first refugees were mostly Croats displaced by fighting, many of whom returned home after the UN-brokered cease-fire. Today the majority of refugees are from Bosnia or Kosovo. They can be divided into six groups:

- *de facto* refugees who have fled from the conflict but are staying in Britain on visitor's, au pair's or student's visas;
- Bosnians who arrived by themselves and have applied for political asylum;
- Bosnians who were brought to Britain by voluntary organisations on convoys. Most of them have applied for political asylum;
- former prison camp detainees, plus medical evacuees who have been admitted as part of a British government programme administered by the Refugee Council and the British Red Cross;
- Kosovo Albanians;
- other asylum-seekers, including small numbers of Serbian peace activists, conscientious objectors and Roma.

Refugees from former Yugoslavia encounter most of the problems faced by other groups of refugees. It has become increasingly difficult to reach Britain: on 7th November 1992 Britain imposed a visa requirement on nationals from Serbia, Montenegro, Macedonia and Bosnia-Hercegovina. There is no British consulate in Bosnia-Hercegovina, and those who have fled to Croatia are regularly having visas refused in Zagreb.

The British government has also returned at least 46 Bosnian asylum-seekers to other European countries, stating that they should claim asylum in those countries. After pressure from the German government — Germany has received 250,000 asylum-seekers from former Yugoslavia — the British government agreed to accept Bosnian asylum-seekers who had travelled via other EC countries.

The Home Office has, to date, made very few decisions on asylum applications. This means that most Bosnians remain as asylum-seekers, their future in limbo.

Like other asylum-seekers in Britain those from former Yugoslavia find it difficult to achieve family reunion.

The geographical distribution of refugees from former Yugoslavia is very different from other refugee communities. With the exception of the Kosovo Albanians, the majority of Bosnian refugees are living outside Greater London. The convoy groups are particularly widely dispersed. Some refugees are living in areas far from experienced immigration lawyers and refugee support agencies. Many refugee families have felt very isolated.

The situation faced by some convoy groups has been of concern to the Refugee Council. About 50 groups of people organised convoys to Bosnia in 1992 and brought back about 1,200 refugees. Many of the group leaders were based in churches or mosques and most had no prior experience of working with refugees. Some groups made adequate arrangements for support of the refugees, but there were also many disasters. Accommodation was inadequate and the organisers of a few convoys tried to discourage contact with outside agencies such as social services or immigration lawyers. The Refugee Council is calling for government funding for support services for the convoy groups and other Bosnian refugees outside Greater London.

One group of Bosnian refugees has received government funding: the former Serbian prison camp detainees admitted as part of a government programme. In November 1992 the British government granted temporary protection to 1,000 former prison camp detainees, plus their dependants. The refugees were to be given temporary visas to enter Britain and accommodated by the Refugee Council and the British Red Cross. These organisations set up reception centres in London, Cambridge, Rugby, Dewsbury and Edinburgh. The refugees spend up to two months in the reception centre before being moved into housing association accommodation. Housing is chosen to enable the refugees to stay near each other. Red Cross and Refugee Council staff are available to assist the Bosnian refugees once they have moved into permanent accommodation.

To date about 800 people have arrived on this programme — fewer than anticipated. That the British government initially operated very stringent criteria on who constitute a family may have discouraged many refugees from travelling to Britain.

Refugees from former Yugoslavia have formed community organisations which are offering advice and support. A London- based group is working with Kosovo Albanians.

☐ Refugees From Zaire

About 15,000 refugees from Zaire have arrived in Britain since 1988.

The Republic of Zaire has a population of 38 million, of whom 40 per cent are living in urban areas. The capital is Kinshasa.

Ethnic Groups

There are over 200 ethnic groups in Zaire, of whom about 80 per cent speak Bantu languages. Other peoples, mainly living in north east Zaire, speak Nilotic languages. The main ethnic groups are:

The Kikongo — about six million people mostly in western Zaire, who speak the Kikongo language. Other Kikongo live in Angola and the Republic of Congo.

The Luba — about seven million people who live in south east Zaire and speak Tshiluba. At present there is conflict between Luba from Kasai province and Luba from Shaba province. During colonial times, Luba from Kasai were taken as indentured labour to work in the Shaba mines. Some of the Kasai Luba became successful in commerce, arousing resentment among the Shaba Luba. At least 40,000 Kasai Luba fled from Shaba Province in Autumn 1992, some of them to western Europe. Communal conflict between the Kasai Luba and the Shaba Luba is being exploited by President Mobutu and Nguza Karl-I-Bond, in order to undermine Etienne Tshisekedi who is a Kasai Luba.

The Mongo — about five million people mostly living in central Zaire.

The Goma (Rwandans) — about one million Goma people in eastern Zaire, on the border with Rwanda. This is a very tense area and there are reports of Goma businesses being looted in 1993. Media sympathetic to the government has scapegoated the more prosperous Goma community, blaming them for the deteriorating economic situation.

Nearly four million people belonging to Sudanese ethnic groups live in north east Zaire about one million Bwaka people (pygmies) and in central and eastern Zaire.

Languages

French is the official language and the language of government. All teaching is through the medium of French, although teachers frequently use the local language in classrooms. Fluency in French will obviously depend on how long a person has spent at school in Zaire.

There are four other languages given official status: Kiswahili, Tshiluba, Kikongo and Lingala. Each is the language of trade and commerce in a particular region and all four are Bantu languages.

In addition to the five national languages there are about 200 other languages and dialects. A Zairean who has completed secondary education will probably be able to speak at least three languages.

Mostly living in the eastern parts of Zaire along the border with Tanzania and Uganda are about three million people who speak Kiswahili. The dialect of Kiswahili spoken in Zaire is known as Kingwana and is written using the Roman alphabet, but without the letters c, q and x. Like other Bantu languages, the grammatical inflections occur at the beginning of the word, for example *Kitabu* means 'a book' and *Vitabu* means 'books'.

Tshiluba is spoken by about three million people in southern Zaire. Lingala is spoken by about 1.5 million people in northern and north west Zaire and also in the Republic of Congo. Kikongo is spoken by about two million people in western Zaire, around the mouth of the Congo river, and in the Republic of Congo and Angola. Tshiluba, Lingala and Kikongo are also written using the Roman alphabet, although Lingala has two additional letters.

Names

Zairean refugees usually have French first names and African family names, although some have African first and family names.

Religion

About 50 per cent of the population follow traditional Zairean beliefs. Some 40 per cent, mostly town dwellers, are Roman Catholic. Protestant and Kimbanguist (local) churches are also represented and there is a Muslim minority in northern Zaire. Zairean Muslims are also known as Kindu Manyema. Jehovah's Witnesses are not allowed to practice their religion. The churches play an important role in the provision of services such as healthcare and education, and in implementing socio-economic development programmes.

Education System

During the colonial period the Roman Catholic church ran most schools and played a major role in formulating educational policy. Education was basic; it reinforced gender roles and deliberately sought to avoid creating an educated Zairean middle class.

Primary education starts at six years, although not all pupils enrol at this age. As in many African countries, students may remain in a class for more than one year or miss parts of their education, so age is not always a realistic gage to the numbers of years a pupil has spent in school. Primary education is theoretically compulsory, although only 60 per cent of boys and 40 per cent of girls enrol at primary schools. Parents have to pay for both state and private education.

The medium of instruction in primary schools is French. The primary school curriculum includes French, maths, moral and religious education, physical and natural sciences, PE, art and African languages. Classes are numbered from one to six. A *Certificat d'Etudes Primaires* is awarded to pupils who do well in the *Examen de Fin de Cycle.*

Secondary education is not compulsory and students have to sit an entrance examination in order to enrol at secondary school. There are two parts to secondary education: a two year *Cycle d'Orientation* and a three or four year *Cycle Superieur.* As in primary schools the medium of instruction is French.

During the *Cycle d'Orientatiion* students study the same subjects as in primary schools, plus technology and sociology. On completion of the second year students take an examination that leads to the *Brevet du Cycle d'Orientation.*

There are two types of course in the *Cycle Superieur: Court* and *Long.* The *Cycle Court* consists of two or three years of technical and vocational education, at the end of the which students are awarded a *Brevet de Fin d'Etudes Secondaires* or a *Diplome de Fin d'Etudes Secondaires.*

The *Cycle Long* lasts four years. Students study French, English, history, geography, religious, moral and civic education and mathematics and can select options in classics, sciences and economics. At the end students take the *Diplome d'Etat d'Etudes Secondaires du Cycle Long*. Students wishing to go on to higher education must take a university entrance examination (British Council, 1991).

About half of all boys progress to secondary education but only a third of girls. In rural areas and among the poor, girls are kept at home to look after siblings or work in the fields. The overall literacy rate is 53 per cent.

Teaching is much more formal than in Britain and Zairean children will have had little experience of using a laboratory or other practical aspects of education. The schools are badly equipped; wealthy Zaireans send their children to private schools. Teachers of Zairean refugee children should make every effort to extend the children's French. Schools should, for example, purchase French literature and newspapers.

Economy

Zaire's main exports are copper, palm oil and coffee. It is the world's largest producer of copper and has considerable resources of other minerals such as zinc and tin, mostly located in Shaba Province. Zaire could become a rich country, but its wealth gives little benefit to the majority of its people. At least 80 per cent of the population live below the poverty line and Zaire is one of the poorest countries in the world.

Corruption is rife. In order to obtain basic services, almost everyone has to pay bribes to government officials. There has also been very little investment in infrastructure and basic services. Transport is appalling. There is little investment in primary healthcare and malaria is widespread.

As a result of corruption, political mismanagement and lack of infrastructure the Zairean economy is in shambles. Inflation is running at 7000 per cent and the purchasing power of ordinary people is being constantly and dramatically eroded.

A Chronology of Events

Before colonisation, Zaire was a collection of small states along the River Congo. Information about Zaire reached Europe between 1840 and 1870, through the journalistic coverage of David Livingstone and Henry Stanley's expeditions. The latter was financed by a Belgian trading company, who signed trading agreements with local leaders.

1884

The Berlin Conference draws up the borders of the Free State of Congo decreeing that the country is the personal property of the King of Belgium.

1908

Congo formerly becomes a Belgian colony. The Belgians extract the country's timber and mineral resources but do very little to develop the infrastructure of the Congo. The native population is subject to very harsh working conditions in the mines and forests, and all anti-colonial opposition is is brutally suppressed.

1957-59

African political parties are allowed to operate for the first time but many draw support on a narrow ethnic basis. Only Patrice Lumumba's Mouvement Nationale Congolaise achieved a national outlook. In 1959 violent unrest follows the police repression of a peaceful political demonstration. King Badouin of Belgium promises independence in a move to avert further bloodshed.

1960

Independence is won and Patrice Lumumba becomes Prime Minister. Within days the army mutinies and Colonel Joseph-Desire Mobutu seizes power. A secession crisis starts in the Shaba region, due to local resentment over the extraction of the region's mineral resources. Belgium gives support to the secessionist movement. UN troops are sent to the Congo to maintain order.

1961

Mobutu returns power to Joseph Kasavubu. Patrice Lumumba is arrested by Kasavubu and delivered to Belgian mercenaries in Shaba, who kill him. A new government is formed in August 1962.

1963-64

The secessionist movement in Shaba ends, but unrest flares up in Kwilu.

1965

Mobutu seizes power in a coup d'etat and declares himself head of state.

1967

A new constitution is adopted and Mobutu forms a political party — Le Mouvement Populaire de la Revolution. By 1972 this is the sole legal political party and all citizens are automatically members of it.

1970

Mobutu is elected President in an election where there is no opposition. Thousands of opponents are arrested, tortured or killed.

1971

Mobutu institutes 'Zairisation'. The Democratic Republic of Congo is renamed the Republic of Zaire, and Mobutu becomes known as Mobutu Sese Seko. Place names are changed and people are encouraged to change their personal names. The copper mines are nationalised but their wealth benefits only the elite. This latter measure causes unease among western leaders. Mobutu later announces that he has uncovered a US-funded conspiracy to overthrow his leadership. But all this is rhetoric: in the context of Cold War politics, Mobutu continues to receive support from the US, who see Zaire as an ally in the region.

1977-78

The Fronte Nationale de Liberation de Congo invade Shaba province in 1977 and 1978 with support from the Angolan MLPA, a pro-Soviet liberation movement in Angola. Both invasions are repulsed by the Zairean army, with western support. Large numbers of refugees flee to Zambia. Mobutu and Augustina Neto of the MPLA sign a peace treaty in 1978, with the latter agreeing not to support secessionist forces in Zaire.

President Mobutu is re-elected in 1977 for another seven year term.

1982

A new party, Le Union pour la Democratie et la Progres Social (UDPS) is formed by thirteen former members of the National Legislative Council. The founders are imprisoned, then sent into internal exile. The formation of the UDPS is followed by the founding of the FCD, a coalition of opposition groups with Nguza Karl-I-Bond its main spokesperson.

1983

Amnesty International publishes a report condemning human rights abuse in Zaire. The Zairean government is criticised for extra-judicial executions, the arbitrary arrest and torture of opponents and the torture, rape and ill-treatment of prisoners. Following the publication of the report some political prisoners are released.

1984

There is further unrest in Shaba, brutally put down by the army. Mobutu is re-elected for a further seven years.

1986

A further report from Amnesty International highlights continued human rights violations. Opposition parties continue to be banned and members are constantly under the threat of detention. Newspapers which criticise the government are promptly closed. Forcibly repatriated refugees are also prime targets for detention and mistreatment. The incidence of extra-judicial executions and secret detention seem to be on the increase in the late 1980s. Local church organisations and Amnesty International find it increasingly difficult to trace detainees. Amnesty International is also concerned about the violent suppression of demonstrations, often resulting in death and injuries.

1987

A number of Jehovah's Witnesses are detained without trial.

1988

Etienne Tshisekedi of the UDPS holds a political meeting at which three people are shot and 50 disappear. Tshisekedi is also detained and banished. Women are ordered to wear traditional dress.

Relations with the Belgian government break down after the Belgian press publishes reports on corruption in Zaire. Mobutu orders Zaireans living in Belgium to return. Diplomatic relations are not resumed until 1990, when Belgium signs a treaty of co-operation with Zaire.

1989

Student demonstrations are held in Kinshasa and Lubumbashi against increases in the cost of living. Up to 50 students are killed when the security services try to disperse the demonstrators. Kinshasa University and four other institutes are closed. UDPS members are arrested and beaten at a meeting to commemorate the assassination of Patrice Lumumba. Other arrests of UDPS members increase.

There is increasing unrest in the Kivu region, bordering Rwanda, and numerous arrests.

1990

Mobutu announces reforms, including the right to form political parties and trade unions. But these are hollow promises. In May 1990 students at Lubumbashi University stage an anti-government demonstration. Between 50 and 150 students are subsequently killed and many others flee to Zambia.

1991

Student demonstrations and UDPS meetings are violently disrupted by security forces. Mobutu tries to appoint Tshisekedi as Prime Minister but he refuses. The National Conference, a forum to draft a new constitution, is opened then closed again.

In September 1991 the devaluation of the currency leads to massive price increases. The army riots and there is extensive damage to shops and businesses.

The US and IMF suspend aid. French and Belgian armed forces intervene to protect expatriate communities. The reopened National Conference appoints Tshisekedi, leader of the UDPS, as Prime Minister, but Mobutu sacks him and installs his own candidate. This causes further riots and bloodshed.

In November 1991 Tshisekedi establishes a parallel government. The National Conference resumes. Mobutu appoints Nguza Karl-I- Bond as Prime Minister.

1992

The National Conference is suspended again. A peaceful demonstration calling for its resumption is violently dispersed by security services, at the cost of 45 lives. In April 1992 the National Conference opens and declares its own sovereignty. It appoints Tshisekedi as Prime Minister in August 1992 and Karl-I-Bond resigns.

In September 1992 Kasai Luba living in Shaba are attacked by Shaba Luba. At least 60 people are killed and 40,000 flee Shaba. Some politicians call for the expulsion of all Kasai Luba. The riots are suspected of being an attempt to destabilise Tshisekedi's parallel government.

In December 1992 the National Conference is dissolved and replaced by a 'Council of Wise Men', but most people regard it as too conciliatory.

1993

Mobutu issues a 5,000,000 Zaire note despite opposition from Tshisekedi, who declares the note illegal tender. Mobutu issues the note as payment to the army but retailers reject it. The army riots and shops and businesses are looted in Kinshasa. Mobutu sends in his security forces and up to 1,000 people are killed, including the French Ambassador. It is alleged that Mobutu ordered the riots, to conceal house-to-house searches for opposition members. Mobutu surrounds Parliament with his security forces.

In May and June 1993 Rwandan minorities in Goma become the target of attack. Increased numbers of Kasai Luba flee from their homes in May 1993, after their houses are burned or property confiscated. By June 1993 nearly 700,000 people leave Kasai Province, many suffering from malnutrition. Refugees also flee to Angola, Zambia, France, Britain and Belgium.

President Mobutu's position is maintained by security forces which report to him. The most powerful are the *Division Special Presidentielle*, and '*les Hiboux*', who work at night and are responsible for night-time arrests.

Zairean Refugees in Britain

Statistics

Year	Asylum Applications	Refugee Status	ELR	Refusal
1986	26	1	0	2
1987	53	0	0	6
1988	157	3	10	9
1989	525	130	5	25
1990	2,590	10	5	95
1991	7,010	10	5	1,095
1992	880	10	10	4,810
1993	635	5	10	1,700

Zaireans were the largest group of refugees entering Britain in 1991, with over 7,000 asylum applications lodged with the Home Office. Until 1989 the numbers of Zaireans claiming asylum in Britain was low and those who did flee to Europe tended to claim asylum in Francophone countries — France and Belgium — where a they would have historical and linguistic ties.

Although it is very expensive to fly to a European country, many Zaireans see Europe as the only safe destination. There are well documented instances of the SIE, President Mobutu's external intelligence service, seeking out Zairean refugees in Rwanda and Angola, and murdering or kidnapping them. Neighbouring countries have mutual agreements with the Zairean government to return refugees. Any refugee returned to Zaire is likely to be detained and tortured; the act of claiming asylum is judged as evidence in itself of dissent.

There are three reasons why more Zaireans have fled to Britain. Firstly, refugees who flee from ethnic conflict in Shaba travel via Zambia. There are more flights from Zambia to London than to Brussels or Paris. It is also believed that the SIE operates in France and Belgium, where there are reports of refugees being harassed or kidnapped by them. Many Zaireans also say that they believe racial harassment is worse in France and Belgium than in England.

The treatment of Zairean refugees by the Home Office is of great concern to the Refugee Council and other human rights organisations. Proportionally larger numbers of Zaireans are detained on arrival in Britain than other refugee groups. The Home Office gives no reasons why Zaireans are more likely to be detained, but it might be prejudice — recent press articles have hardly enhanced the reputation of Zairean asylum-seekers.

Many Zaireans are also forced to buy false passports in order to escape. Presentation of false travel documents may make British immigration officers suspicious, thus increasing the asylum-seeker's chances of being detained. The reason for the need for false documents is obvious: in Zaire all passports are held by

Zairean immigration officers. On re-entering the country people have to give up their passports in exchange for a receipt. A Zairean who is being sought by security services and needs to leave the country will not wish to draw attention to him/herself by applying for the return of a passport from the Zairean authorities.

It is also believed that the British government uses detention as a deliberate deterrent. Detainees rarely receive information about their legal rights or when they will be released. Detention can be a profoundly disorientating experience, particularly if the detainee has been imprisoned in the home country.

Very few Zaireans speak English when they arrive, which makes applications for asylum difficult. Asylum applications are conducted sometimes in English and sometimes in French, on the assumption that all Zaireans speak French. In fact by no means all do: fluency in French depends on the number of years spent in school.

Very few Zairean asylum-seekers are being awarded full refugee status. The proportion of Zaireans being refused is higher than almost every other refugee group. Despite a grave deterioration in the security situation in Zaire, the Home Office is continuing to refuse requests for political asylum. Zairean asylum-seekers are also being refused asylum under Rule 101 of the Immigration Rules, for failure to attend for an interview or failure to provide additional information to corroborate claims of persecution. It should be noted that in Zaire detention usually takes place without trial and often in secret detention centres, not prisons. For some asylum-seekers additional evidence of detention can be hard to obtain.

In 1991 and 1992 sections of the British press seized on isolated cases of social security fraud by Zaireans. Several national tabloid newspapers used this in a campaign to vilify asylum-seekers, in the run-up to the Asylum Bill. There is no doubt that the reputation of Zaireans has suffered as a result of the convictions and subsequent press coverage. About ten Zairean asylum-seekers have served prison sentences as a result of DSS fraud. This figure should be viewed objectively: it is a tiny minority of Zairean asylum-seekers that has been involved in criminal activity of this kind. As there is virtually no rule of law in Zaire, it is not surprising that some Zaireans have little understanding of British law.

Most Zairean asylum-seekers are living in Greater London. They tend to be young, often under 30. The majority are well-educated, often holding first and higher degrees. Housing is a major concern, with many Zairean families spending protracted periods in bed and breakfast hotels.

Most Zairean refugees hold hopes of returning to Zaire to rebuild the country. But most believe that Mobutu must relinquish power before it is safe to go home.

☐ Other Refugee Groups

The Armenians

Britain's Armenian community numbers about 15,000. Most have arrived in Britain in the last 20 years.

The Armenian homeland is located in the mountains of eastern Turkey and the Caucasus. The Armenians were converted to Christianity around 300 AD and have their own church and patriarch. The Armenian church was formed after an early schism from the church if the Roman Empire.

Most Armenians speak Armenian as a first or second language. It constitutes a separate branch of the Indo-European language family, although it has borrowed many Persian words. Armenian uses a distinct script and is written from left to right.

Eastern Turkey has never experienced long periods of peace and the Armenians have been ruled by many different empires over the centuries. In the 15th century a large part of Armenia became part of the Ottoman Empire. By 1827, and the Russian conquest of the Caucasus, large numbers of Armenians found themselves living in the Russian Empire. But the most tragic event in Armenian history was the genocide of 1915. In 1908 there was a coup d'etat in Turkey and the Sultan was overthrown. The coup was led by the Young Turks who were extremely nationalistic. There was then increased repression of Turkey's minority groups and the Armenians were one group suspected of sympathies with enemy powers.

Violent attacks on the Armenians started after the military setbacks in the First World War. Nationalists used the Armenians as a scapegoat. Starting in the summer of 1915 over 1,500,000 Armenians were shot or died of starvation and disease. Thousands were deported from their homelands and died on death marches. One third of all Armenians died in this holocaust. The perpetrators of this crime were never brought to justice and even today the Turkish government denies the entire outrage.

Some 500,000 Armenians fled into exile to Russia, other Middle Eastern countries, France and the US. Many of those who fled to Russia and the Middle East have had to face another exile. Since 1965 some 410,000 Armenians have fled from their homes in Cyprus, Iran, Lebanon and Syria. Another 200,000 Armenians fled from Azerbaijan in 1990-91 after inter-ethnic conflict and war between the two new republics of Armenia and Azerbaijan.

Today there are about five million Armenians. About four million live in Armenia and small minorities live in other parts of the former Soviet Union. Another 500,000 live in the Middle East, in Lebanon, Turkey, Syria and Iran. Some 500,000 Armenians live in the US and about 250,000 in France.

Britain's Armenian community numbers about 15,000, of whom about 12,000 live in London, mostly in west London, in Ealing, Kensington and Chelsea and Hammersmith. Recent refugees have settled around an old established community.

The Armenians are probably the oldest refugee community in Britain: in the 13th century some refugees settled in distant Britain after Mongols invaded parts of Armenia. Later Armenian textile merchants settled in Plymouth, Liverpool and Manchester and they were joined at the beginning of the 20th century by refugees escaping massacres in Turkey. But the greatest numbers of Britain's Armenians have arrived in the last 20 years, fleeing civil war and human rights abuse in Cyprus, Lebanon and Iran.

The Armenian community is very diverse. Some members have achieved great success in commercial life. Other more recent arrivals are struggling to make new lives and face most of the problems common to refugees. There a large number of elderly Armenian refugees in Britain.

The Centre for Armenian Information and Advice (CAIA) is an active community group working to support refugees. It offers an advice service, giving information on immigration law, welfare rights and housing. There are several ESL classes and a playgroup for children. The CAIA also runs Armenian classes for young people born in Britain or married to Armenians. It runs training and careers advice for Armenian women, and produces a newsletter which goes to virtually every Armenian living in Britain. An Armenian radio programme is broadcast once a week and there is a unique library of information about Armenia. The CAIA also collects funds for refugees displaced by fighting in the Caucasus.

Refugees from Colombia

About 1,500 Colombian asylum-seekers have arrived in Britain since 1990. They have joined an existing Colombian community numbering about 25,000 people in Greater London.

Colombia has experienced much political violence in the 19th and 20th century. The years 1949-1953 were the most bloody. For many years the Liberal Party and Conservative Party had monopolised political power and in 1946 political rivalries erupted into civil war that lasted until 1958. Local conflicts, reflecting a complex mixture of personal, village, class and ethnic divisions were channelled into an inter-party conflict of intense brutality. The Conservatives controlled the army. The Liberal Party organised peasant guerrilla armies which retaliated savagely. Some 200,000 people were killed and two million displaced between 1949 and 1957.

By the early 1950s some guerrilla armies were beginning to operate independently of the Liberal Party and the communists began to build their own armed units. These developments prompted attempts to end the conflict.

In 1958 Conservative and Liberal leaders signed the National Front pact, in an attempt to end political rivalry. The presidency was to be alternated between the two parties, and posts in the cabinet, judiciary and civil service were to be divided. Although the pact overcame the traditional conflict, it meant that no third party could challenge the Liberals or Conservatives.

Rising poverty and the sense of political powerlessness led some rural people to support left-wing guerrilla organisations. Large landowners responded by giving support to death squads which also had close links with the armed forces. During the 1960s and 1970s Colombia's narcotics trade grew. The drug barons also lent support to death squads. This triple alliance of the army, landowners and drugs barons are at the root of much of today's displacement. At the same time left-wing guerrillas have resorted to extortion, kidnapping and drugs profiteering in order to feed and arm themselves. Some 300,000 people are internally displaced and many more have left the country. Any trade unionist or human rights activist who dares challenge the system is at risk.

Although the number of actual asylum-seekers in Britain is small, many Colombians have fled persecution but not sought asylum, entering Britain instead with tourist or student's visas. Most Colombians live in the inner London boroughs and work in the hotel and catering industry. The Migrant Resource Centre estimates that 80 per cent of Colombians in Britain are visa overstayers — people whose legal permission to remain in Britain has expired. As a consequence many Colombians may be fearful of authority.

There is a community organisation working with Colombian refugees and migrants in London.

Refugees from India

The numbers of Indian asylum-seekers has risen since 1988. Their numbers include those fleeing violence in the Punjab and Kashmir. Indian asylum-seekers are living in many parts of Britain, usually where there are existing communities from their region. Very few are given refugee status or exceptional leave to remain.

Refugees from Kenya

About 1,000 Kenyans have sought asylum in Britain in the last ten years. They fall into two groups: political opponents of Daniel arap Moi's government, and recent arrivals fleeing inter-ethnic conflict in western Kenya. Most Kenyan refugees live in Greater London.

Refugees from Pakistan

Pakistan has experienced numerous changes of government in the 1980s and 1990s and at certain times asylum-seekers from opposition parties have fled to Britain. Many returned when the situation changed. Very few asylum-seekers from Pakistan have received refugee status or exceptional leave to remain in Britain.

Refugees from Romania

About 1,500 Romanians have applied for asylum in Britain, the majority since 1990. Most asylum-seekers are active opponents of the National Salvation Front. Since the 1989 revolution human rights violations have continued. Roma (gypsies), human rights activists and Hungarian political activists seem most at risk. Several Roma have been killed in racially motivated murders.

Further Resources

Books and Articles

☐ General

Amnesty International (1993) *The Amnesty International Report.* AI

The British Council International Guide to Qualifications and Education 1991. Routledge

Joint Council for the Welfare of Immigrants (1992) *The Immigration and Nationality Law Handbook.* London, JCW.

Katzner, Kenneth (1986) *The Languages of the World.* Routledge. A 375-page guide to languages spoken throughout the world.

Minority Rights Group (1992) *Female Genital Mutilation.* London, MRG.

☐ Refugee Issues

Refugee Council

The following leaflets are free and may be obtained by writing to the Publications Department at the Refugee Council address. A fuller publications list can be obtained from the Refugee Council.

Who is a Refugee

Refugees in the New Europe

Asylum Seeking in the UK

The Asylum and Immigration (Appeals) Bill

Advice Leaflets

Leaflets for asylum-seekers and refugees in English, Arabic, French, Somali, Amharic (add new languages) and Serbo-Croat

How to Get Advice
How to Claim Income Support
Advice for Women
Advice on Health
Advice on Women and Benefits
Advice on HIV/AIDS
Advice on Housing
Advice on Pregnancy
Advice on Women and Health
Advice on Racial Harassment

Refugee Council (1993) *The Refugee Adviser's Handbook*
Aimed at advice workers it is the definitive work on all immigration, protection and settlement issues. £3 from the Refugee Council.

Refugee Council (1992) *Asylum Statistics 1982-1992*

World University Service (1994) *Refugee Education Handbook*
Details the rights of refugees to school-based, further and higher education and gives information on professional requalification, grants and other sources of finance for education. £10 from World University Service.

☐ Afghanistan

Arney, George (1989) *Afghanistan.* Mandarin

Dupree, Louis (1980) *Afghanistan.* Princeton University Press

Hiro, Dilip (1988) *Islamic Fundamentalism.* Paladin

Minority Rights Group (1992) *Afghanistan: a nation of minorities.* MRG

Roy, Olivier (1986) *Islam and Resistance in Afghanistan.* Cambridge University Press

Ruthven, Malise (1984) *Islam in the World.* Penguin

School of Oriental and African Studies (1989) *Courtesy and Survival in Pashto and Dari.* London, SOAS.

☐ Angola

Catholic Institute of International Relations (1991) *Angola.* CIIR

Jamba Sousa (1992) *Patriots.* Viking
Novel about post-independence Angola.

☐ Armenians

Minority Rights Group (1991) *The Armenians.* MRG

☐ Eritrea

Cliffe, L and Davidson, B (1988) *The Long Struggle of Eritrea.* Spokesman Books

Keneally, T (1989) *Towards Asmara: an African novel*. Paladin

Legum, C and Firebrace, J (1983) *Eritrea and Tigray.* Minority Rights Group

Warner, R (1992) *Voices from Eritrea.* Minority Rights Group

☐ Iran

Hiro, Dilip (1985) *Iran under the Ayatollahs.* Paladin

☐ The Kurds

Chaliand, Gerard (Ed) (1994) *A People Without a Country: The Kurds and Kurdistan.* Zed Press

Laizer Sheri (1991) *Into Kurdistan, Frontiers Under Fire.* Zed Press

McDowall David (1991) *The Kurds: A Nation Denied.* Minority Rights Group

Minority Rights Group Report (1991) *The Kurds.* MRG

Refugee Council (1994) *Gulf Information Pack*

☐ Somalia

Cawl, Faarax (1982) *Ignorance is the Enemy of Love.* Zed Press

Minority Rights Group Report (1991) *Somalia: a Nation in Turmoil.* MRG

Haan Publishers (1993) *Understanding Somalia.* Haan Publishers

☐ Sri Lanka

Hensman, Rohini (1993) *Journey without a Destination.* Refugee Council

Minority Rights Group (1988) *The Tamils of Sri Lanka.* MRG

Refugee Council *Sri Lanka Monitor*

☐ Sudan

Panos Institute (1989) *War Wounds: Sudanese People Report their War.* Panos

☐ Uganda

Amnesty International (1989) *Uganda: the Human Rights record 1986-89.* AI

Karugire (1980) *A Political History of Uganda.* Heinemann

Minority Rights Group Report (1989) *Uganda.* MRG

☐ Viet Nam

Ashworth, Georgina (1979) *The Boat People and the Road People.* Sunbury: Quartermaine House

Maclear, Michael (1981) *The Ten Thousand Day War: Vietnam 1945-1975.* Harvard University Press

Mares, Penny (1982) *The Vietnamese in Britain: a handbook for health workers.* National Extension College

Refugee Council (1993) *Vietnamese Refugee Reception and Resettlement 1979-88*

Robinson, Uaporn Ang (1992) *South East Asian New Year's Celebrations.* Smithsonian Institution, Washington DC

☐ Former Yugoslavia

Glenny, Misha (1993) *The Fall of Yugoslavia.* Penguin

Poulton (1991) *The Balkans.* Minority Rights Group

Thompson, Mark (1992) *A Paper House: the ending of Yugoslavia.* Paladin

☐ The Education of Refugee Children

AIDS Education Research Trust (1990) *AIDS: Working With Young People*

Commission for Racial Equality (1989) *Code of Practice for the Elimination of Racial Discrimination in Education.* CRE

Commission for Racial Equality (1989) *From Cradle to School: a practical guide to race equality and childcare.* CRE

Community Service Volunteers (1993) *Lunchtime Link.* CSV

Cummins, Jim (1984) Bilingualism and Special education: issues in assessment and pedagogy. *Multilingual Matters* no 6

Eggleston J., Dunn D.K. and Anjali M. (1986) *Education for Some: the Educational and Vocational Experiences of 15-18 Year Old Members of Minority Ethnic Groups.* Trentham Books.

Gravelle, Maggie (1993) Case study or cause? The role of Section 11 teachers. *Multicultural Teaching* 12 (1)

Guy, W and Menter, I (1992) Local management of resources who benefits? in Gill, D, Mayor, B and Blair, M (1992) *Racism and Education: structures and strategies.* Sage

Harvard Programme in Refugee Trauma (1992) *A Community Study of Health, Mental Health and Social Functioning of Khmer.* Harvard University Press

DES (1985) *Education for All: the report of the Committee of Inquiry into the Education of Children from Ethnic Minority Groups.* (Swann Report) HMSO

Klein, Gillian (1993) *Education Towards Race Equality.* Cassell

McCallin, M (1993) *Living in Detention: a review of the psychological well-being of Vietnamese children in the Hong Kong detention camps.* International Catholic Child Bureau

Maksoud, Mona (1992) Assessing War Trauma in Children; a case study of Lebanese children. *Journal of Refugee Studies* 5 (1)

Marshall, Tony (1992) *Careers Guidance with Refugees.* Refugee Council.

Marshall, Tony (1991) *Cultural Aspects of Job-Seeking.* Refugee Council.

Melzak and Warner (1992) *Integrating Refugee Children into Schools.* Medical Foundation for the Care of Victims of Torture and Minority Rights Group. (Single copies of this useful leaflet are available for free from the Minority Rights Group).

National Association for Pastoral Care in Education (1993) *Children and Bereavement, Death and Loss: What Can a School Do?* Available from NAPCE, c/o Education Department, University of Warwick, Coventry CV4 7AL.

NAPCE (1993) *Refugee Children in School*

National Children's Bureau (1992) *Religion, Ethnicity and Sex Education.* NCB

Northamptonshire County Council (1992) *Dealing with Harassment and Racist Incidents in Schools*

Refugee Council (1989) *Supplementary Schools Directory*

Refugee Council (1994) *Refugee Children in Schools.* (free booklet outlining ideas for good practice).

Ressler, E, Boothby, N and Steinbock, D (1988) *Unaccompanied Children.* Oxford University Press

Richman, Naomi (1993) *Communicating with Children.* (This small book is highly recommended. It contains much useful advice and ideas for training activities, written in accessible language. £4.50 from the Save the Children Fund).

Runneymede Trust (1993) *Equality Assurance in Scho*ols. Stoke-on-Trent, Trentham Books

Scottish Council for Research in Education (1993) *Supporting Schools against Bullying*

Siraj-Blatchford Iram (1994) *The Early years: laying the foundations for race equality.* Stoke-on-Trent, Trentham Books

Troyna, B and Hatcher, R (1992) Racist Incidents in Schools: a framework for analysis. in Gill, D, Mayor, B and Blair, M (1992) *Racism and Education.* Sage

Wiles, Sylvaine (1985) Learning a Second Language. *The English Magazine.* London, English Language and Media Centre

Yule and Gold (1993) *Wise Before the Event: Coping with Crises in Schools.* Calouste Gulbenkian Foundation. Explains how schools can support children who have been involved in disasters.

☐ Audio Visual Resources for School Students

International Broadcasting Trust (1992) *Refugees in Today's Europe: An Action Video Pack.* (video and accompanying activities aimed at 14-18 year old students. £3.25 from Academy TV, 104 Kirkstall Road, Leeds LS3 1JS.

Refugee Council (1988) *Africa, Asia, Central America and Refugee Children* (A set of four videos in VHS format. The first three are suitable for students over 11 years. 'Refugee Children' may be used in primary schools. The set of four, or single videos are available on free hire from the Refugee Council).

George Orwell School (1994) *Safe in Another Country* (video made by refugee children in a London school — an excellent training resource). Obtainable from George Orwell School.

☐ Books for School Students

Alexander, Sue (1983) *Leila.* Hamish Hamilton

Centre for Education in World Citizenship (1993) *The Disintegration of Yugoslavia*

Christian Aid (1993) *Eritrea: Africa's Newest Country.*

Christian Aid (1991) *An Ethiopian Calendar.*

Dejong, Meidert (1956) *The House of Sixty Fathers.* (story about a refugee child aimed at 11-13 year olds.) Puffin

Filipovic, Zlata (1994) *Zlata's Diary.* Heinemann

Harbour, Bernard (1993) *The Conflict in Eastern Europe.* Wayland

Harrow LEA (1992) *English Somali Phrase Book*

Hillier, S and Gerlach, L (1987) *Whose Paradise? Tea and the Plantation Tamils of Sri Lanka.* MRG

Hounslow Language Service (1991) *Multilingual Topic Words*

Kerr, Judith (1974) *The Other Way Round.* Harper Collins

Kerr, Judith (1971) *When Hitler Stole Pink Rabbit.* Harper Collins (autobiographical accounts of a small girl fleeing from Nazi Germany).

King, John (1992) *The Kurds.* Wayland

Laird, Elizabeth (1991) *Kiss the Dust.* (story about an Iraqi Kurdish family forced to flee their home). Heinemann

Rutter, Jill (1992) *Refugees: A Resource Book for 8-13 Year Olds.* £3 from the Refugee Council.

Rutter, Jill (1991) *Refugees: We left Because We Had To.* Refugee Council. (for 14-18 year old students: background information, testimonies and activities. £5 from the Refugee Council).

Save the Children Fund (1993) *New Faces, New Places* (resource pack on refugees for four to seven year olds. £9 from Save the Children Fund).

Serraillier, Ian (1956) *The Silver Sword.* Puffin

Strachan, Ian (1980) *Journey of a Thousand Miles.* MacMillan

Sulieman, A. (1991) *Somali Studies: Land of the People, Early History, Stories from the Land of Punt, Somali Nomads, Food and Somali People of the Horn of Africa* (six booklets). Haan Publishers

Sulieman, A. (1991) *Words lists for Geography, Mathematics, Science, Technology and Social Science.* Haan Publishers

Vallely, Paul (1993) *Daniel and the Mischief Boy.* Christian Aid. (story of an Eritrean family).

Warner, Rachel (1992) *Voices from Eritrea, Voices from Kurdistan, Voices from Somalia.* (Three books of testimonies of refugee children, in dual language texts. Set of three £7.95 from Minority Rights Group).

Organisations

☐ International Organisations and Government Departments

Commission for Racial Equality
Elliot House
10 Allington Street
London SW1H 5EH
0171-828-7022

Office of the United Nations High Commissioner for Refugees
7 Westminster Palace Gardens
Artillery Row
London SW1P 1RL
0171-222-3065

☐ Local Education Authority Contacts

In addition to the Refugee Council (see p. 274) and the Medical Foundation for the Care of Victims of Torture (p. 272) the following people may be able to provide in-service training about refugee children in schools.

Rocky Deans
Travellers and Displaced Person's Team
Teacher's Centre
Brentfield Road
London NW10
0181-963-0735

Betty Davies
Anson School, Anson Road
London NW2 4AB
0181-452-8552

Sheila Kasabova
Refugee Liaison Teacher
Camden Language Development Service
136 Charlton Street, London NW1
0171-388-7458

Elaine Noden
Support Team for International Children
Elthorne Education Centre
Westlea Road
London W7 2AD
0181-840-4050

Hounslow Language Service
Education Centre
Martingdale Road
Hounslow
Middlesex TW4 7HE
0181-570-2392
(has produced a wide selection of multilingual topic words and stories).

Caroline Lodge
George Orwell School
Turle Road, London N4 3LS
0171-263-1465

Roger Hancock
Learning by Design
Tower Hamlets Professional Development Centre
English Street
London E2
(has produce dual language fold stories in Somali and Kurdish Sorani).

Bill Bolloten and Tim Spafford
Refugee Support Teachers
Multicultural Development Service
Markhouse School
Markhouse Road
London E17 8BD
0181-520-4878

☐ Non-Governmental Organisations

Advisory Centre for Education
1b Aberdeen Studios
22 Highbury Grove
London N5 2EA
0171-354-8321
ACE offers free advice to parents of children in maintained schools and produces a wide range of publications on all aspects of education.

Africa Education Trust
38 King Street
London WC2E 8JS
0171-836-5075
AET offers advice and a limited number of scholarships for refugees from Africa.

AIMER
Access to Information on Multicultural Education Resources
Bulmershe Court
University of Reading
Earley
Reading RG6 1HY
0734-875123

Amnesty International British Section
99-119 Rosebery Avenue
London EC1R 4RE
0171-814-6200
Amnesty International is a world-wide human rights organisation. In Britain AI presents information about the risks that individual refugees could face in their countries of origin and it may provide statements of support for asylum applicants. AI produces a wide range of published material and is engaged in human rights education.

Asylum Aid
244a Upper Street
London N1 1RU
0171-359-4026
Asylum Aid provides free advice and support for refugees and asylum-seekers in the UK.

British Red Cross Society
9 Grosvenor Crescent
London SW1X 7EJ
0171-235-5454

The British Red Cross operates a tracing and family message service to enable people separated by conflict or disaster to make contact with other members of their family. It also deals with family reunion cases. Runs reception centres for Bosnian programme refugees in Rugby, Cambridge and Oxford.

Catholic Fund for Overseas Development
2 Romero Close
Stockwell Road
London SW9 9TY
0171-733-7900
CAFOD is organising a two year refugee campaign lasting until 1996. Its education unit produces information useful in Roman Catholic schools.

Children's Legal Centre
20 Compton Terrace
London N1 2UN
0171-359-6251
Offers free advice and information on all aspects of law affecting children and young people.

The Daycare Trust
Wesley House
4 Wild Court
London WC2B 4AU

Detention Advisory Service
244a Upper Street
London N1 1RU
0171-704-8007
DAS provides advice and support for people held under Immigration Act powers in London and southern England.

Development Education Association
3rd Floor
29-31 Cowper Street
London EC1R 4AP
0171-490-8108
The DEA has a list of local development education centres across the UK.

Early Years Trainers Anti-Racist Network
1 The Lyndens
51 Granville Road
London N12 0JH

FORWARD
The Africa Centre
38 King Street
London WC2E 8JT
0171-379-6889

Immigration Law Practicioner's Association
115 Old Street
London EC1V 9JR
0171-250-1671
ILPA has a list of solicitors who are experienced in immigration law.

Institute of Race Relations
2-6 Leeke Street
London WC1X 9HS
0171-837-0041

Joint Council for the Welfare of Immigrants
115 Old Street, London EC1V 9JR
0171-251-8706
JCWI produces information materials on legal matters and advise individuals.

Haan Associates
PO Box 607
London SW16 1EB
Haan publishes information about Somalia.

Law Centres Federation
Duchess House
18 Warren Street
London W1P 5DB
0171-387-8570
Law centres give free advice, and this organisation will give information about their location.

Letterbox Library
Unit 2D, Leroy House
436 Essex Road
London N1 3QP
0171-226-1633
Distributes non-sexist and multicultural books for children.

London Black Women's Health Action Group
Cornwall Community Centre
1 Cornwall Avenue, London E2
0181-980-3503

Mantra Publishers
5 Alexandra Grove
London N12 8NU
0181-445-5123
Mantra produces a wide range of dual language children's story books including many in Arabic, Turkish, Somali and Vietnamese.

Medical Foundation for the Care of Victims of Torture
96 Grafton Road
London NW5 5ET
0171-284-4321
Sheila Melzak Child Psychotherapist
The Medical Foundation provides support for survivors of torture and their families. It employs a wide range of staff including psychotherapists, social workers and doctors. Its offers specialist services for children. A child psychotherapist is engaged in assessment and casework and offers in-service training for teachers and runs a drop-in session for those with concerns about individual children.

Midlands Refugee Council
Unit 204 The Argent Centre
60 Frederick Street
Hockley
Birmingham B1 3HS
021-212-1435
Offers a wide range of support to refugees, and information for those working to support refugees.

Minority Rights Group
379 Brixton Road
London SW9 7DE
0171-978-9498
MRG produces many useful reports and also works with teachers.

Multicultural Teaching
Trentham Books Ltd
Westview House
734 London Road
Oakhill
Stoke on Trent ST4 5NP
0782-745567
Journal for practitioners.

North East Refugee Services
Swinburne House
Swinburne Street
Gateshead NE8 1AX
091-490-6314

308 Lindthorpe Road
Middlesborough
Cleveland TS1 3QX
0642-211117

NERS support refugees living in the north east.

Northern Refugee Centre
Jew's Lane, off Fitzalan Square
Sheffield S1 2BE
0742-701429
Offers support services to refugees living in the Yorkshire and Humberside region.

Ockenden Venture
Head Office
Guildford Road
Woking, Surrey GU22 7UU
0483-772012

Oxfam
274 Banbury Road
Oxford OX2 7DZ
0865-311311

Positive Options Barnados
345 Goswell Road
London EC1V 7LQ
0171-278 5039

Refugee Action
The Offices
The Cedars
Oakwood
Derby DE2 4FY
0332-833310

240a Clapham Road
London SW9 0PZ
0171-735-5361

Woodville
Shirley Road
Cheetham, Manchester M8 7NE
061-740-6711
Refugee Action support refugees from Viet Nam. In Manchester it also gives support to other groups of refugees.

Refugee Arrivals Project
Room 2005, 2nd Floor
Queen's Building
Heathrow Airport
Hounslow, Middlesex TW6 1DL
0181-759-5740
Offers advice for asylum-seekers at Heathrow Airport or those detained nearby.

Refugee Housing Association
47-49 Durham Street
London SE11 5JA
0171-582-0038

The Refugee Council
3 Bondway
London SW8 1SJ
0171-582-6922
A team of advice workers gives help newly-arrived refugees. Team includes an accommodation officer and an outreach worker supporting single parents in bed and breakfast hotels. The advice service is open on Monday, Tuesday, Thursday and Friday from 9.30-1pm. Police registration fees can be reclaimed. The Refugee Council's National and Community Development teams work to support refugee community organisations, statutory and voluntary organisations who are working with refugees. Produces a wide range of publications and has a library open to the public. It also has a training division. There are several specialist services for schools including:

answering individual inquiries requesting information;
providing in-service training about refugees and educational provision for refugee students;
providing advice and curriculum support for teachers;
speaking to school students;
running workshops for voluntary agencies;
producing and distributing publications and audio-visual resources.

Refugee Legal Centre
Sussex House
39 Bermondsey Street
London SE1 3XF
0171-827-9090
Out of hours emergency number 0831-598057
Provides free legal advice and representation for asylum-seekers including those in detention.

Refugee Support Centre
King George's House
Stockwell Road
London SW9 9EJ
0171-733-1482
Offers a free, confidential counselling service for asylum-seekers and refugees who are experiencing emotional distress.

Refugee Studies Programme
Queen Elizabeth House
St Giles
Oxford OX1 3LA
0865-270722
RSP is an academic research institute.

Runneymede Trust
11 Princelet Street
London E1 6QH
0171-375-1496
Monitors race relations; publishes books on race issues.

Save the Children Fund
17 Grove Lane
London SE5
0171-703-5400

Scottish Refugee Council

43 Broughton Street	73 Robertson Street
Edinburgh EH1 3JU	Glasgow G2 8QD
031-557-8083	041--221-8793

Provides advice and information for refugees in Scotland and works to raise awareness about refugees' needs.

Sickle Cell Society
54 Stattion Road
London NW10 4UX
0181-961-4006

Southern Voices
300 Oxford Road
Manchester M13 9NS
061-273-2228

UK Thalassaemia Society
107 Nightingale Lane
London N8 7QY
0181-348-0437

Welsh Refugee Council
c/o South Glamorgan Race Equality Council
Unit 8
Williams Copurt
Trade Street
Cardiff CF1 5DQ
0222-666250

World University Service
20 Compton Terrace
London N1 2UN
0171-226-6747
WUS offers training to people working with refugees in further and higher education, runs an educational advice service for refugees and offers small grants to refugee students.

Roy Yates Books
Rudgewick
Horsham
West Sussex RH12 3DE
Distributes a wide range of bilingual children's books.

☐ Refugee Community Organisations

The addresses for refugee community organisations may change from time to time. The Refugee Council keeps an up-to-date list that can be obtained from their Public Information Section.

Greater London

Society of Afghan Residents in UK
West Acton Youth and Community Centre
Churchill Gardens
London W3 0JN
0181-993-8168

OCA-RU Organisation of the Angolan Community in the United Kingdom
Christ Church
Mowll Street
London SW9 6DF
0171-587-1679

Arab Line
3 Cameron House
12 Castlehaven Road
London NW1 8ZN
0171-284-2580

Centre for Armenian Information and Advice
105a Mill Hill Road
London W3
0181-992-4621

Assyrian Cultural and Advice Centre
PO Box 1314
London W5 5QH
0181-579-0192

Bosnia-Hercegovina Advice Centre
10 Rosslyn Court
Ornan Road
London NW3 4PU
0171-435-4180

Bromley Refugee Network
28a Beckenham Road
Beckenham
Kent BR3 4LS
0181-658-1490

Chile Democratico
15 Wilkin Street
London NW5
0171-284-2400

Colombian Community Association
12 Thornton Street
London SW9 0BL
0171-761-9072

East European Advice Centre
240 King Street
London W6
0181-748-3085

Eritrean Community in Haringey
Selby Centre
Selby Road
London N7 8JN
0181-365-01819

Eritrean Community in UK
266 Holloway Road
London N7 6NE
0171-700-7995

Ethiopian Community in Britain
66 Hampstead Road
London NW1 2NT
0171-388-4944

Eritrean Support Group
1 Thorpe Close
London W10 5XL
0181-964-3856

Ghana Refugee Welfare Group
2nd Floor
5 Westminster Road
London SE1 7XW

Greenwich Refugee Association
Suite D, Building B
Mc Bean Street
London SE18 6LW
0181-317-3461

Haringey Refugee Consortium
Selby Centre
Selby Road
London N7 8JN
0181-885-5511

Kosova Information Centre
132 Buckingham Palace Road
London SW1V 9SA
0171-730-1050

Kurdish Cultural Centre
14 Stannary Street
London SE11 4AA
0171-735-0918

Kurdistan Workers Association
Fairfax Hall
11 Portland Gardens
London N4 1HU
0181-809-0743

Kurdish Information Centre
Caxton House
129 St John's Way
London N19
0171-272-9499

Iranian Community Centre
266 Holloway Road
London N7 6HP
0171-700-0477

Iraqi Community Association
5 Bradbury Street
London N16 8JN
0171-249-3788

Latin America House
Priory House
Kingsgate Place
London NW6 4TA
0171-372-5244

Latin American Women's Rights Service
The London Women's Centre
Wesley House
Wild Court
London WC2B 5AV

Oromo Relief Association
1 Amwell Street
London EC1R 1VL
0171-833-0715

Romania Refugee Association
92 Brook Green
London W6
0171-602-9154

Somali Advice and Information Office
Unit 4
8 West Bute Street
Cardiff CF1 7HQ

Somali Arts Project
Oxford House
Derbyshire Street
London E2
0171-739-9001

Somali Community and Cultural Association
54 Cemetery Road
Sheffield S11

Somali Refugee Counselling Programme
24a Chain Walk
Birmingham B19 1SJ
021-554-8900

Somali Counselling Project
South Bank House, Black Prince Road
London SE1
0171-582-3472

Somali Refugee Women's Group
373 Greenrigg Walk
Chalkhill Estate
Wembley
Middlesex
0181-908-6274

Ealing Somali Welfare and Cultural Organisation
Northfields Community Centre
Northcroft Road
London W13
0181-567-1914

Health Counselling for Somali Refugees
16 Askew Crescent
London W12
0181-740-7241

Sudanese Community Information Centre
14 Newton Road
London W2
0171-229-4338

Sudan Relief and Rehabilitation Association
1a St Martin's House
Polygon Road
London NW1 1BQ
0171-383-5846

Sudanese Women's Association — Brighton
23 Prestonville Court
134 Dyke Road
Brighton BN1 3UG
0273-776571

Sudanese Women's Group
The Bayswater Centre
14 Newhorn Road
London W2 5LT
0171-221-3290

South London Refugee Project
South Norwood AE Centre
Sandown Road
London SE25 4XE
0181-656-4560

Tamil Information Centre
720 Romford Road
London E12 6BT

Tamil Refugee Action Group
3rd Floor
Grays Inn Road
London WC1
0171-833-2020

West London Tamil School
Station House
Stonebridge Park
London NW10

Tigrayan Community in Britain
The Print House
18 Ashwin Street
London E8 3DL
0171-923-2400

Uganda Community Relief Association
Selby Centre, Selby Road
London N7 8JN
0181-808-6221

Uganda Refugee Welfare Association
176 Clapton Common
London E5 9AG
0181-802-3992

Uganda Welfare Action Group
700 Harold Road, London E13 0ES
0181-470-5541

ZACA
(Community Organisation for Zairean Refugees)
Selby Centre, Selby Road
London N17 8JC
Tel: 0181-365-1665

Terminology

Asylum-seeker — someone who has fled from his or her home country in search of safety and has applied for political asylum in another country.

Bilingual student — a student who has access to, or needs to use, two or more languages at home and school. Does not imply fluency in the languages and includes students who are beginning to learn English.

ELR — Exceptional Leave to Remain. An immigration status granted at the discretion of the Home Secretary, for 'humanitarian or administrative reasons'. Many asylum-seekers are now granted ELR instead of full refugee status. ELR does not afford the same rights as refugee status. In this book, people with ELR are referred to as refugees except when it is important to distinguish between those with full refugee status and ELR — for example when describing rights to grants for higher education.

ESL — English as a second language: classes or teacher support to help bilingual students learn English.

LEA — local education authority.

Refugee — a person who has been given full refugee status, according to the provisions of the 1951 UN Convention and 1967 UN Protocol Relating to the Status of Refugees, after having been judged to have fled from his or her home country or to be unable to return to it 'owing to a well-founded fear of being persecuted for reasons of race, religion, nationality, membership of a particular social group or political opinion'.

UNHCR — The United Nations High Commissioner for Refugees. The UN organisation responsible for giving legal protection to asylum-seekers and refugees and for co-ordinating relief.

Index